EXTRAORDINARY ACCLAIM FOR

# Are You My Mother?

"Not only a probing and mordantly funny inquiry of Bechdel's intellectually curious but distant mother . . . but also a profound look at intimacy, sexuality, art and religion. Bechdel ties it all together with her touching and sometimes haunting images, crimson-hued drawings that convey an astonishing range of emotions."  — *San Francisco Chronicle*

"Inventive . . . In her quiet, rigorous, self-deprecating way, [Bechdel] succeeds at creating a world in which we are bound to recognize some part of ourselves, and our mothers."  — *Washington Post*

"*Are You My Mother?* offers an improbably profound master class in how to live an examined life . . . More moving and illuminating than *Fun Home.*"  — *Elle*

"Bechdel, for whom the self is psychoanalytic subject, is remarkably able to translate her internal universe onto the page."  — *New York Magazine*

"A stunning, psychologically astute, and sophisticated masterwork."  — *Philadelphia Inquirer*

"Depicts moments of stunning emotional charge . . . Bechdel captures moments of striking intimacy . . . Rich with thought."  — *Milwaukee Journal-Sentinel*

"*Are You My Mother?* is a work of the most humane kind of genius, bravely going right to the heart of things: why we are who we are. It's also incredibly funny. And visually stunning. And page-turningly addictive. And heartbreaking."
  —Jonathan Safran Foer, author of *Extremely Loud and Incredibly Close* and *Everything is Illuminated*

"Many of us are living out the unlived lives of our mothers. Alison Bechdel has written a graphic novel about this; sort of like a comic book by Virginia Woolf. You won't believe it until you read it—and you must!"
— Gloria Steinem

"This book is not so much the sequel to Alison Bechdel's captivating memoir *Fun Home,* as the maternal yin to its paternal yang. Bravely worrying out the snarled web of missed connections that bedevil her relationship with her remarkable mother from the very start, Bechdel deploys everyone from Virginia Woolf to D.W. Winnicott (the legendary psychoanalytic theorist who comes to serve as her quest's benign fairy godfather) to untie the snares of a fraught past. She arrives, at long last, at something almost as shimmering as it is simple: a grace-flecked accommodation and an affirming love."
— Lawrence Weschler, author of *Everything that Rises: A Book of Convergences* and *Uncanny Valley: Adventures in the Narrative*

"A staggering achievement . . . a masterwork that gracefully documents the torture that sensitive people can put themselves through while searching for the causal movers of their lives."
— *Daily Beast*

"Bechdel's intellectual curiosity and generosity toward her mother make this a complex, transcendent work of art that will resonate whether or not you relate to its specifics . . . Perfect for anyone who has experienced a dysfunctional family dynamic (i.e., everyone)."
— *Bitch*

"As layered and complex a memoir as you are going to read this year."
— *Austin American-Statesman*

"Now Bechdel does herself one better with a tender and wide-ranging examination of her relationship with her living mother . . . *Are You My Mother?* is all the more erudite, subtle and charming . . . engaging, sly and amusing . . . We come to know these two dynamic and vulnerable women. We root for them to recognize each other. When at last the analytical Mother, reading chapters we've already read, decides, "It coheres . . . It is a Meta Book," we celebrate."
— *Oregonian*

"Her genius is that she takes very particular experiences and crafts them into something universal." — *The Stranger*

"Breathtaking . . . Stunning." — *Curve*

"In her inimitable style as graphic alchemist, Bechdel has created another audacious book: insightful, engrossing, entertaining, and courageous." — *Burlington Free Press*

"A fiercely honest work about the field of combat that is family." — *Publishers Weekly,* starred review

"[Bechdel's] lines and angles are sharper than in *Fun Home,* and yet her self-image and her views of family members, lovers, and analysts are thorough, clear, and kind. Mothers, adult daughters, literati, memoir fans, and psychology readers are among the many who will find this outing a rousing experience . . . This may be the most anticipated graphic novel of the year." — *Booklist,* starred review

"A psychologically complex, ambitious, illuminating successor to the author's graphic-memoir masterpiece." — *Kirkus,* starred review

"The best writers, whether they are creating fiction or nonfiction, are trying to find out what makes people human for better and for worse. A taut, complex book within several books, Bechdel's investigation of her relationship with her mother and the work of pioneering psychoanalyst Donald Winnicott offers the most articulate answer you're likely to ingest. You'll feel like Alice climbing your way out the jagged rabbit hole to limbo." — *Library Journal*

# Are You
# My
# Mother?

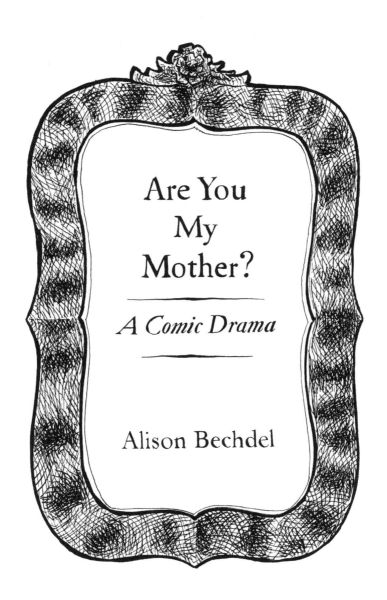

# Are You My Mother?

*A Comic Drama*

Alison Bechdel

Mariner Books

HOUGHTON MIFFLIN HARCOURT

BOSTON • NEW YORK

*FOR MY MOTHER,*
*WHO KNOWS WHO SHE IS.*

FIRST MARINER BOOKS EDITION 2013
COPYRIGHT © 2012 BY ALISON BECHDEL
ALL RIGHTS RESERVED

FOR INFORMATION ABOUT PERMISSION TO REPRODUCE SELECTIONS FROM THIS BOOK,
WRITE TO PERMISSIONS, HOUGHTON MIFFLIN HARCOURT PUBLISHING COMPANY,
215 PARK AVENUE SOUTH, NEW YORK, NEW YORK 10003.

WWW.HMHCO.COM

LIBRARY OF CONGRESS CATALOGING-IN-PUBLICATION DATA
BECHDEL, ALISON, DATE.
ARE YOU MY MOTHER? : A COMIC DRAMA / ALISON BECHDEL.
P.  CM.
ISBN 978-0-618-98250-9  ISBN 978-0-544-00223-4 (PBK.)
1. BECHDEL, ALISON, DATE.—COMIC BOOKS, STRIPS, ETC.
2. CARTOONISTS—UNITED STATES—COMIC BOOKS, STRIPS, ETC.
3. GRAPHIC NOVELS. I. TITLE.
PN6727.B3757Z46 2012
741.5'973—DC23  [B]  2012010582

PRINTED IN THE UNITED STATES OF AMERICA
DOC 10 9 8 7 6 5 4 3 2

"LIAISONS" FROM *A LITTLE NIGHT MUSIC*. WORDS AND MUSIC BY STEPHEN SONDHEIM © 1973 (RENEWED)
RILTING MUSIC, INC. ALL RIGHTS ADMINISTERED BY WB MUSIC CORP. ALL RIGHTS RESERVED. USED BY PERMISSION.
REPRINTED BY PERMISSION OF HAL LEONARD CORPORATION.

"THE GLAMOROUS LIFE" FROM THE FILM VERSION OF *A LITTLE NIGHT MUSIC*.
WORDS AND MUSIC BY STEPHEN SONDHEIM © 1973 (RENEWED) RILTING MUSIC, INC. ALL RIGHTS ADMINISTERED
BY WB MUSIC CORP. ALL RIGHTS RESERVED. USED BY PERMISSION.
REPRINTED BY PERMISSION OF HAL LEONARD CORPORATION.

For nothing was simply one thing.
~*Virginia Woolf*

# CONTENTS

# The Ordinary Devoted Mother

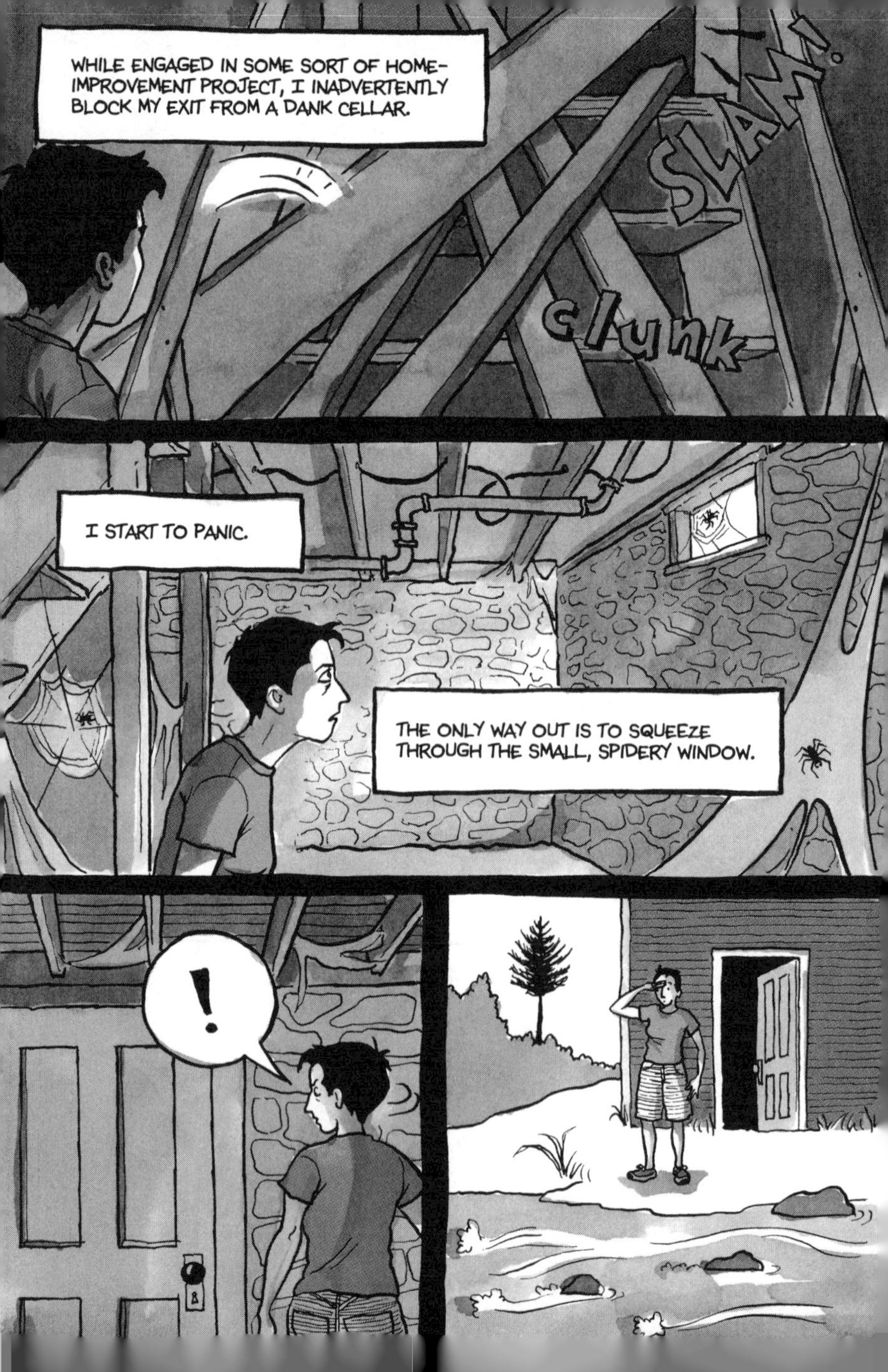
WHILE ENGAGED IN SOME SORT OF HOME-IMPROVEMENT PROJECT, I INADVERTENTLY BLOCK MY EXIT FROM A DANK CELLAR.
SLAM!
clunk
I START TO PANIC.
THE ONLY WAY OUT IS TO SQUEEZE THROUGH THE SMALL, SPIDERY WINDOW.
!

I WALK ALONG THE BROOK, LOOKING FOR A PLACE TO CROSS.

THE STEPPING STONES ARE UNDERWATER.

THE POOL IS DEEP AND MURKY. IT'S WARM OUT. I'M NOT WEARING ANYTHING I NEED TO WORRY ABOUT GETTING WET.

I HAVE SOME CONCERN ABOUT THE DIRTY WATER...

..BUT THIS ONLY SLIGHTLY DIMINISHES A SUBLIME FEELING OF SURRENDER.

This story begins when I began to tell another story.

I had the dream about the brook right before I told my mother I was writing a memoir about my father.

...I HAVE SOMETHING TO TELL YOU.

MOM, I WANT TO TELL YOU SOME-THING.

THE EMOTION OF THE DREAM STUCK WITH ME FOR DAYS. I HAD GOTTEN MYSELF OUT OF A DEAD PLACE AND PLUNGED WITH BLIND TRUST INTO A VITAL, SENSUOUS ONE.

OKAY. THEN SHE'LL SAY, "WHAT?"

AND I'LL SAY...

WHAT? WHAT WILL YOU SAY, ALISON?

YOU SMARMY, SELF-INDULGENT, SOLIPSISTIC PIECE OF *SHIT*.

OKAY.

I'LL SAY, "I'M WRITING A BOOK ABOUT DAD."

AND SHE'LL SAY, **"WHAAAAT?!!"**

I'D HAD SOME PRACTICE IN TELL-ING MY MOTHER DIFFICULT THINGS.

I FELT KIND OF LIKE I DID TWENTY YEARS EARLIER, WHEN I WAS PREPARING TO TELL HER I WAS A LESBIAN.

WHY AM I TELLING HER AT ALL?

AND KIND OF LIKE I DID FIVE YEARS BEFORE THAT, WHEN I WAS WORKING UP THE COURAGE TO TELL HER I'D GOTTEN MY FIRST PERIOD. THAT HAD TAKEN ME SIX MONTHS.

OKAY, SO SHE MIGHT FREAK OUT AT FIRST, BUT THEN SHE'LL SAY, "WHY?"

THIS STORY--A MEMOIR ABOUT MY MOTHER--COULD BEGIN WITH EITHER OF THOSE SCENES.

UHH...IT'S JUST SOMETHING I NEED TO DO.

... AND SHE'LL SAY, "WHY?"

I WANT TO GIVE HIM A PROPER FUNERAL. I WANT TO TELL THE TRUTH.

BUT AS I CONSIDER MOVING THE BEGINNING FURTHER BACK IN TIME, BEFORE THE COMING OUT, BEFORE THE FIRST PERIOD...

"THE **TRUTH**?!"

Scranton

...I SEE THAT PERHAPS THE REAL PROBLEM WITH THIS MEMOIR ABOUT MY MOTHER IS THAT IT HAS NO BEGINNING.

YEAH. HIS BISEXUALITY, THE SUICIDE. YOU DON'T MIND, DO YOU?

SORT OF LIKE HOW I'D UNDERSTOOD HUMAN REPRODUCTION AS A CHILD. I WAS AN EGG IN-SIDE MY MOTHER WHEN SHE WAS STILL AN EGG INSIDE HER MOTHER, AND SO FORTH AND SO ON.

A DIZZYING, INFINITE REGRESS.

I DON'T WANT TO HURT YOU BUT I HAVE TO DO THIS.

THERE'S A CERTAIN RELIEF IN KNOWING THAT I AM A TERMINUS.

EVEN IF I'D EVER HAD THE SLIGHTEST URGE TO REPRODUCE, IT'S TOO LATE NOW. I'M RUNNING OUT OF EGGS.

MY CLOCKWORKLIKE MENSTRUAL CYCLE SKIPPED ITS FIRST BEAT THE VERY WEEK, IN MY FORTY-FIFTH YEAR, THAT I SAT DOWN TO BEGIN WRITING ABOUT MY MOTHER.

I HOPE THAT IN TIME YOU'LL COME TO UNDERSTAND...

OF COURSE, THE POINT AT WHICH I BEGAN TO WRITE THE STORY IS NOT THE SAME AS THE POINT AT WHICH THE STORY BEGINS.

OH, THAT'S GOOD. SANCTIMONIOUS AND PATRONIZING.

YOU CAN'T LIVE AND WRITE AT THE SAME TIME.

?

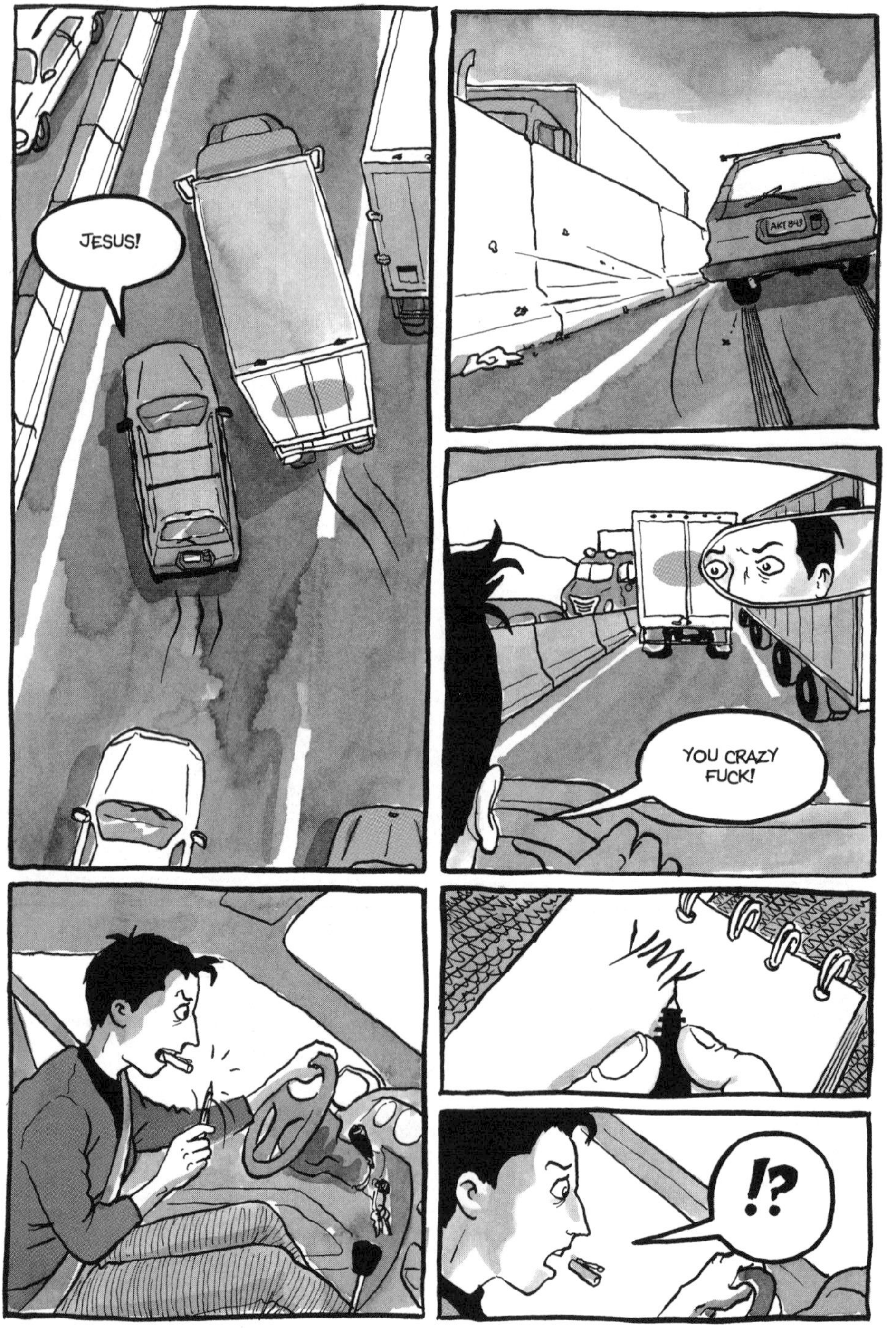
JESUS!
YOU CRAZY FUCK!
!?

IT HAD BEEN A STROEHMANN SUNBEAM BREAD TRUCK THAT KILLED MY FATHER...

...THAT MY FATHER LIKELY JUMPED IN FRONT OF.

AFTER SUCH A CURIOUSLY LITERAL AND FIGURA-TIVE BRUSH WITH DEATH, TELLING MY MOTHER ABOUT THE BOOK LOOMED RATHER SMALLER.

AND A FEW DAYS LATER, RETURNING WITH HER FROM A STRING OF ERRANDS, I DID IT.

YOU MEAN, THIS IS SOMETHING YOU HAVE TO DO?

WELL, YEAH.

I CAN'T HELP YOU. YOU'RE ON YOUR OWN.

ON THE WHOLE, IT WENT AS WELL AS I COULD HAVE HOPED. MOM'S BOYFRIEND, BOB, CAME OVER FOR DINNER THAT NIGHT.

SHE SAYS IT'S SOMETHING SHE HAS TO DO.

AND YOU'RE OKAY WITH IT?

I FEEL RECKLESS. TELL EVERYONE.

I'M GONNA GO DO MY PUZZLE.

BOB IS A RETIRED PSYCHIATRIST. HE HAD SOME INSIGHT INTO MY BROOK DREAM.

WATER IS USUALLY ABOUT CREATIVITY. THAT SEEMS AUSPICIOUS FOR YOUR PROJECT.

I JUST HOPE IT WON'T BE ALL ANGRY, ALL ABOUT HOW AWFUL YOUR FATHER WAS.

THIS IS ONE OF MY DIFFICULTIES NOW...

...MY FEAR THAT MOM WILL FIND THIS MEMOIR ABOUT HER "ANGRY." ANOTHER DIFFICULTY IS THE FACT THAT THE STORY OF MY MOTHER AND ME IS UNFOLDING EVEN AS I WRITE IT.

DID YOU SEE DANIEL MENDELSOHN'S ARTICLE ON MEMOIR IN *THE NEW YORKER*?

IT'S GOOD. ISN'T HE THE ONE WHO BEAT YOU FOR THAT PRIZE?

UH...NO.

UH... YEAH.

YET ANOTHER DIFFICULTY IS THE FACT THAT MY MOTHER CONSIDERS MEMOIR A SUSPECT GENRE. THIS ADDS A CONFUSING OBSERVER EFFECT TO THE WHOLE PROCESS.

WHAT'S IT ABOUT?

OH, YOU KNOW. INACCURACY, EXHIBITIONISM, NARCISSISM, THOSE FAKE MEMOIRS.

INDEED, MY FOREMOST DIFFICULTY IS THE EXTENT TO WHICH I HAVE INTERNALIZED MY MOTHER'S CRITICAL FACULTIES.

AS OF THIS MOMENT, I'VE BEEN STRUGGLING FOR FOUR YEARS WITH THE WRITING OF THIS BOOK, THIS MEMOIR ABOUT MY MOTHER.

DID I TELL YOU I'M ORDERING THAT CHLORINE-RESISTANT SWIMSUIT?

I TALK TO MY MOTHER ALMOST EVERY DAY. THAT IS, I CALL, SHE TALKS, I LISTEN. THAT'S OUR PATTERN.

IT COSTS A HUNDRED DOLLARS, BUT I GO THROUGH SEVERAL SPEEDOS A YEAR.

I MUST CONFESS THAT I HAVE TAKEN TO TRANSCRIBING WHAT SHE SAYS. I DON'T THINK SHE KNOWS I'M DOING IT, WHICH MAKES IT A BIT UNETHICAL.

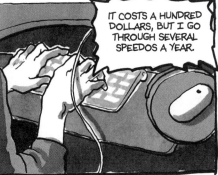

1/29/2010, 4:15pm
article in New Yorker on memoir
Isn't daniel mendelsohn the one who be

A new chlorine-resistant swimsuit, for $1
Maybe I'll decide to spring for it. I go thr
not sure about size. Sizes don't mean anything any more?

THE ARCHITECTURAL REVIEW BOARD SAID SHE COULDN'T PUT UP VINYL SID-ING, BUT THE TOWN OVERRULED THEM BECAUSE SHE'S A POOR WIDOW.

somebody bought that house down the street when it was up for auction, and th
flipped it. They covered up the original painted brick and slapped on vinyl siding
They ruined it. You know how it was when I moved up here. A woman wanted t
up vinyl siding and the arch. review board said no, but the town overruled them

BUT I WANT TO CAPTURE HER VOICE, HER PRECISE WORDING, HER DEADPAN HUMOR. I DON'T THINK I COULD POSSIBLY RE-CREATE IT ON MY OWN.

WELL, I'M A POOR WIDOW, TOO, AND I DON'T WANT TO LOOK AT VINYL SIDING!

I'M TRYING SO HARD TO GET DOWN WHAT SHE'S SAYING THAT I'M NOT REALLY LISTENING PROPERLY.

UH HUH...

I WOULD HAVE MORE SCRUPLES ABOUT THIS, I LIKE TO THINK, IF I DIDN'T SUSPECT THAT SHE WAS NOT SO MUCH TALKING TO ME AS DRAFTING HER OWN DAILY JOURNAL ENTRY OUT LOUD.

MY MOTHER HAS ALWAYS KEPT A JOURNAL. SHE INSISTS THIS IS JUST A RECORD OF THINGS SHE'S DONE. OF EXTERNAL, AS OPPOSED TO INTERNAL, EXPERIENCE.

I SHARE THIS COMPULSION FOR KEEPING TRACK OF LIFE.

MY MOTHER LOGS HER DAILY ACTIVITIES IN HER JOURNAL. AND EVERY DAY SHE READS ANOTHER JOURNAL—THE NEW YORK TIMES.

IF YOU'RE GOING OUT, CAN YOU GET ME A COPY OF TO-DAY'S PAPER?

NOT ONLINE. THE NEWSPRINT, THE THING ITSELF.

THE TRUCK DIDN'T GET HERE BECAUSE OF THE BLIZZARD, SO NO ONE HAS IT.

YOU WANT ME TO MAIL TODAY'S *NEW YORK TIMES* FROM VERMONT TO PENNSYLVANIA?

I KNOW! IT'S MY OCD. BUT I HATE MISSING ANY NEWS. AND THE PUZZLE.

I OFTEN THINK OF THIS PASSAGE FROM VIRGINIA WOOLF'S DIARY: "WHAT A DISGRACEFUL LAPSE! NOTHING ADDED TO MY DISQUISITION, & LIFE ALLOWED TO WASTE LIKE A TAP LEFT RUNNING. ELEVEN DAYS UNRECORDED."

I STARTED MY OWN DIARY AS A CHILD. AND WHEN A SPELL OF OBSESSIVE-COMPULSIVE DISORDER MADE MY ENTRIES TOO TIME-CONSUMING, MY MOTHER SAT ON MY BED AND TOOK DICTATION.

MOTHER WENT TO SCHOOL TO SUBSTITUTE TEACH. MARY-JO BROUGHT IN A LOVE TEST THAT WE DID ON THE BUS.

GETTING HER UNDIVIDED ATTENTION WAS A RARE TREAT. IT FELT MIRACULOUS, ACTUALLY--LIKE PERSUADING A HUMMINGBIRD TO PERCH ON YOUR FINGER.

I DIDN'T GET MUCH DONE. I WENT TO MY PIANO LESSON. I GOT BACH'S MINUET.

SHE WAS LISTENING TO ME. WHATEVER I SAID, SHE WROTE DOWN.

I FOUND THIS CALMING. COMPOSING.

MY MOTHER COMPOSED ME AS I NOW COMPOSE HER.

SHE LIKES TO USE SCRUBBING BUBBLES, BUT I TOLD HER TO USE THE COMET.

THE RUNNING TAP OF HER LIFE FLOWS THROUGH MY FINGERS.

SOMETIMES THERE WILL BE A LULL AND MY MOTHER WILL ASK ME THIS QUESTION:

HOW ARE YOU DOING?

MY CONSIDERABLE VERBAL APTITUDE OFTEN FAILS ME COMPLETELY WHEN I'M TALKING TO MY MOTHER.

When she cleans the bathroo to use the comet.

She asks how I'm doing.

THROUGHOUT MY TWENTIES AND THIRTIES, SHE NEVER ASKED ME ABOUT MY LIFE.

EVEN NOW, WHEN SHE POSES THE QUESTION POINT-BLANK, I KNOW HER ATTENTION FOR MY ANSWER IS LIMITED.

UHH...

THE PRESSURE TO BE CONCISE, ENTERTAINING, AND APPOSITE IN THIS SMALL WINDOW IS FIERCE. MORE OFTEN THAN NOT, I PASS WITH A "FINE. NOTHING NEW TO REPORT."

I...

BUT I KNOW I CAN'T BLAME HER FOR DOMINATING OUR CONVERSATIONS IF I REFUSE TO PARTICIPATE. SO SOMETIMES, LIKE TODAY, I DIVULGE SOMETHING.

I HAVE TO REWRITE MY BOOK.

WHAT?!

I HAVE TO START OVER. I...I FEEL LIKE I'M WRITING AROUND SOMETHING.

HA!

SHE'S LAUGHING IN WHAT SEEMS LIKE AN UNDERSTANDING WAY. SHE DOESN'T ASK ME WHAT IT IS THAT I'M WRITING AROUND.

YOU HAVE TOO MANY STRANDS!

SHE KNOWS THIS BOOK IS ABOUT MY RELATIONSHIP WITH HER, AND SHE SEEMS TO FEEL ABOUT IT ROUGHLY THE WAY SHE FELT ABOUT THE BOOK ON MY FATHER--RESIGNED.

WELL, I READ IT IN THE WRONG ORDER. I COULDN'T FIGURE OUT THE PAGINATION. I'LL HAVE TO LOOK AT IT AGAIN.

I HAD RECENTLY SENT HER WHAT I THOUGHT WAS THE FIRST CHAPTER. WE DISCUSSED IT, FOR ABOUT THREE MINUTES, DURING MY CHRISTMAS VISIT.

THE CHAPTER HAD BEEN A TURGID ABSTRACTION ABOUT THE SELF AND DESIRE THAT BARELY MENTIONED MY MOTHER.

ALISON, YOU SHOULD JUST WRITE WHATEVER YOU WANT TO WRITE.

HER TONE WAS WEARY BUT NOT UNKIND. SHE SEEMED TO BE SAYING, "WRITE ABOUT ME IF YOU MUST, BUT DON'T ASK ME TO APPROVE IT."

WELL... THANK YOU.

TWO NIGHTS AFTER RECEIVING THIS MIXED BLESSING, I HAD AN ECHO OF THE BROOK DREAM I'D HAD TEN YEARS EARLIER. I WAS SOMEWHAT BETTER EQUIPPED THIS TIME.

I WAS INSIDE A CAVE, ON AN UNDERGROUND LAKE.

THE ONLY WAY OUT WAS TO DIVE INTO THE WATER AND SWIM UNDERNEATH THE ROCK LEDGE. IF I DID THIS, I'D COME UP ON THE OTHER SIDE, UNDER THE OPEN SKY.

I KNEW I COULD MAKE IT, BUT AT THE SAME TIME I WAS TERRIFIED OF GETTING STUCK DOWN THERE. I STALLED, FUSSING WITH MY MASK TO GET A GOOD SEAL.

FINALLY, I HAD DETERMINED TO JUMP...

...WHEN I WOKE UP.

I TOOK THIS DREAM, LIKE THE EARLIER ONE, AS A GOOD SIGN, AN INDICATION THAT I WAS GETTING SOMEWHERE WITH MY WRITING.

BUT WITHIN A FEW DAYS, IT BECAME CLEAR THAT "GETTING SOME-WHERE" MEANT STARTING OVER. THIS FELT ODDLY ENCOURAGING.

Thursday, January 28
week 4 of 2010

173days

7

8AM Write

IT HAD BEEN FIVE MONTHS SINCE THIS BOOK WAS DUE, AND SIX SINCE MY LAST PERIOD.

LIKE MY MOTHER, I KEEP A LOG OF THE EVENTS OF DAILY, EXTERNAL LIFE. BUT UNLIKE HER, I ALSO RECORD A GREAT DEAL OF INFOR-MATION ABOUT MY INTERNAL LIFE.

ALTHOUGH I'M OFTEN CONFUSED ABOUT PRECISELY WHERE THE DEMARCATION LIES.

VIRGINIA WOOLF SEEMS TO HAVE CONSIDERED HER OWN DIARY TO BE MORE OF AN EXTERNAL RECORD, AN ACCOUNT OF "LIFE" RATHER THAN "THE SOUL."

Monday 19 February

How it would interest me if this diary were ever to become a real diary: something in which I could see changes, trace moods developing; but then I should have to speak of the soul, & did I not banish the soul when I began? What happens is, as usual, that I'm going to write about the soul, & life breaks in. Talking of diaries sets me thinking of old Kate, in the dining room at 4 Rosary Gardens; & how she opened the cabinet (wh. I remember) & there in a row on a shelf were her diaries from Jan 1 1877.[13] Some were brown; others red; all the same to a t. And I made her read an entry; one of many thousand days, like pebbles

WOOLF'S DISMISSAL OF "THE SOUL" REMINDS ME A BIT OF MY MOTHER'S INSISTENCE THAT HER OWN JOURNAL IS LITTLE MORE THAN A COMPLETED TO-DO LIST, THAT SHE NEVER RE-READS IT...

...THAT IN FACT SHE'S THROWN WHOLE CHUNKS OF IT AWAY.

To the Lighthouse
Virginia Woolf

MOMENTS of BEING

AUTOBIOGRAPHICAL WRITING

Virginia WOOLF

The DIARY of VIRGINIA WOOLF

VOLUME TWO
1920-1923

NOON

I'M SURE THESE THINGS ARE TRUE.

BUT THE WAY SHE SAYS THEM FEELS LIKE AN IMPLIED CRITICISM. AS IF SHE'S COMPARING HER OWN SELFLESS-NESS TO MY SELF-ABSORPTION.

BUT OF COURSE THAT'S JUST EVIDENCE OF MY SELF-ABSORPTION. MY MOTHER IS PROBABLY NOT THINKING ANYTHING LIKE THIS.

IN FACT, MY DESIRE TO THINK THAT SHE'S THINKING OF ME AT ALL IS A BIT PATHETIC.

SHE LOOMS MUCH LARGER IN MY PSYCHE THAN I LOOM IN HERS. WOOLF SAYS THAT HER OWN MOTHER, WHO DIED WHEN VIRGINIA WAS THIRTEEN, OBSESSED HER UNTIL SHE WAS FORTY-FOUR.

when I was thirteen, until I was forty-four. Then one day walking round Tavistock Square I made up, as I sometimes make up my books, *To the Lighthouse*; in a great, apparently involuntary, rush. One thing burst into another. Blowing bubbles out of a pipe

LET'S LEAVE ASIDE THE ANNOYING RAPIDITY WITH WHICH SHE DISPATCHED THIS MASTERPIECE. THE POINT IS, WHAT HAPPENED AFTERWARD.

when it was written, I ceased to be obsessed by my mother. I no longer hear her voice; I do not see her. I suppose that I did for myself what psycho-analysts do for their patients. I expressed some very long felt and deeply felt emotion. And in expressing it I explained it and then laid it to rest. But what is

I'VE BEEN IN THERAPY FOR NEARLY MY ENTIRE ADULT LIFE AND HAVE NOT LAID MY DEEPLY FELT EMOTIONS ABOUT MY MOTHER TO REST.

MY LIFE IS A MESS. I'VE BEEN IN A REALLY SOLID RELATIONSHIP FOR EIGHT YEARS...

BUT I KEEP GET-TING ATTRACTED TO OTHER PEOPLE.

I STARTED SEEING MY CURRENT THERAPIST, CAROL, TEN YEARS AGO.

I'M WRITING THIS MEMOIR ABOUT MY DAD'S SUICIDE AND FOR EVERY SENTENCE I PUT DOWN, I DELETE TWO.

I JUST FEEL LIKE I'M IN MY OWN FUCKING WAY ALL THE TIME.

IT'S LIKE...LIKE I'M HOBBLED SOMEHOW.

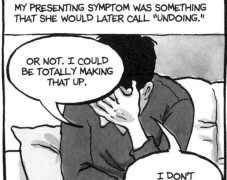

MY PRESENTING SYMPTOM WAS SOMETHING THAT SHE WOULD LATER CALL "UNDOING."

OR NOT. I COULD BE TOTALLY MAKING THAT UP.

I DON'T KNOW!

BUT LONG BEFORE CAROL, THERE WAS JOCELYN. I STARTED SEEING HER WHEN I WAS TWENTY-SIX.

WHEN I WAS LITTLE, I'D GET MY MOM TO PLAY THE "CRIPPLED CHILD" GAME WITH ME.

SANTA FE
CHAMBER MUSIC FESTIVAL

I HAD, LIKE, FLAT FEET OR SOMETHING, AND HAD TO WEAR CORRECTIVE SHOES. AND EVERY SO OFTEN I'D GO TO THE HOSPITAL FOR A CHECKUP.

I'D SEE ALL THESE OTHER KIDS THERE WITH BRACES AND CRUTCHES AND STUFF, Y'KNOW? REALLY DISABLED.

I WAS FASCINATED WITH THEM.

ACTUALLY, I KIND OF ENVIED THEM.

I'D PRETEND I WAS A "CRIPPLED" CHILD, AND MOM WOULD PLAY ALONG WITH IT.

YOU'LL NEED THESE CRUTCHES.

IT WAS SO FUN. WHER- EVER I WENT WITH THE FANTASY, SHE WAS RIGHT THERE.

FOR MY FIRST TWO YEARS WITH CAROL, I JUST SAT ON THE COUCH. BUT THEN I BEGAN LYING DOWN ON IT. IN THE TIME I'VE BEEN SEEING HER, SHE HAS BECOME A PSYCHOANALYST.

WHY AM I LYING HERE?

ANALYSIS AND THERAPY ARE DIFFERENT IN MANY WAYS, BUT THE SEATING ARRANGE- MENT IS A BIG ONE.

I SHOULD BE WORKING.

IN THIS POSITION THE PATIENT CAN'T SEE THE ANALYST. AND LYING DOWN, IN THEORY, ALLOWS MORE READY ACCESS TO THE UNCONSCIOUS.

I'M NEVER GONNA GET THIS FUCKING BOOK DONE.

ANALYSIS IS IN NO HURRY TO GET TO THE BOTTOM OF THINGS. THERAPY IS USUALLY A SHORTER-TERM PROPOSITION, MORE FOCUSED ON SYMPTOM RELIEF.

I CAN'T TELL WHETHER IT'S NORMAL CREATIVE STRIFE OR MENOPAUSAL INSANITY.

ALSO, A PSYCHOANALYST MUST UNDERGO A TRAINING ANALYSIS OF THEIR OWN.

ONE REASON THIS MEMOIR IS TAKING ME SO LONG IS THAT I'M TRYING TO FIGURE OUT––FROM BOTH SIDES OF THE COUCH––JUST WHAT IT IS THAT PSYCHO-ANALYSTS DO FOR THEIR PATIENTS.

IN PARTICULAR, I HAVE BEEN STUDYING THE WORK OF THE BRITISH PSYCHOANALYST AND PEDIATRICIAN DONALD WINNICOTT.

PLUS I STILL CAN'T FIGURE OUT HOW TO FIT WINNICOTT IN.

IT HAS TAKEN ME SEVERAL YEARS TO FEEL AS IF I HAVE EVEN A SLENDER GRASP OF HIS CURIOUSLY COMPELLING IDEAS.

WHAT IS IT ABOUT HIM THAT YOU'RE SO DRAWN TO?

I WANT HIM TO BE MY MOTHER.

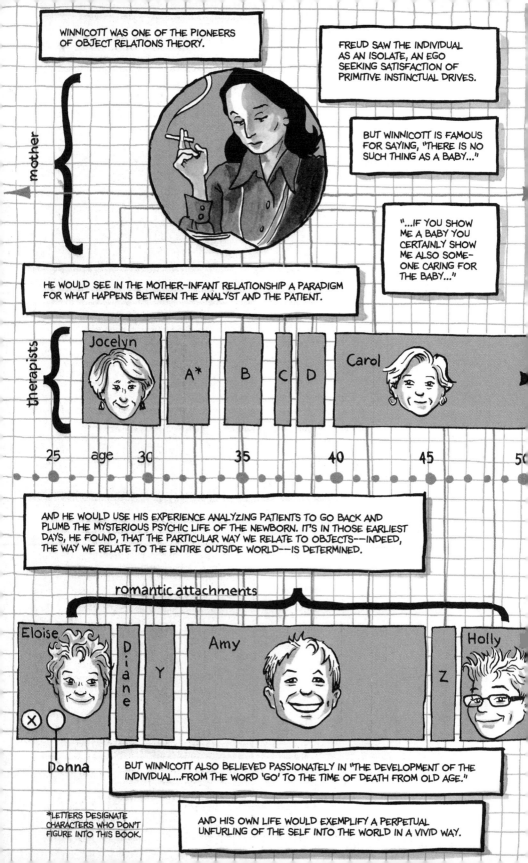

WINNICOTT WAS ONE OF THE PIONEERS OF OBJECT RELATIONS THEORY.

FREUD SAW THE INDIVIDUAL AS AN ISOLATE, AN EGO SEEKING SATISFACTION OF PRIMITIVE INSTINCTUAL DRIVES.

BUT WINNICOTT IS FAMOUS FOR SAYING, "THERE IS NO SUCH THING AS A BABY..."

"...IF YOU SHOW ME A BABY YOU CERTAINLY SHOW ME ALSO SOME-ONE CARING FOR THE BABY..."

mother

HE WOULD SEE IN THE MOTHER-INFANT RELATIONSHIP A PARADIGM FOR WHAT HAPPENS BETWEEN THE ANALYST AND THE PATIENT.

therapists

Jocelyn

A*

B

C

D

Carol

25    age    30    35    40    45    50

AND HE WOULD USE HIS EXPERIENCE ANALYZING PATIENTS TO GO BACK AND PLUMB THE MYSTERIOUS PSYCHIC LIFE OF THE NEWBORN. IT'S IN THOSE EARLIEST DAYS, HE FOUND, THAT THE PARTICULAR WAY WE RELATE TO OBJECTS--INDEED, THE WAY WE RELATE TO THE ENTIRE OUTSIDE WORLD--IS DETERMINED.

romantic attachments

Eloise

Diane

Y

Amy

Z

Holly

⊗  ○
Donna

BUT WINNICOTT ALSO BELIEVED PASSIONATELY IN "THE DEVELOPMENT OF THE INDIVIDUAL...FROM THE WORD 'GO' TO THE TIME OF DEATH FROM OLD AGE."

*LETTERS DESIGNATE CHARACTERS WHO DON'T FIGURE INTO THIS BOOK.

AND HIS OWN LIFE WOULD EXEMPLIFY A PERPETUAL UNFURLING OF THE SELF INTO THE WORLD IN A VIVID WAY.

WHY DO YOU WANT HIM TO BE YOUR MOTHER?

I DUNNO.

BUT I KNOW THAT IF HE HAD BEEN MY MOTHER, I WOULDN'T BE SUFFERING OVER THIS BOOK.

I'D BE DOING SOMETHING USEFUL.

THE THING IS, I CAN'T WRITE THIS BOOK UNTIL I GET HER OUT OF MY HEAD.

BUT THE ONLY WAY TO GET HER OUT OF MY HEAD IS BY WRITING THE BOOK!

IT'S A PARADOX.

MY MOTHER'S EDITORIAL VOICE--PRECISIAN, DISPASSIONATE, ELEGANT, ADVERBLESS--IS LODGED DEEP IN MY TEMPORAL LOBES.

OR A DILEMMA OR SOMETHING.

I DON'T KNOW.

I DON'T KNOW ANYTHING.

HOW I ENVY THE INVOLUNTARY TORRENT OF WORDS AND IMAGES THAT CAME TO VIRGINIA WOOLF THAT DAY IN TAVISTOCK SQUARE.

IT WAS SOMETIME BETWEEN OCTOBER 1924 AND THE FOLLOWING SPRING.

WOOLF NEVER UNDERWENT PSYCHOANALYSIS. HER BROTHER ADRIAN DID, THOUGH.

VIRGINIA WROTE RATHER SNIDELY TO HER SISTER, "I GATHER THAT HIS TRAGEDY—AS THE DR. CALLS IT—IS ALL OUR DOING. HE WAS SUPPRESSED AS A CHILD."

WOOLF WOULDN'T REALLY READ FREUD FOR ANOTHER TEN YEARS OR SO...

...THOUGH THE HOGARTH PRESS, WHICH SHE FOUNDED WITH HER HUSBAND, LEONARD, HAD JUST PUBLISHED HIS COLLECTED PAPERS.

THESE HAD BEEN TRANSLATED BY JAMES AND ALIX STRACHEY, THE BROTHER AND SISTER-IN-LAW OF VIRGINIA'S CLOSE FRIEND LYTTON.

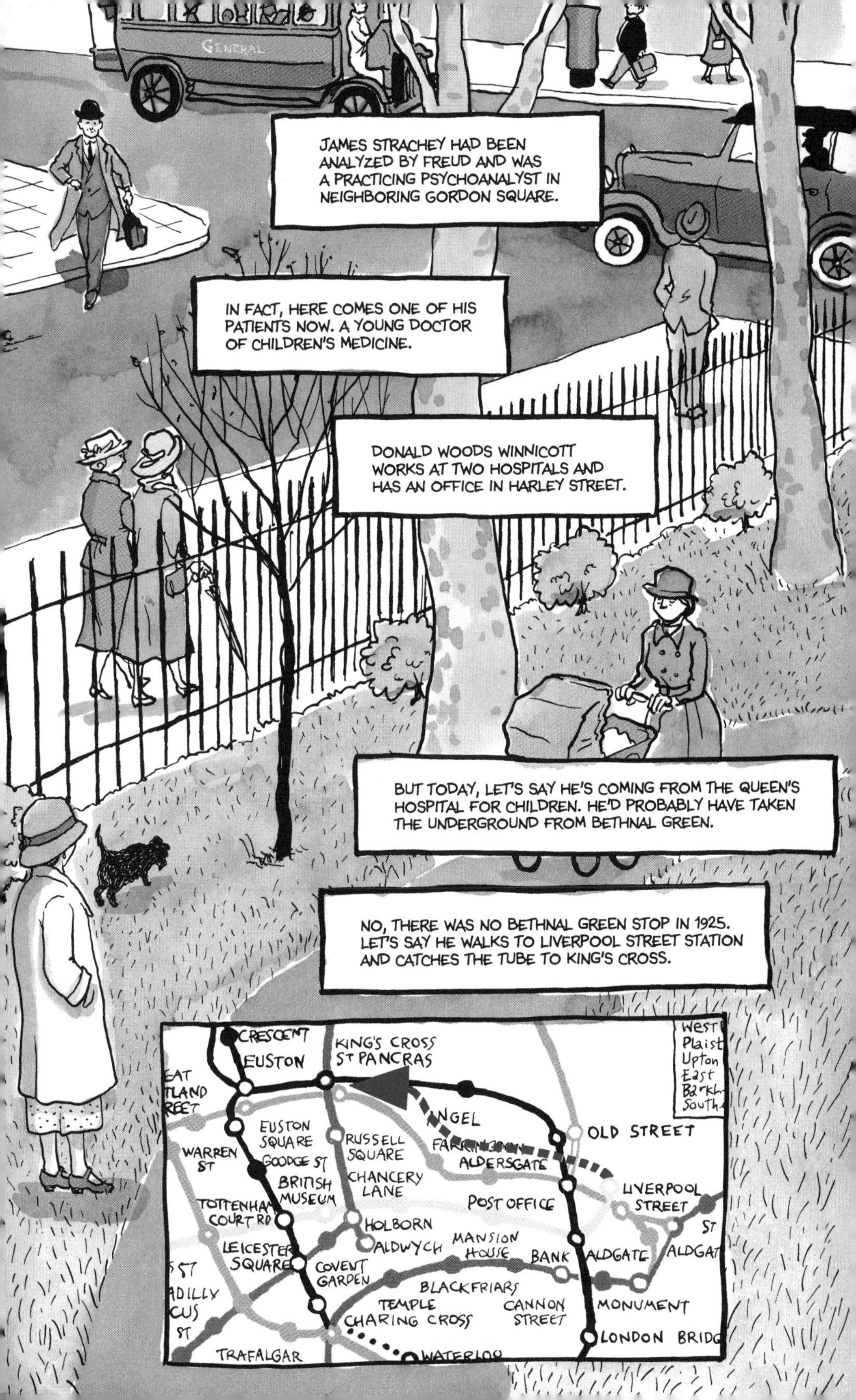
GENERAL
JAMES STRACHEY HAD BEEN ANALYZED BY FREUD AND WAS A PRACTICING PSYCHOANALYST IN NEIGHBORING GORDON SQUARE.
IN FACT, HERE COMES ONE OF HIS PATIENTS NOW. A YOUNG DOCTOR OF CHILDREN'S MEDICINE.
DONALD WOODS WINNICOTT WORKS AT TWO HOSPITALS AND HAS AN OFFICE IN HARLEY STREET.
BUT TODAY, LET'S SAY HE'S COMING FROM THE QUEEN'S HOSPITAL FOR CHILDREN. HE'D PROBABLY HAVE TAKEN THE UNDERGROUND FROM BETHNAL GREEN.
NO, THERE WAS NO BETHNAL GREEN STOP IN 1925. LET'S SAY HE WALKS TO LIVERPOOL STREET STATION AND CATCHES THE TUBE TO KING'S CROSS.
CRESCENT
EUSTON
KING'S CROSS ST PANCRAS
OLD STREET
EUSTON SQUARE
RUSSELL SQUARE
WARREN ST
GOODGE ST
ALDERSGATE
CHANCERY LANE
BRITISH MUSEUM
LIVERPOOL STREET
TOTTENHAM COURT RD
POST OFFICE
HOLBORN
ALDWYCH
MANSION HOUSE
LEICESTER SQUARE
BANK
ALDGATE
COVENT GARDEN
BLACKFRIARS
TEMPLE
CANNON STREET
MONUMENT
CHARING CROSS
LONDON
TRAFALGAR

PERHAPS HE PLOTS THIS TRAJECTORY TO STRACHEY'S HOUSE:

AS HE REACHES THE TOP OF TAVISTOCK SQUARE, SO DOES VIRGINIA WOOLF.

DESPITE THE STRACHEY CONNECTION, IT'S DOUBTFUL THEY KNOW ONE ANOTHER.

DONALD IS TWENTY-NINE, THE SON OF A MERCHANT, IN AWE OF HIS ANALYST'S CULTIVATED BLOOMSBURY WORLD.

WOOLF IS AT THE CENTER OF THAT WORLD, MIDDLE-AGED AND BECOMING FAMOUS.

WINNICOTT WILL EVENTUALLY BE PUBLISHED BY THE HOGARTH PRESS, BUT NOT UNTIL SOME TIME AFTER VIRGINIA'S DEATH.

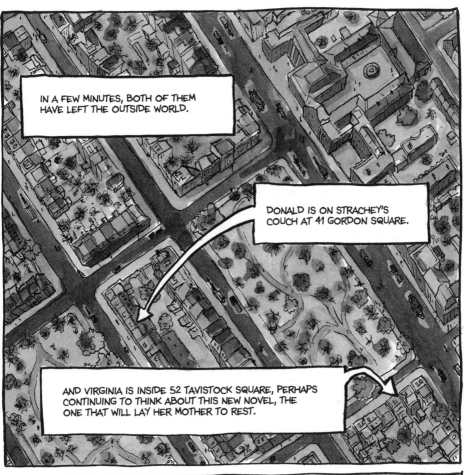

IN A FEW MINUTES, BOTH OF THEM HAVE LEFT THE OUTSIDE WORLD.

DONALD IS ON STRACHEY'S COUCH AT 41 GORDON SQUARE.

AND VIRGINIA IS INSIDE 52 TAVISTOCK SQUARE, PERHAPS CONTINUING TO THINK ABOUT THIS NEW NOVEL, THE ONE THAT WILL LAY HER MOTHER TO REST.

DONALD IS VERY POSSIBLY THINKING ABOUT HIS MOTHER, TOO. SHE HAS EITHER JUST DIED, OR WILL DIE BEFORE 1925 IS OUT. I CAN'T FIND THE EXACT DATE.

MY MOTHER WAS DISGUISED IN A BEARSKIN. THEN HER PENIS POPPED OUT AND CASTRATED ME.

THIS WAS AN ACTUAL DREAM OF WINNICOTT'S. ALTHOUGH I AM ENJOYING THIS LITTLE FORAY INTO FICTION, I FEEL THE NECESSITY OF "CLINGING AS TIGHT TO FACTS AS I CAN," AS WOOLF WROTE IN HER 1923 DIARY ABOUT HER PROGRESS ON *MRS. DALLOWAY.*

BUT I AM NOT ULTIMATELY INTERESTED IN WRITING FICTION. I CAN'T MAKE THINGS UP. OR RATHER, I CAN ONLY MAKE THINGS UP ABOUT THINGS THAT HAVE ALREADY HAPPENED.

I HAVE TO REWRITE MY BOOK.

WHAT?!

I HAVE TO START OVER.

ONCE MY MOTHER TOLD ME SHE WISHED I HAD WRITTEN THE BOOK ABOUT MY FATHER AS FICTION.

ON THE THEORY THAT IT WOULD NOT HAVE EXPOSED OUR FAMILY IN THE WAY MEMOIR DID.

I EXPLAINED THAT THE WHOLE POINT OF THE BOOK WAS THAT IT WAS TRUE, AND THAT EVEN IF I HAD FICTIONALIZED IT, PEOPLE WOULD ASSUME IT WAS AUTOBIOGRAPHICAL.

HA! YOU HAVE TOO MANY STRANDS!

THIS HAD NOT SWAYED HER. *TO THE LIGHTHOUSE* IS FICTION, OF COURSE, BUT HEAVILY AUTOBIOGRAPHICAL.

I DO. I JUST NEED TO TELL A STORY.

IN THE SAME WAY VIRGINIA WOOLF DISTINGUISHES BETWEEN "LIFE" AND "THE SOUL" IN HER DIARY, SHE DISTINGUISHES BETWEEN "TWO KINDS OF TRUTH" IN WRITING BIOGRAPHY.

YES. NARRATIVE IS WHAT THEY WANT.

BUT IT'S HARD TO FIGURE OUT WHAT THE STORY IS.

"LET THE BIOGRAPHER PRINT FULLY, COMPLETELY, ACCURATELY, THE KNOWN FACTS WITHOUT COMMENT; THEN LET HIM WRITE THE LIFE AS FICTION."

IN *TO THE LIGHTHOUSE*, THE CHARACTER LILY BRISCOE HAS A BRIEF VISION AS SHE WATCHES MR. AND MRS. RAMSAY PLAYING CATCH WITH THEIR CHILDREN.

ing catches. And suddenly the meaning which, for no reason at all, as perhaps they are stepping out of the Tube or ringing a doorbell, descends on people, making them symbolical, making them representative, came upon them, and made them in the dusk standing, looking, the symbols of marriage, husband and wife. Then, after an instant, the symbolical outline which transcended the real figures sank down again, and they became, as they met them, Mr. and Mrs. Ramsay watching the children throwing catches. But still for a mo-

THIS "SYMBOLI-CAL" QUALITY THAT TRANSCENDS MERE "REAL FIGURES" SEEMS TO BE WHAT FICTION ACHIEVES FOR WOOLF--A DEEPER TRUTH THAN FACTS.

PERHAPS THAT'S WHY SHE FOUND IT "DIFFICULT TO GIVE ANY CLEAR DESCRIPTION" OF HER ACTUAL, NONFICTIONAL MOTHER. SHE WAS "ASTONISHINGLY BEAUTIFUL..."

But apart from her beauty, if the two can be separated, what was she herself like? Very quick; very direct; practical; and amusing. I say at once offhand. She could be sharp, she disliked affectation. "If

ALL THESE THINGS WILL DO VERY WELL TO DESCRIBE MY MOTHER, TOO.

BUT IT'S HARD TO FIGURE OUT WHAT THE STORY IS.

I'M READING SYLVIA PLATH'S DIARIES. *SHE* PUT HER *HEAD* IN THE OVEN.

MOM MEANS THIS KINDLY, COMMISERATINGLY. "OH, THE WRITER'S LIFE." STILL, I THINK OF MY OWN OVEN AND AM GLAD IT'S ELECTRIC.

OH! I FOUND MY LOST POEM!

GREAT! I WAS GONNA TELL YOU HOW TO SEARCH THE COMPUTER.

I FIGURED IT OUT MYSELF!

MOM STARTED WRITING POETRY IN HER YOUTH, STOPPED FOR ALL THE YEARS OF MARRIAGE, CHILDREN, AND HER CAREER TEACHING HIGH SCHOOL. NOW SHE'S TAKEN IT UP AGAIN.

OH, THE JEHOVAH'S WITNESS LADY IS AT THE DOOR. I HAVE TO GO.

UH...OKAY.

SHE INSISTS THAT SHE'S NOT A POET.

BYE.

I HAVE NEVER READ SYLVIA PLATH. MY MOTHER HAS NEVER READ VIRGINIA WOOLF. IN GENERAL, WE HAVE STAYED OUT OF ONE ANOTHER'S WAY LIKE THIS.

WHEN SHE WAS EXACTLY THE AGE I AM NOW, AND I WAS IN MY EARLY TWENTIES, MOM RESPONDED TO A LETTER I'D WRITTEN TO HER ABOUT A DREAM I'D HAD.

...will probably hear from him since he wants to stay over with you on his way home.

I have puzzled over your dream. I don't know what it means. I dream about brain tumors and babies. I am staring out my dirty windows at the lilac buds. Now I am trying to analyze why I put those two things together. <u>Why do you and I do that?</u> Patterns are my existence. Everything has significance. Everything must fit. It's enough to drive you crazy.

Today I gave one class a list of wo... your enemy. Sycophant, philandere... little rash, but I didn't have tim...

BRAIN TUMORS AND BABIES.
DIRTY WINDOWS AND LILAC BUDS.

THIS SEARCH FOR MEANINGFUL PATTERNS MAY VERY WELL BE CRAZY, BUT TO BE ENLISTED WITH HER IN IT THRILLS ME. "WHY DO YOU AND I DO THAT?"

I AM CARRYING ON HER MISSION.

I'VE ALWAYS BEEN FASCINATED BY THIS SNAPSHOT OF THE TWO OF US.

BUT I DIDN'T REALIZE UNTIL RELATIVELY RECENTLY THAT IT WAS ONE OF A SEQUENCE.

FIVE OTHER SHOTS HAD BEEN SCATTERED ABOUT IN DIFFERENT ALBUMS AND BOXES.

I CALLED MOM A FEW DAYS AFTER THE HEAD-IN-THE-OVEN CONVERSATION.

HEY, MOM. JUST CHECKING IN. WHERE ARE YA? CALL ME.

I DON'T HAVE THE NEGATIVES, SO THERE'S NO WAY TO KNOW THEIR CHRONOLOGICAL ORDER. BUT I'VE ARRANGED THEM ACCORDING TO MY OWN NARRATIVE.

MOM IS MAKING FACES AND PRESUMABLY SOUNDS AT ME. IN EACH SHOT, I REFLECT HER EXPRESSION AND THE SHAPE OF HER MOUTH WITH UNCANNY PRECISION.

BUT "THERE IS NOTHING MYSTICAL ABOUT THIS," SAYS DONALD WINNICOTT, IN *THE ORDINARY DEVOTED MOTHER.*

agrees, that *ordinarily* the woman enters into a phase, a phase from which she *ordinarily* recovers in the weeks and months after the baby's birth, in which to a large extent she is the baby and the baby is her. There is nothing mystical about

FOR A LONG TIME I RESISTED INCLUDING MY PRESENT-DAY INTERACTIONS WITH MOM IN THIS BOOK PRECISELY BECAUSE THEY'RE SO "ORDINARY."

DRRINNG!

MOM!

HI. I WAS AT THE GYM. HAD TO GET MY LAPS IN.

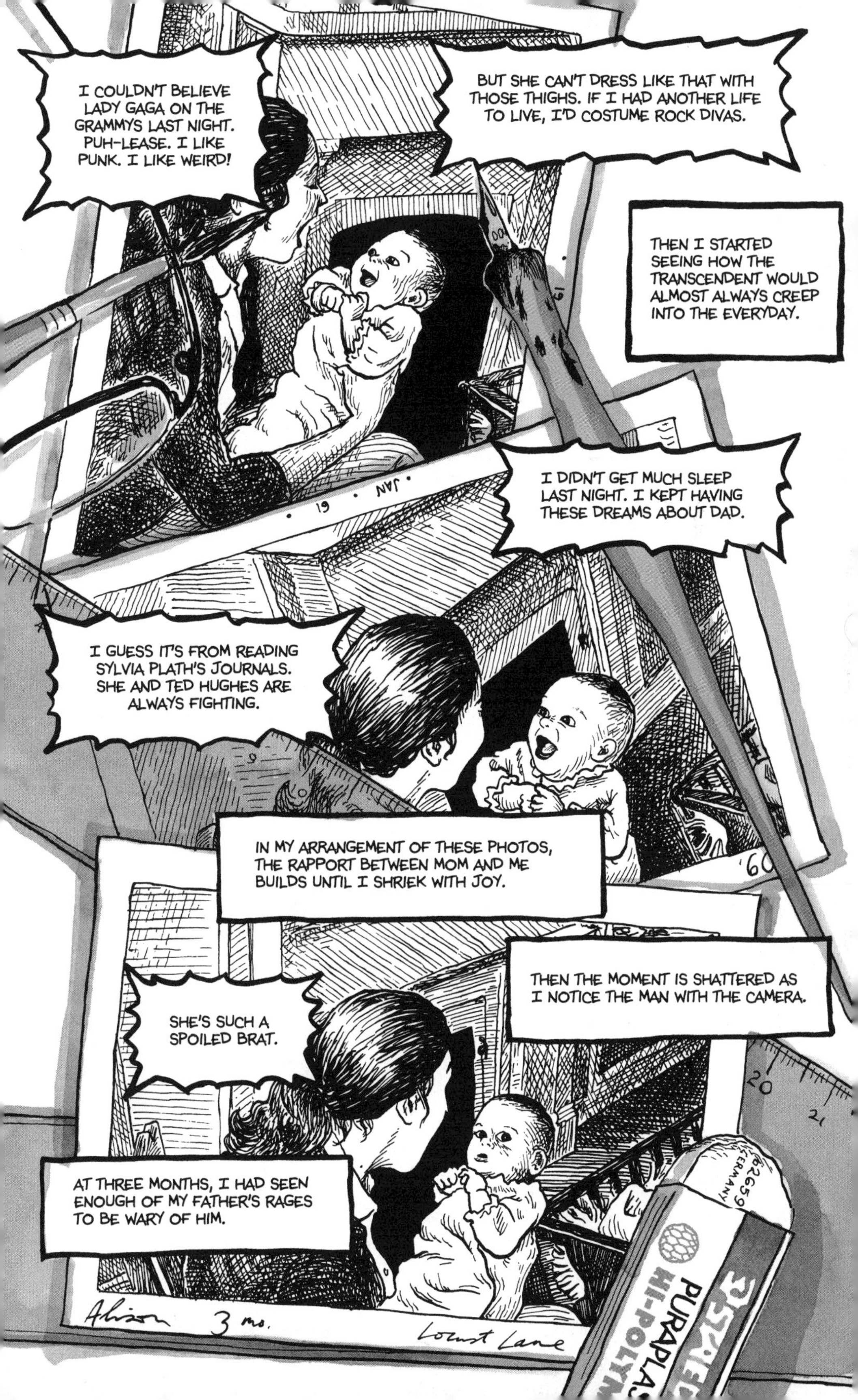
I COULDN'T BELIEVE LADY GAGA ON THE GRAMMYS LAST NIGHT. PUH-LEASE. I LIKE PUNK. I LIKE WEIRD!
BUT SHE CAN'T DRESS LIKE THAT WITH THOSE THIGHS. IF I HAD ANOTHER LIFE TO LIVE, I'D COSTUME ROCK DIVAS.
THEN I STARTED SEEING HOW THE TRANSCENDENT WOULD ALMOST ALWAYS CREEP INTO THE EVERYDAY.
I DIDN'T GET MUCH SLEEP LAST NIGHT. I KEPT HAVING THESE DREAMS ABOUT DAD.
I GUESS IT'S FROM READING SYLVIA PLATH'S JOURNALS. SHE AND TED HUGHES ARE ALWAYS FIGHTING.
IN MY ARRANGEMENT OF THESE PHOTOS, THE RAPPORT BETWEEN MOM AND ME BUILDS UNTIL I SHRIEK WITH JOY.
THEN THE MOMENT IS SHATTERED AS I NOTICE THE MAN WITH THE CAMERA.
SHE'S SUCH A SPOILED BRAT.
AT THREE MONTHS, I HAD SEEN ENOUGH OF MY FATHER'S RAGES TO BE WARY OF HIM.
Alison 3 mo.
Locust Lane

THE PHOTOS WERE TAKEN RIGHT ABOUT THE TIME MOM REALIZED THAT SHE WAS PREGNANT AGAIN.

SHE'S A SNOB, TOO. A SNOB AND A BRAT.

I THOUGHT YOU LIKED HER.

THERE ARE THREE MAIN REASONS, WINNICOTT SAYS, WHY A MOTHER MIGHT NOT BE ABLE TO "GIVE HERSELF OVER TO THIS PREOCCU- PATION WITH THE CARE OF HER INFANT."

SHE'S ALWAYS ASKING HER THERAPIST FOR PERMISSION TO HATE HER MOTHER.

ONE, SHE DIES. TWO, SHE "STARTS UP A NEW PREGNANCY BEFORE THE TIME THAT SHE HAD THOUGHT OUT AS APPROPRIATE." THREE...

THE ORDINARY DEVOTED MOTHER

ing. Or a mother becomes depressed and she can feel herself depriving her child of what the child needs, but she cannot help the onset of a mood swing, which may quite easily be reactive to something that has impinged in her private life. Here she is causing trouble, but no one would blame her.

In other words there are all manner of reasons why some children do get let down before they are able to avoid being wounded or maimed in personality by the fact.

Here I must go back to the idea of blame. It is necessary for us to be able to look at human growth and development, with all its complexities that are internal or personal to the child, and we must be able to say; here the ordinary devoted mother factor failed, without blaming anyone. For my part I have no interest whatever in apportioning blame. Mothers

"AM I ALLOWED TO HATE MY MOTHER?"

"NO!"

OH, SERENA'S GRANDDAUGHTER JUST GOT HER PERIOD. SHE'S ONLY TWELVE. THAT'S SO SAD. TWELVE IS TOO YOUNG.

UHH...I THINK TWELVE IS KINDA NORMAL.

I HAVE NOT BEEN MAIMED, ONLY WOUNDED, AND PERHAPS NOT IRREPARABLY.

her baby and in his or her care. At three or four months after being born the baby may be able to show that he or she knows what it is like to be a mother, that is a mother in her state of being devoted to something that is not in fact herself.

THE PICTURE OF ME LOOKING AT THE CAMERA FEELS LIKE A PICTURE OF THE END OF MY CHILDHOOD.

WELL, I'M HEARTBROKEN. SHE WON'T BE A CHILD ANYMORE.

"SHE IS THE BABY AND THE BABY IS HER." I DISAGREE THAT THERE IS NOTHING MYSTICAL ABOUT THIS.

No! (mom, as if she's SP's therapi
Serena's granddaughter just got h
is too young....
Well I'm heartbroken.
She won't be a child anymo|

FOR TWO SEPARATE BEINGS TO BE IDENTICAL—TO BE ONE...

oung....

heartbroker

n't be a child

...THIS SEEMS TO ME AS MYSTICAL, AS TRANSCENDENT OF THE LAWS OF EVERYDAY REALITY, AS IT GETS.

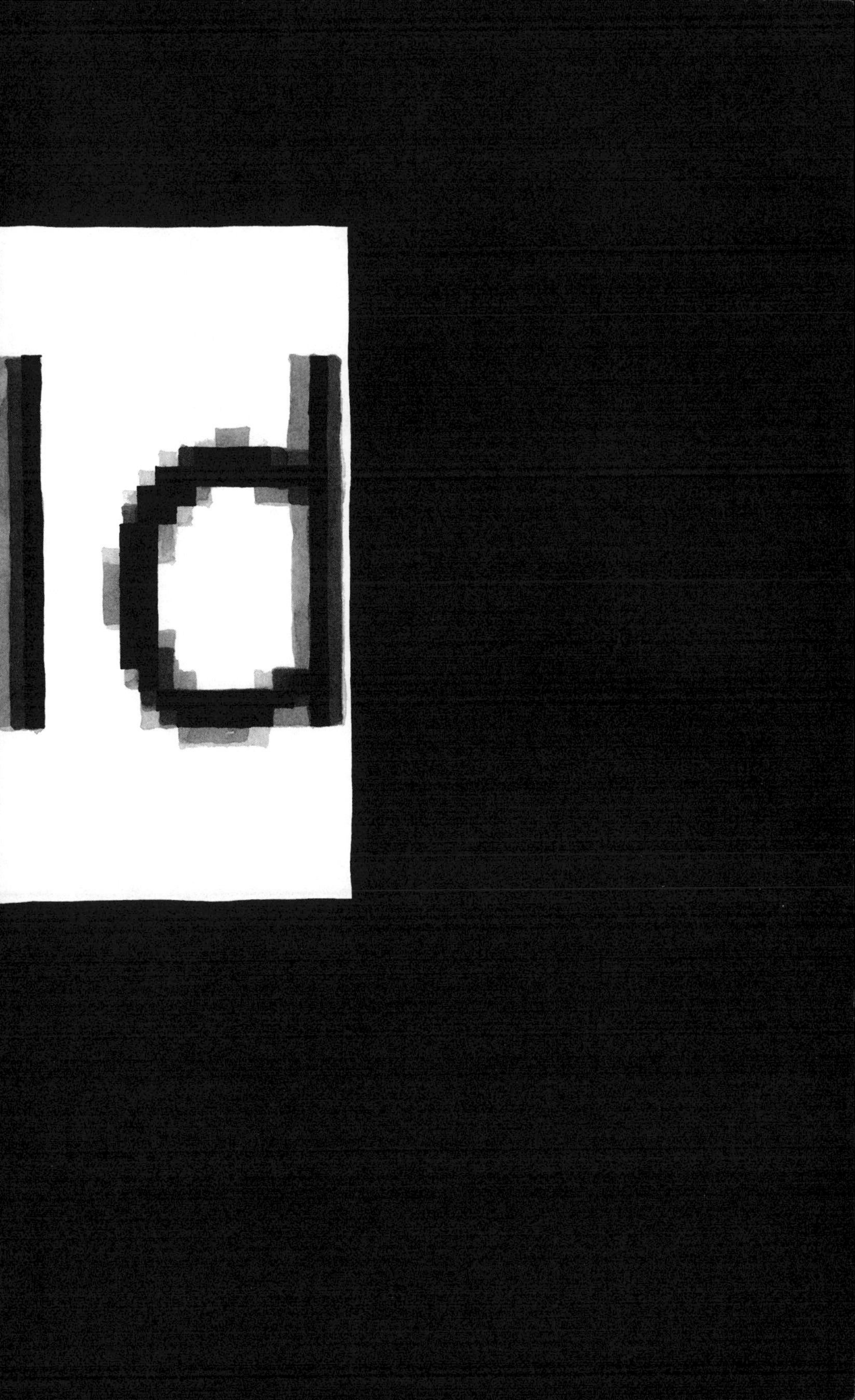

# 2

# Transitional Objects

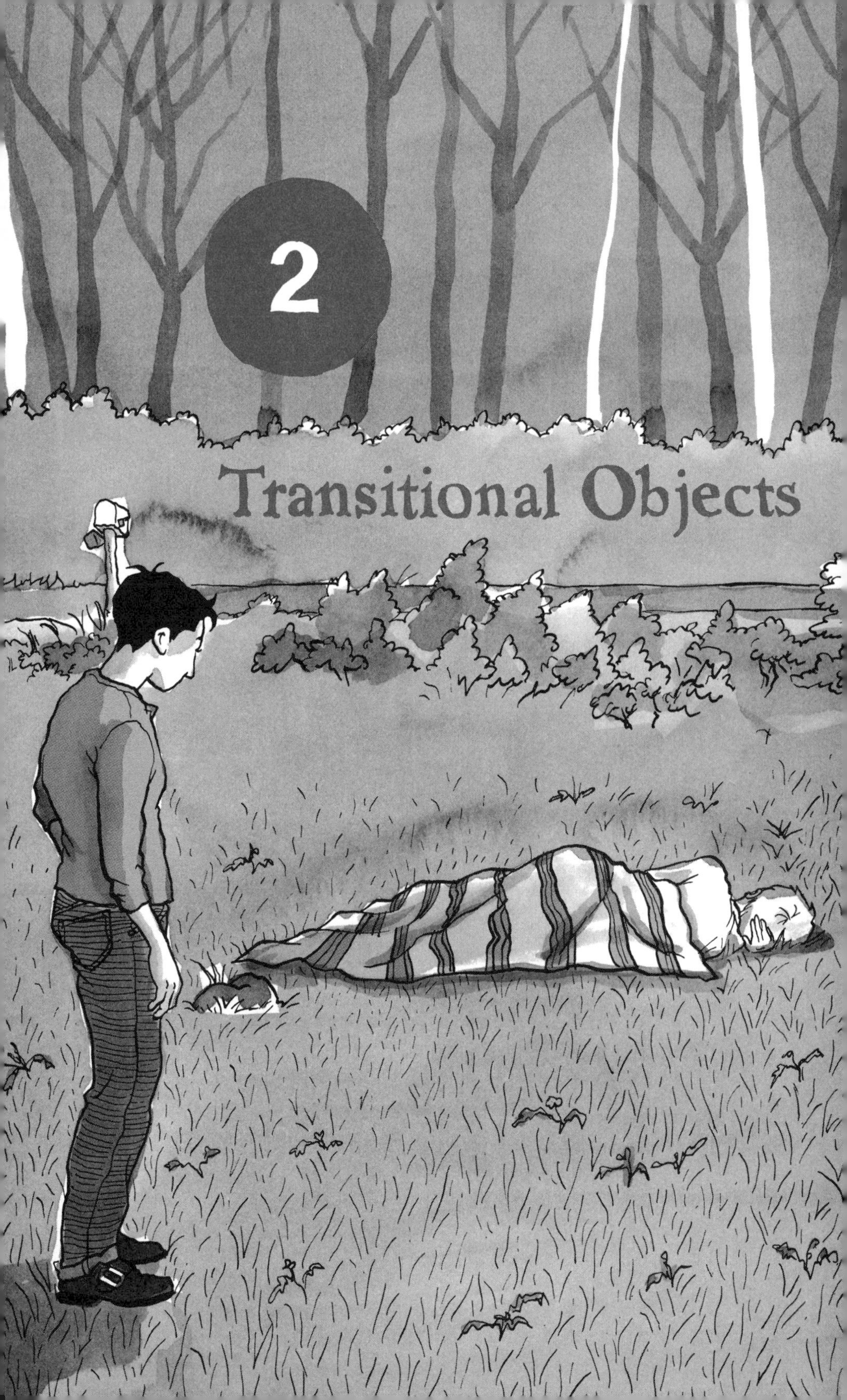

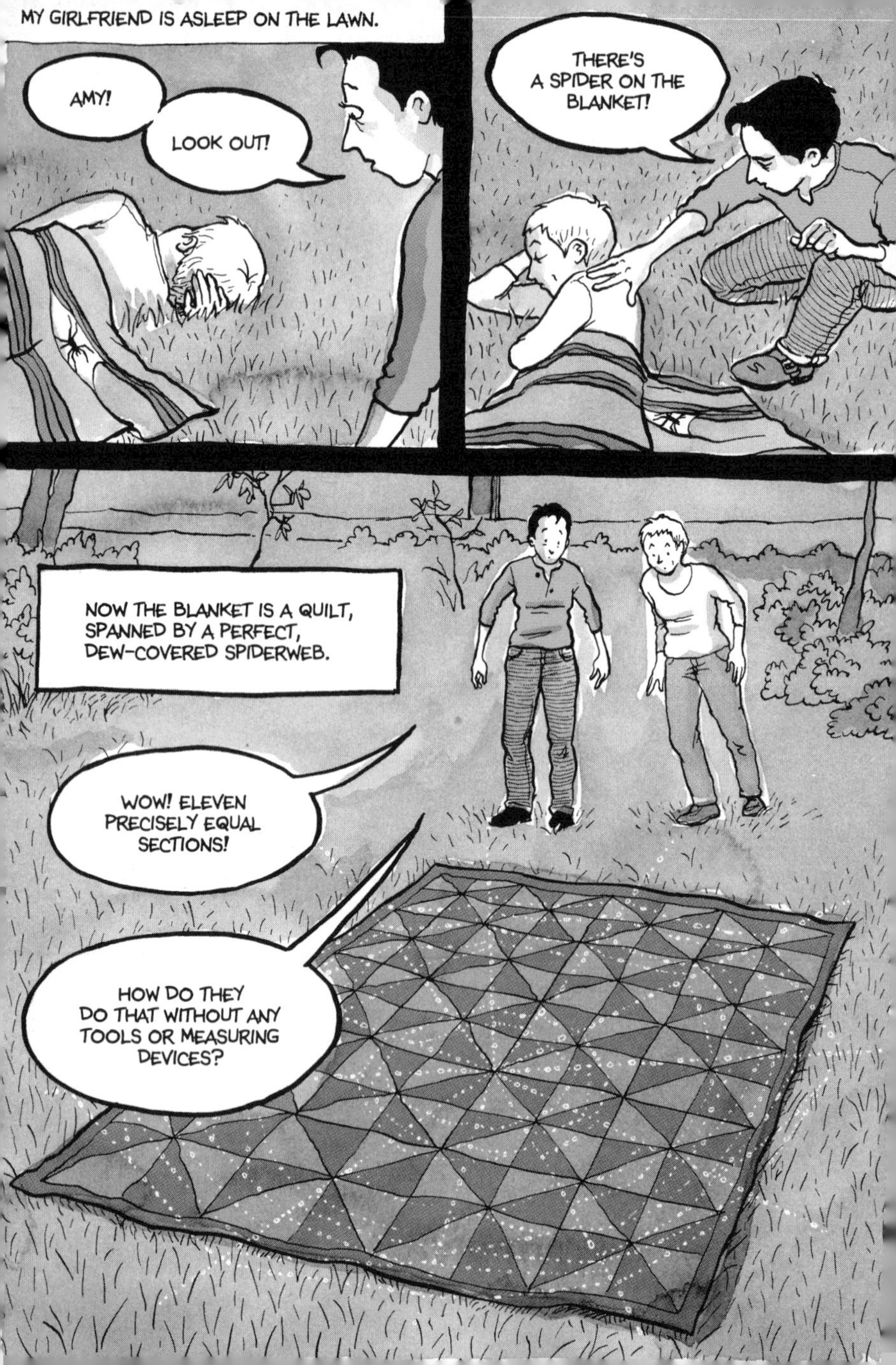
MY GIRLFRIEND IS ASLEEP ON THE LAWN.
AMY!
LOOK OUT!
THERE'S A SPIDER ON THE BLANKET!
NOW THE BLANKET IS A QUILT, SPANNED BY A PERFECT, DEW-COVERED SPIDERWEB.
WOW! ELEVEN PRECISELY EQUAL SECTIONS!
HOW DO THEY DO THAT WITHOUT ANY TOOLS OR MEASURING DEVICES?

I HAD A BAD HABIT OF INTERRUPTING AMY, APPARENTLY EVEN WHEN I WAS ASLEEP.

IF WE WEREN'T RATIONAL BEINGS, WE COULDNT BE *IRRATIONAL!*

LIKE, IT'S OUR VERY CAPACITY FOR SELF-CON-SCIOUSNESS THAT MAKES US SELF-DESTRUCTIVE!

IN THE DREAM, THIS PLATITUDE STRUCK ME AS PROFOUND. I FELT A TINGLING EXHILARATION.

I HAD THE SPIDERWEB DREAM TWO YEARS AFTER THE ONE ABOUT THE BROOK, AND IMMEDIATELY AFTER STARTING TO READ FREUD'S *INTERPRETATION OF DREAMS.*

I WAS IN THE THICK OF WRITING THE BOOK ABOUT MY FATHER.

I WAS CARVING OUT TIME FOR THIS FROM MY JOB WRITING AND DRAWING A COMIC STRIP.

I'D BOUGHT THE COPY OF FREUD A FEW WEEKS EARLIER, AFTER A POWERFUL THERAPY SESSION.

AMY AND I WERE DRIVING HOME FROM THE GROCERY STORE ON CHRISTMAS EVE, HAVING THIS BIG FIGHT ABOUT MONEY.

I'D BEEN DOING THE COMIC STRIP--ABOUT A GROUP OF LESBIAN FRIENDS--SINCE MY EARLY TWENTIES, BUT IT WAS GETTING HARDER AND HARDER TO EARN A DECENT LIVING FROM IT.

WHEN WE PASSED THE CATHOLIC CHURCH, ALL THESE PEOPLE WERE GOING IN. SO I SAID, "LET'S GO TO MASS!"

MAYBE THIS'LL SNAP US OUT OF THE FIGHT.

I'D BEEN RAISED CATHOLIC BUT HADN'T BEEN IN A CHURCH FOR A LONG TIME.

CAN I PUT MY COAT IN HERE?

AMY WAS JEWISH.

THAT'S THE CONFESSIONAL!

WE TRIED TO STIFLE OUR SACRILEGIOUS LAUGHTER. THE SERVICE HAD ALREADY BEGUN.

BUT SOON, AS I REALIZED THAT THE PEW IN FRONT OF US WAS FILLED WITH CHILDREN IN COSTUMES, I WAS FIGHTING BACK TEARS.

ACROSS THE AISLE WAS ANOTHER PEW FULL OF ANGELS. THE CHOIR ABOVE US BEGAN SINGING.

...echoing their joyous strain

WHAT DO YOU THINK YOU WERE SO SAD ABOUT?

UNDER CAROL'S QUESTIONING, THE IMPULSE TO CRY RETURNED. AGAIN, I RESISTED IT.

I DUNNO... THEY WERE ALL JUST SO...

...YOU KNOW. INNOCENT.

I DIDN'T CRY, BUT THEN I STARTED WORRYING THAT SOMEONE MIGHT THROW UP, OR I'D CATCH FLU GERMS.

LET'S GO.

JUST THEN, THE SHEPHERDS BEGAN FILING OUT OF THEIR PEW AND WE COULDN'T MOVE.

SHUFFLE

SQUEAK

THEN A WOMAN RUSHED OUT, FOLLOWED BY A MAN.

ARE YOU GONNA BE SICK?

MY ANXIETY INTENSIFIED. THE ONLY WAY OUT WAS THROUGH THE FRONT DOOR, WHERE THIS WOMAN WAS POSSIBLY THROWING UP.

WE EXITED AT THE NEXT OPPORTUNITY, AND TO MY GREAT RELIEF, THE WOMAN AND ANY SIGN OF HER WERE GONE.

GOD!

WHAT WAS IT ABOUT THE CHILDREN'S INNOCENCE THAT MADE YOU WANT TO CRY?

GOD, HOW TRITE IS THAT?

I DUNNO. IT MAKES ME THINK OF THIS NEWSPAPER CLIPPING OF A CHRISTMAS PAGEANT I WAS IN WHEN I WAS TEN.

I LOOK DIFFERENT FROM THE OTHER KIDS.

HOW?

UH...SELF-CONSCIOUS?

I WONDER IF YOU WERE FEELING EVEN THEN THAT THE PAGEANT WAS "TRITE."

YEAH, PROBABLY!

THAT YOU COULDN'T LET YOURSELF BE PART OF IT BECAUSE YOU KNEW YOUR PARENTS FOUND THAT SORT OF THING SILLY AND SENTIMENTAL.

YOUR ANXIETY ATTACK IN THE CHURCH SOUNDS LIKE A COMPROMISE FORMATION.

A WHAT?

YOUR UNCONSCIOUS WANTS TO EXPRESS THE PAIN YOU FEEL ABOUT YOUR OWN LOST INNOCENCE. BUT YOUR EGO WANTS TO KEEP IT REPRESSED.

SO THE COMPROMISE IS ANXIETY.

IT WAS AFTER THE SESSION THAT I DECIDED I NEEDED TO LEARN MORE ABOUT PSYCHOANALYSIS.

USED BOOKS

FREUD

HEADACHE FROM NOT-CRYING FOR FIFTY MINUTES.

AT HOME, I DUG OUT THE CLIPPING OF THE PAGEANT.

MAYBE PART OF WHY I SEEM SO OUT OF PLACE IS THAT MY TINSEL HALO GIVES THE EFFECT OF A YARMULKE.

I LOOK LIKE A JEWISH BOY ON THE WRONG SET.

OLD THEME IN TODAY'S SETTING — This is the Christmas story, portrayed by public school elementary students of the Lock Haven Catholic churches, who study religion in Saturday classes. Last week this class, meeting in the Immaculate Conception Church hall, gave a play. The drama marked the last Confraternity of Christi... Catholic pupils until I...

AT ANY RATE, I APPEAR TO SENSE THE ARROW (DRAWN BY MY PATERNAL GRANDMOTHER) AT THE BACK OF MY HEAD, SINGLING ME OUT.

FREUD HAD BEEN OUT OF FASHION WHEN I WAS IN COLLEGE. I'D READ ONLY ONE THING BY HIM, *PSYCHOPATHOLOGY OF EVERYDAY LIFE*, FOR A LINGUISTICS CLASS.

THE BASIC WRITINGS of SIGMUND FREUD
Modern Library

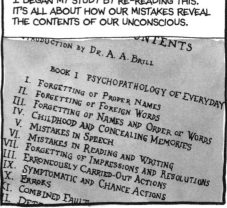

I BEGAN MY STUDY BY RE-READING THIS. IT'S ALL ABOUT HOW OUR MISTAKES REVEAL THE CONTENTS OF OUR UNCONSCIOUS.

CONTENTS

INTRODUCTION BY DR. A. A. BRILL

BOOK I   PSYCHOPATHOLOGY OF EVERYDAY

I. FORGETTING OF PROPER NAMES
II. FORGETTING OF FOREIGN WORDS
III. FORGETTING OF NAMES AND ORDER OF WORDS
IV. CHILDHOOD AND CONCEALING MEMORIES
V. MISTAKES IN SPEECH
VI. MISTAKES IN READING AND WRITING
VII. FORGETTING OF IMPRESSIONS AND RESOLUTIONS
VIII. ERRONEOUSLY CARRIED-OUT ACTIONS
IX. SYMPTOMATIC AND CHANCE ACTIONS
X. ERRORS
XI. COMBINED FAULTS
I. DET...

I REMEMBERED ONE EXAMPLE VERY CLEARLY FROM MY INITIAL READING TWENTY YEARS EARLIER. FREUD KNOCKS THE COVER OF HIS INKWELL TO THE FLOOR AND BREAKS IT.

JUST A FEW HOURS EARLIER HIS SISTER HAD OBSERVED THAT THE INKSTAND DIDN'T MATCH THE OTHER THINGS ON THE DESK.

WAS HE OBLIGING HER BY GETTING RID OF IT? SO THAT PERHAPS SHE COULD GIVE HIM A NEW ONE AS A GIFT?

HE MAINTAINS THAT HIS APPARENT BLUNDER, WHICH DID NOT DIS-TURB ANY OF THE MORE VALUABLE FIGURINES CLOSE TO THE INK-STAND, WAS IN FACT A MANEUVER "MOST SKILLFUL AND DESIGNED."

THE IDEA THAT OUR UNCONSCIOUS POSSESSES SUCH SURE AIM EXCITED ME. I BECAME MORE ATTUNED TO MY OWN "ERRONEOUSLY CARRIED OUT ACTIONS."

TEN DAYS AFTER BUYING THE FREUD BOOK, I WAS SECURING A BOARD TO MY CAR AT THE HARDWARE STORE.

IT WAS COLD AND I WAS MOVING QUICKLY.

I CINCHED THE KNOT AND HUSTLED BACK TO THE DRIVER'S SIDE.

Tonk! ★

THE PLANK CAUGHT ME RIGHT BETWEEN MY EYES.

?

TWICE A DAY FOR A YEAR I'D BEEN TAKING HERBAL TABLETS FROM MY ACUPUNCTURIST CALLED "BRIGHTEN THE EYES." NOW WHEN I LOOKED AT THE BOTTLE, I SAW THIS:

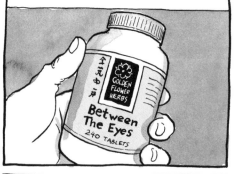

GOLDEN FLOWER HERBS

Between The Eyes

240 TABLETS

ALSO, FOR A FEW DAYS A PIMPLE HAD BEEN SWELLING BETWEEN MY EYEBROWS.

THE "THIRD EYE," OR BROW CHAKRA IN INDIAN MEDICINE, IS WHERE WE LOOK NOT OUT, BUT IN.

The Holistic Health Handbook

PERHAPS MY UNCONSCIOUS WAS TELLING ME TO PAY MORE ATTENTION TO MY UNCONSCIOUS.

I WAS PLAGUED THEN, AS NOW, WITH A TENDENCY TO EDIT MY THOUGHTS BEFORE THEY EVEN TOOK SHAPE.

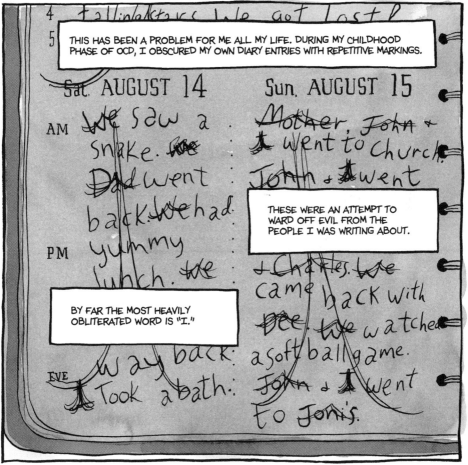

THIS HAS BEEN A PROBLEM FOR ME ALL MY LIFE. DURING MY CHILDHOOD PHASE OF OCD, I OBSCURED MY OWN DIARY ENTRIES WITH REPETITIVE MARKINGS.

THESE WERE AN ATTEMPT TO WARD OFF EVIL FROM THE PEOPLE I WAS WRITING ABOUT.

BY FAR THE MOST HEAVILY OBLITERATED WORD IS "I."

49

FREUD SHEDS SOME LIGHT ON MY BEHAVIOR IN *THE PSYCHOPATHOLOGY OF EVERYDAY LIFE.*

IV. Whoever has had the opportunity of studying the concealed feelings of persons by means of psychoanalysis can also tell something new concerning the quality of unconscious motives, which express themselves in superstition. Nervous persons afflicted with compulsive thinking and compulsive states, who are often very intelligent, show very plainly that superstition originates from repressed hostile and cruel impulses. The greater part of superstition signifies fear of impending evil, and he who has frequently wished evil to others, but because of a good bringing up, has repressed the same into the unconscious, will be particularly apt to expect punishment for such unconscious evil in the form of a misfortune threatening him from without.

MY FIRST THERAPIST, JOCELYN, SUBSCRIBED TO THIS THEORY AS WELL. IN OUR INITIAL SESSION SHE ASKED ME A STRANGE QUESTION.

I DON'T THINK SO.

I DIDN'T CONSIDER MYSELF THE SORT OF PERSON WHO NEEDED THERAPY. BUT SOMETHING FRIGHTENING HAD BEEN GOING ON.

EVERYTHING'S GONE FLAT. NOTHING INTERESTS ME, I'VE LOST MY APPETITE.

FOR EVERYTHING.

LIFE HAS BECOME JUST... JUST THIS DRUDGING EFFORT OF WILL.

AFTER LEAVING JOCELYN'S OFFICE, MY DEPRESSION IMMEDIATELY BEGAN TO LIFT. I MET WITH TWO OTHER THERAPISTS, AS FRIENDS HAD ADVISED ME TO DO. BUT THERE WAS NO COMPARISON.

Friday May 29, 1987

So I want Jocelyn to be my mother. Totally. I completely admit it. How can I have such a strong desire when I've only spent 2 hours with her?

MY LIFE BEGAN REVOLVING AROUND TUESDAYS AT THREE O'CLOCK. ALTHOUGH THE TERRIBLE FLAT FEELING HAD DISSIPATED, I WAS STILL ANXIOUS AND HAD TROUBLE SLEEPING.

I WOULD TRANQUILIZE MYSELF BY WALKING MILES THROUGH DODGY NEIGHBORHOODS IN THE MIDDLE OF THE NIGHT TO GAZE AT JOCELYN'S HOUSE.

JOCELYN AGREED WITH MY THEORY THAT THE DEPRESSION HAD BEEN A GOOD THING, A CRUMBLING OF MY DEFENSES--AND THAT MY SECURE RELATIONSHIP WITH MY GIRLFRIEND, ELOISE, HAD ENABLED IT.

ELOISE AND I HAD BEEN TOGETHER FOR THREE-AND-A-HALF YEARS AT THAT POINT. WE'D JUST MOVED FROM THE EAST COAST TO THE TWIN CITIES WITH SOME OF HER COLLEGE FRIENDS.

I MET ELOISE AFTER SHE'D GRADUATED FROM BRYN MAWR, AND BEFORE SHE WENT ON TO GET A DEGREE IN AUTO MECHANICS.

AREN'T YOU WORRIED THE GUYS WILL SEE US?

THOSE NIMRODS. THEY THINK YOU'RE MY *BOYFRIEND*.

YOU LOOK EXHAUSTED.

I HAVE TO GET OUTTA THAT PLACE BEFORE I TAKE A BOLT CUTTER TO ONE OF THOSE ASSHOLES.

BUT THE BEGINNING OF MY RELATIONSHIP WITH JOCELYN WOULD BE THE BEGINNING OF THE END OF MY RELATIONSHIP WITH ELOISE.

WHAT'D YOU DO TODAY?

HAD THERAPY. AND BOUGHT A BOOK ABOUT THERAPY.

I'M NOT SURE HOW I STUMBLED ONTO THIS SLENDER VOLUME. IT WASN'T THROUGH JOCELYN. PERHAPS A FRIEND RECOMMENDED IT. PERHAPS THE TITLE CAUGHT MY EYE.

APPARENTLY, IT WAS SOME KIND OF SACRED TEXT.

WELL, KISS LIFE AS YOU KNOW IT GOODBYE.

ELOISE WAS PATIENT WITH MY INCREASED SELF-ABSORPTION IN THOSE EARLY DAYS OF THERAPY.

...SO THIS GUY'S STARTING UP A GARAGE!

THE BOOK DESCRIBED PERFECTLY THE STRANGELY INVERTED RELATIONSHIP I'D ALWAYS FELT I HAD WITH MY MOTHER...

WHO EVER HEARD OF A GAY MECHANIC? IT'S AN OXYMORON. BUT I MET HIS BOYFRIEND.

REALLY.

...THIS SENSE THAT I WAS HER MOTHER.

HE HAS THIS GREAT, FUNKY OLD GAS STATION. THERE'S NO LIFT, THOUGH. JUST A PIT.

tively from the type of talent that is needed by an analyst. His sensibility, his empathy, his intense and differentiated emotional responsiveness, and his unusually powerful "antennae" seem to predestine him as a child to be used—if not misused—by people with intense narcissistic needs.

Of course, there is the theoretical possibility that a child

HUH.
NO LIFT.

THE BOOK WAS WRITTEN FOR ANALYSTS, SO A LOT OF IT WENT OVER MY HEAD.

IT'D BE LIKE WORKING OUT OF MY OWN GARAGE.

BUT I WAS VERY TAKEN WITH THE RECURRING REFERENCES ALICE MILLER MADE TO THE IDEAS OF SOMEONE NAMED WINNICOTT. PARTICULARLY RESONANT WAS THE NOTION OF A "TRUE SELF" THAT HAD TO BE KEPT HIDDEN AT ALL COSTS.

perienced for the first time during analysis.

The true self has been in "a state of noncommunication," as Winnicott said, because it had to be protected. The patient never needs to hide anything else so thoroughly, so deeply, and for so long a time as he has hidden his true self. Thus it is like a miracle each time to see how much individuality has survived behind such dissimulation, denial, and self-alienation, and can reappear as soon as the work of mourning brings freedom from the introjects. Nevertheless, it would be wrong to understand Winnicott's words

IN MY CURSORY READING, I ASSUMED THAT WINNICOTT WAS A WOMAN.

HOW LONG ARE YOU GONNA READ?

I DUNNO. I'M ANXIOUS. I NEED TO WIND DOWN.

I'LL WIND YOU DOWN.

SWEETIE.

NONE OF THE MENTIONS INCLUDED A PRONOUN, AND THE IDEAS THEMSELVES HAD A NURTURING, MATERNAL ASPECT.

ALSO, THOUGH I KNEW IT WAS A SURNAME, "WINNICOTT" JUST SOUNDED LIKE A GIRL'S NAME. LIKE "WINNIE."

IF YOU GO OUT FOR ONE OF YOUR MIDNIGHT WALKS, TAKE THE DOG.

NOT THAT I KNEW ANYONE NAMED WINNIE, EXCEPT FOR WINNIE-THE-POOH.

OF COURSE, THERE WAS SOME GENDER AMBIGUITY ABOUT WINNIE-THE-POOH AS WELL.

## CHAPTER 1

WHICH *We Are Introduced to Winnie-the-Pooh and Some Bees, and the Stories Begin*

BUT I WOULDN'T LEARN FOR MANY YEARS THAT DONALD WINNICOTT WAS A SMALL MAN, HIGH-VOICED AND "FEY"...

*HERE is Edward Bear, coming down-stairs now, bump, bump, bump, on the back of his head, behind Christopher Robin. It is, as far as he knows, the only way of coming down stairs, but some-times he feels that there really is another way, if only he could stop bumping for a moment and think of it. And then he feels that perhaps there isn't. Anyhow, here he is at the bottom, and ready to be introduced to you, Winnie-the-Pooh.*

*When I first heard his name, I said, just as you are going to say, "But I thought he was a boy?"*

*"So did I," said Christopher Robin.*

*"Then you can't call him Winnie?"*

*"I don't."*

*"But you said ——"*

*"He's Winnie-ther-Pooh. Don't you know what 'ther' means?"*

...WHO STRUGGLED WITH IMPOTENCE, DISPLAYED "A MOTHERLY DISPOSITION," AND HAD "ASTON-ISHING POWERS WITH CHILDREN."

7

IT WOULD ALSO BE MANY YEARS BEFORE I LEARNED ABOUT HIS PRIMARY CONTRIBUTION TO PSYCHOANALYSIS, THE CONCEPT OF THE "TRANSITIONAL OBJECT."

BABIES OFTEN MAKE USE OF A SPECIAL POSSESSION AS THEY LEARN THAT THEY'RE SEPARATE FROM THEIR MOTHER.

IT OCCUPIES A "TERRITORY BETWEEN THE SUBJECTIVE AND THE OBJECTIVE."

IT'S NOT "ME," BUT NOT "NOT-ME," EITHER.

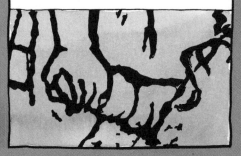

IN THE INTRODUCTION TO *THE WORLD OF POOH*, A.A. MILNE EXPLAINS MORE ABOUT THE STUFFED BEAR'S NAME--AND INCIDENTALLY, ABOUT THE NATURE OF THE TRANSITIONAL OBJECT.

IF YOU happen to have read another book about Christopher Robin, you may remember that he once had a swan (or the swan had Christopher Robin, I don't know which) and that he used to call this swan Pooh. That was a long time ago, and when

WHO, INDEED, HAS WHOM?

WINNICOTT PRESENTED HIS PAPER "TRANSITIONAL OBJECTS AND TRANSITIONAL PHENOMENA" IN 1951, WHEN HE WAS IN HIS FIFTIES.

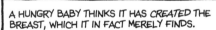

The mother, at the beginning, by an almost 100 per cent adaptation affords the infant the opportunity for the *illusion* that her breast is part of the infant. It is, as it were, under the baby's magical control.

A HUNGRY BABY THINKS IT HAS *CREATED* THE BREAST, WHICH IT IN FACT MERELY FINDS.

THIS "AREA OF ILLUSION" BETWEEN THE MOTHER AND THE BABY IS THE FORERUNNER OF THE TRANSITIONAL OBJECT.

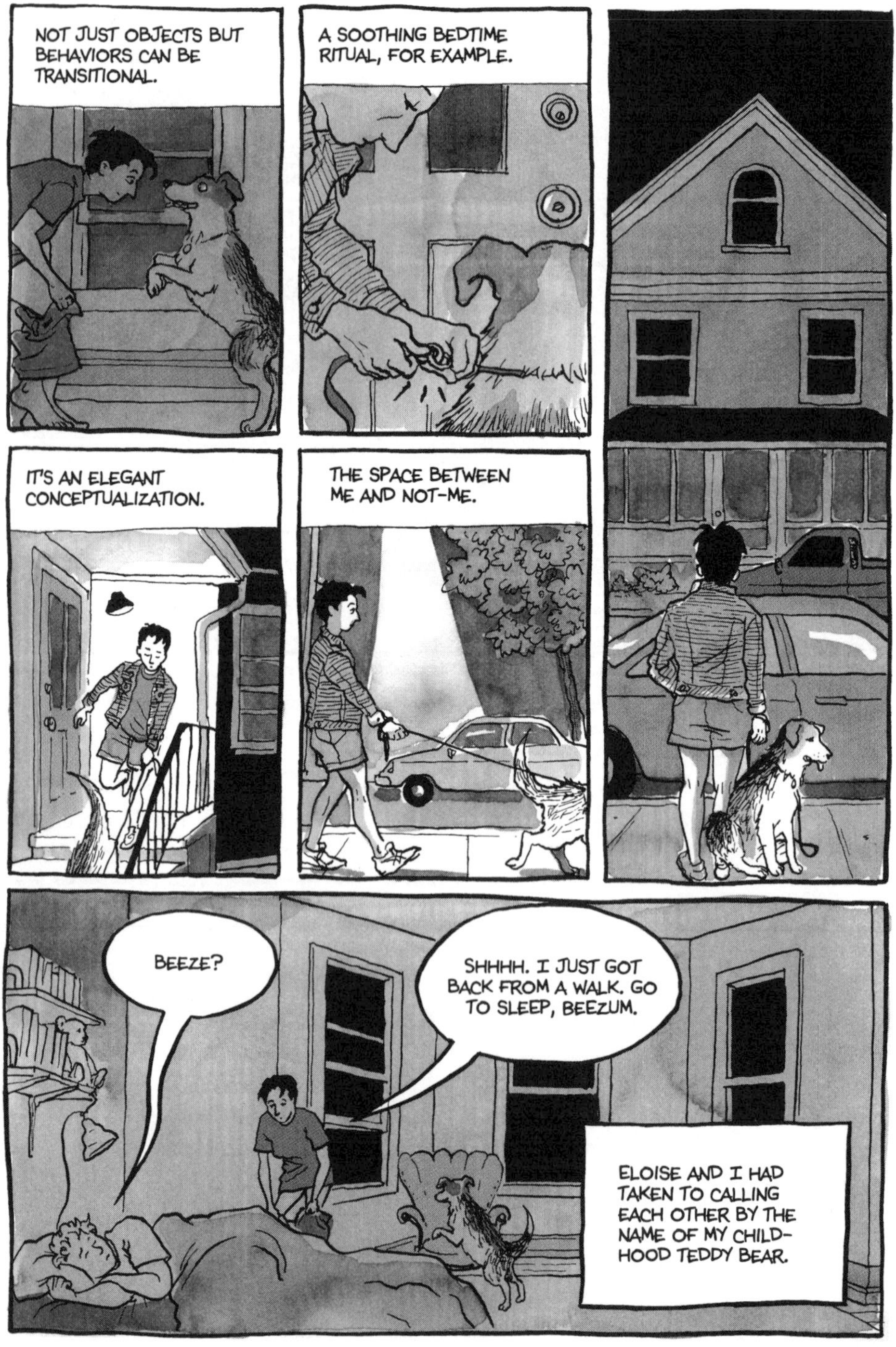
NOT JUST OBJECTS BUT BEHAVIORS CAN BE TRANSITIONAL.
A SOOTHING BEDTIME RITUAL, FOR EXAMPLE.
IT'S AN ELEGANT CONCEPTUALIZATION.
THE SPACE BETWEEN ME AND NOT-ME.
BEEZE?
SHHHH. I JUST GOT BACK FROM A WALK. GO TO SLEEP, BEEZUM.
ELOISE AND I HAD TAKEN TO CALLING EACH OTHER BY THE NAME OF MY CHILD-HOOD TEDDY BEAR.

may appear a 'word' for the transitional object. The name given by the infant to these earliest objects is often significant, and it usually has a word used by the adults partly incorporated in it. For instance, 'baa' may be the name, and the 'b' may have come from the adult's use of the word 'baby' or 'bear'.

THE SIMILARITY OF "BEEZUM" TO "BOSOM" IS PERHAPS NOTABLE.

MOM HAD BREASTFED ME OVER THE OBJECTIONS OF EVERYONE AROUND HER. WE WERE LIVING TEMPORARILY WITH MY FATHER'S PARENTS IN THE FAMILY FUNERAL HOME, A TENSE ARRANGEMENT.

THREE GODDAMN SOLID BRONZE CASKETS?

YOU'D LET THAT SALESMAN TALK YOU INTO ANYTHING, YOU DUMBSHIT.

MY FATHER'S BOISTEROUS OLDER SISTERS DIDN'T UNDERSTAND MOM'S NEED TO BE LEFT ALONE.

DON'T LOOK IN THE BACK SEAT, ED!

HELEN'S NURSING HER BABY!

MOM LATER TOLD ME THAT SHE WOULD WAKE ME TO NURSE IF I WAS ASLEEP, IN ACCORDANCE WITH THE CUSTOM AT THAT TIME OF FEEDING INFANTS ON A RIGID SCHEDULE.

FOR WHATEVER REASON, THE BREASTFEED-ING DID NOT GO WELL. MOM HEARD THAT BEER MIGHT HELP.

BUT AT SIX WEEKS, I WEIGHED NO MORE THAN I HAD AT BIRTH.

I WANT YOU TO SWITCH TO THE BOTTLE. YOU'RE JUST NOT A GOOD COW.

I DON'T THINK IT'S GOING TOO FAR TO CLAIM THAT OUR "FAILURE" MUST HAVE BEEN DEEPLY FRUSTRATING FOR BOTH OF US.

BECHDEL FUNERAL HOME

OR EVEN THAT A PATTERN OF MUTUAL, PRE-EMPTIVE REJECTION COULD HAVE BEEN SET IN MOTION, EACH OF US WITHHOLDING IN ORDER TO FORECLOSE FUTURE REJECTION.

TRUST ME, I AM AWARE OF THE DANGERS OF THIS SORT OF THINKING. EVEN JAMES STRACHEY ROLLED HIS EYES AT DONALD WINNICOTT'S "MEMORIES" OF HIS BIRTH AND INFANCY.

I THINK I ENJOY URINATING INTO THE SEA SO MUCH BECAUSE I MIGHT HAVE URINATED ON MY MOTHER JUST AFTER BIRTH.

WHY STOP THERE? PERHAPS IT WAS IN UTERO!

WINNICOTT'S MOTHER, TOO, STOPPED BREASTFEEDING HIM VERY EARLY.

I SUSPECT SHE COULDN'T BEAR HER OWN EXCITEMENT.

BUT IF SHE'D WEANED HIM MORE GRADUALLY, WOULD HE HAVE EVER COME TO WONDER ABOUT THIS COMPLICATED PLACE "BETWEEN THE SUBJECTIVE AND THE OBJECTIVE"?

WINNICOTT WROTE FAMOUSLY OF THE "GOOD-ENOUGH MOTHER." MOTHERS DO NOT HAVE TO BE PERFECT, JUST GOOD ENOUGH—AND LEFT TO THEIR OWN INSTINCTS, MOST MOTHERS ARE.

pleasure principle to the reality principle or towards and beyond primary identification (see Freud, 1923), unless there is a good-enough mother. The good-enough 'mother' (not necessarily the infant's own mother) is one who makes active adaptation to the infant's needs, an active adaptation that gradually lessens, according to the infant's growing ability to account for failure of adaptation and to tolerate the results of frustration. Naturally, the infant's own mother is more likely to be good enough than some other person, since this active adaptation demands an easy and unresented preoccupation with the one infant; in fact, success in infant care depends on the fact of devotion, not on cleverness or intellectual enlightenment.

I DON'T WANT TO SUGGEST THAT MY OWN HIGHLY CAPABLE MOTHER WAS NOT "GOOD-ENOUGH."

CAN'T YOU KEEP THAT BRAT QUIET?

BUT SOME BABIES CAN "TOLERATE THE RESULTS OF FRUSTRATION" SOONER THAN OTHERS.

AND IT'S TEMPTING, WINNICOTT SAYS, TO LET THEM.

MOM SAYS I WAS A "GOOD BABY."

IN THERAPY WITH JOCELYN, I TRIED TO EXPLAIN OUR PECULIAR RELATIONSHIP.

I ALWAYS CALL HER. SHE NEVER CALLS ME.

I LISTEN TO HER GO ON AND ON ABOUT PEOPLE I DON'T KNOW, I SUPPORT HER, ENCOURAGE HER. BUT SHE DOESN'T WANT TO HEAR ABOUT MY LIFE.

I KNOW IT'S PARTLY THE LESBIAN THING. LIKE SHE'S AFRAID IF I GET A WORD IN EDGEWISE, IT'LL BE "CUNNILINGUS."

BUT IT FEELS DEEPER THAN THAT.

SANTA FE CHAMBER MUSIC FESTIVAL

IT'S LIKE I'M THE MOTHER.

IT WAS RIGHT AROUND THE TIME OF THE CHRISTMAS PAGEANT THAT MY OBSESSIVE-COMPULSIVE PHASE BEGAN.

WHAT HOSTILE IMPULSES, AS FREUD CALLED THEM, COULD I HAVE BEEN REPRESSING AT AGE TEN?

HAD I BEEN ANGRY AT MY MOTHER? DID I WANT TO HURT HER?

WAS I *STILL* ANGRY AT HER?

AND IF SO, IS THAT WHY I WAS WRITING THIS MEMOIR ABOUT MY FATHER? A BOOK THAT WOULD EXPOSE HER INTIMATE SECRETS?

I CONSIDERED THIS DISTURBING POSSIBILITY.

IT WAS ONE WEEK AFTER I'D WALKED INTO THE PLANK.

I OFTEN CLIMBED THIS HILL NEAR MY HOUSE.

BUT TODAY, ON THE STEEPEST PART, AS I LOOKED UP...

FUCK!

...A SHARP TWIG HIT ME NOT BETWEEN THE EYES, BUT SQUARELY IN MY LEFT ONE.

I HAD BADLY SCRATCHED MY CORNEA.

WHAT HAPPENED?!

THE PSYCHO-PATHOLOGY OF EVERYDAY LIFE.

THIS KINDA THROWS MY WHOLE "LISTEN TO YOUR THIRD EYE" THEORY OUT THE WINDOW. WHAT IS THE MESSAGE HERE?!

AM I FAILING TO SEE SOMETHING? SOME-THING THAT'S RIGHT IN FRONT OF ME?

I COULDN'T FIGURE IT OUT. THE INJURY MADE ME TIRED. I LOST TWO DAYS OF WORK ON THE DAD BOOK, JUST WHEN I WAS BEGINNING THE PART ABOUT MY PARENTS' MARRIAGE.

IT ONLY OCCURS TO ME NOW, AS I'M WRITING THIS BOOK ABOUT MY MOTHER, THAT PERHAPS I HAD SCRATCHED MY CORNEA TO PUNISH MYSELF FOR "SEEING" THE TRUTH ABOUT MY FAMILY.

LIKE OEDIPUS GOUGING OUT HIS OWN EYES.

I'D BEEN READING FREUD FOR THE PAST THREE WEEKS AT THAT POINT. AS SOON AS MY EYE WAS HEALED, I BEGAN *THE INTERPRETATION OF DREAMS.*

TO ILLUSTRATE THE TECHNIQUE OF FREE ASSOCIATION, FREUD QUOTES A LETTER THE POET SCHILLER WROTE TO A FRIEND WITH WRITER'S BLOCK.

"The reason for your complaint, it seems to me, is the constraint which your intellect imposes upon your imagination ... you reject too soon and discriminate too severely."

THAT NIGHT I HAD THE SPIDERWEB DREAM. INTERPRETED VIA FREUD'S METHOD, IT SEEMED TO BE *ABOUT* THE UNCONSCIOUS. THE SLEEPING FIGURE OF AMY IS MYSELF, DREAMING

MY FEAR OF THE SPIDER TURNS TO AWE AT THE PERFECTION OF ITS WEB...

...A PERFECTION THAT COULD NOT BE REPLICATED WITH THE "TOOLS OR MEASURING DEVICES" OF THE CONSCIOUS MIND.

THE WEB IS MY UNCONSCIOUS, BUT IT'S ALSO A WISH—A FANTASY OF WHAT MY OWN CREATIVITY MIGHT LOOK LIKE IF I WEREN'T CONSTANTLY IMPEDING ITS FLOW.

SIXTEEN MONTHS AFTER STARTING TO REWRITE THIS BOOK ABOUT MY MOTHER, I'M NOT DONE. NOR HAVE I SHOWN ANY OF IT TO HER.

I FINALLY FINISHED THAT JOYCE CAROL OATES MEMOIR, *A WIDOW'S STORY*.

I'D GET SO MAD I HAD TO KEEP STOPPING. BUT IT WAS DUE AT THE LIBRARY.

JULIAN BARNES JUST REVIEWED IT.

HE TAKES HER TO TASK FOR NOT MENTIONING THAT SHE'D REMARRIED SOMEONE ELSE BY THE TIME THE BOOK CAME OUT.

HE'S RIGHT. IT WAS CALLOUS AND HYPOCRITICAL.

WELL...WRITERS ARE KIND OF MONSTROUS, AREN'T THEY? THEY DON'T HAVE, LIKE, NORMAL HUMAN ETHICS.

I KNOW! SHE WRITES ABOUT THROWING OUT THE SYMPATHY BOUQUETS SHE GOT! HOW WILL THOSE PEOPLE FEEL?

YOU WOULDN'T DO THAT, WOULD YOU?

UHH...I DON'T THINK SO.

AND I DON'T THINK SHE HAD THE RIGHT TO REVEAL ALL THAT STUFF ABOUT HER HUSBAND, LIKE THE NOVEL HE WROTE AND SET ASIDE.

I ALSO JUST READ HER BOOK *BLONDE*, ABOUT MARILYN MONROE.

SHE CHANGES THE SPELLING OF NORMA JEAN, AND SAYS IN THE PREFACE THAT SHE ADAPTED AND INVENTED, THEREFORE IT'S FICTION.

WELL, NO, IT'S NOT! HOW DOES *THAT* GET BY THE LEGAL DEPARTMENT?

MOM, YOU SHOULD WRITE ABOUT ALL THIS!

I KNOW.

IF I WERE GOING TO WRITE ABOUT BEING A WIDOW, WHAT WOULD I SAY? I HAD THREE TEENAGERS, A JOB, THE FUNERAL HOME TO RUN. YOU DIDN'T HEAR ME COMPLAINING.

EXCEPT I DON'T WRITE ABOUT MYSELF. SO THAT'S THAT.

I'LL WRITE ABOUT YOU.

WHAT DID SHE SAY TO THAT? I WAS TOO ENGAGED WITH THE CONVERSATION TO RE-CORD IT. SHE PROBABLY ROLLED HER EYES.

MY NOTES RESUME WHEN SHE CHANGED THE SUBJECT.

BOB AND I ARE GOING INTO PHILADELPHIA NEXT WEEKEND.

IN MY DREAM, THE SPIDERWEB HAD BEEN DIVIDED INTO ELEVEN SECTIONS. "THERE IS NOTHING ARBITRARY OR UNDETERMINED IN THE PSYCHIC LIFE," FREUD INSISTS. NUMBERS IN PARTICULAR.

ELEVEN IS THE FIRST NUMBER THAT CAN'T BE COUNTED ON TWO HUMAN HANDS. IT GOES BEYOND, TRANSGRESSES, AND FOR THAT REASON HAS AN ASSOCIATION WITH SIN.

IT WAS TWO WEEKS AFTER I TURNED ELEVEN THAT MY OCD REACHED ITS CRESCENDO AND MY MOTHER TOOK OVER MY DIARY ENTRIES.

IN FACT, I SEE NOW THAT IT WAS ON ROSH HASHANAH––THE DAY ON WHICH THE BOOKS CONTAINING THE DEEDS OF HUMANITY ARE OPENED FOR REVIEW.

Monday SEPTEMB

Jewish New Year

9
10
11
12

THE RIGHTEOUS ARE INSCRIBED.

THE WICKED ARE BLOTTED OUT.

AND EVERYONE ELSE GETS TEN (NOT ELEVEN) DAYS TO ATONE FOR THEIR SINS.

YOU'LL TAKE ALL NIGHT AT THAT RATE. WHY DON'T YOU TELL ME WHAT YOU WANT TO SAY, AND I'LL WRITE IT DOWN FOR YOU.

68

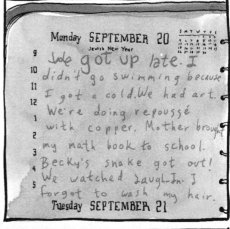

SHE DID THIS EVERY NIGHT FOR SIX WEEKS. WHATEVER I SAID, SHE WROTE DOWN.

COMING HOME FROM SCHOOL THE TURKEYS GOBBLED AND DAD HONKED THE HORN.

THERE WAS ONE WITH A BLIND EYE.

I DIDN'T GET MY PICTURE IN JACK AND JILL.

BOO HOO.

JACK AND JILL MAGAZINE PUBLISHED ART BY THEIR READERS ON THE BACK PAGE. I HAD RECENTLY SUBMITTED A DRAWING.

TWO DAYS AFTER MY DREAM ABOUT THE SPIDERWEB, I HAD A BREAKTHROUGH WITH CAROL.

SO WHEN YOU SEE THIS GAY CARTOONIST'S WORK IN *THE NEW YORKER*...

OH, GOD. IT'S THE WORST FEELING IN THE WORLD.

I WAS SUFFERING AT THIS TIME FROM NEARLY UNBEARABLE SPASMS OF PROFESSIONAL ENVY.

I FEEL... ANNIHILATED.

I'M NOT MAKING ENOUGH MONEY. THE NEWSPAPERS MY STRIP RUNS IN KEEP FOLDING OR MERGING.

OF OTHER CARTOONISTS, OF OTHER GAY AND LESBIAN WRITERS, OF ANYONE WHO WAS AT ALL LIKE ME OR WAS DOING ANYTHING REMOTELY SIMILAR TO WHAT I WAS DOING.

PEOPLE DON'T NEED CARTOONS ABOUT LESBIANS ANYMORE! YOU CAN WATCH THEM ON TV!

I'M SPENDING MORE THAN HALF MY TIME ON THIS CRAZY BOOK ABOUT MY DAD AND I DON'T EVEN KNOW IF IT'LL EVER GET PUBLISHED.

70

SO, YEAH. WHEN ALL OF A SUDDEN *THE NEW YORKER* STARTS RUNNING THESE BLASÉ POST-GAY CARTOONS, I FEEL LIKE, FUCK! WHAT HAVE I BEEN DOING WITH MY LIFE?

AM I GOING TO HAVE TO GET A JOB?

HMM. YOUR OWN ACHIEVEMENTS GET ERASED BY OTHER PEOPLE'S.

ISN'T THAT HOW IT WORKS?

ALL THIS MAKES ME THINK THAT IN YOUR FAMILY THERE WASN'T ENOUGH ROOM UNDER ONE ROOF FOR SEVERAL GENIUSES.

YOU'VE REVERSED YOUR OWN AGGRESSION. YOU FEEL GUILTY FOR WANTING TO ANNIHILATE OTHERS, SO YOU TURN IT ON YOURSELF.

WHOA!

I HAVE TO STOP DOING THAT!

YES, YOU DO.

I THINK YOUR FEAR OF ANNIHILATION MIGHT ALSO BE A KIND OF REACTION FORMATION.

A WHAT?!

IT'S A DEFENSE MECHANISM. IT'S LIKE PEOPLE WHO BECOME HOMOPHOBIC BECAUSE THEY CAN'T ACCEPT THEIR OWN HOMOSEXUAL DESIRE.

REACTION FORMATION!

SOMEHOW THE MERE IDEA THAT I HAD AGGRESSION BROKE THE GRIP OF THE TERRIBLE FEELING.

THIS IS **GREAT!**

I'M GONNA GO **KILL** SOMEONE!

I FOUND A FILE FOLDER IN MY BAG TO TAKE NOTES ON.

YOU GOT THIS FROM YOUR PARENTS. YOU INHERITED THEIR UNMETABOLIZED FEAR AND AGGRESSION.

UH HUH.

THEIR SENSE OF THREAT ABOUT THE ARTISTIC ABILITY OF OTHERS.

UH HUH.

THE CONCEPT OF ORIGINAL SIN HAD PUZZLED ME IN MY RELIGION CLASSES AS A CHILD. HOW COULD AN INNOCENT, FLAWLESS BABY ALREADY HAVE SIN RACKED UP AGAINST IT?

BUT MAYBE THIS IS JUST ANOTHER NAME FOR THE UNMETABOLIZED EMOTIONS WE ABSORB FROM OUR PARENTS, LIKE TRACES OF NICOTINE.

AS I SAID, MY DEPRESSION BEGAN TO LIFT IMMEDIATELY AFTER MY FIRST SESSION WITH JOCELYN.

AFTER OUR SECOND SESSION, I DREAMED THAT MY FATHER HAD DRIVEN OFF WITH NO NOTICE, STRANDING ME AT A PICNIC.

MY DREAM FURY WAS HOT, GALVANIC, PURIFYING. I REHEARSED WHAT I WOULD SAY TO HIM.

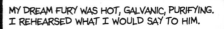

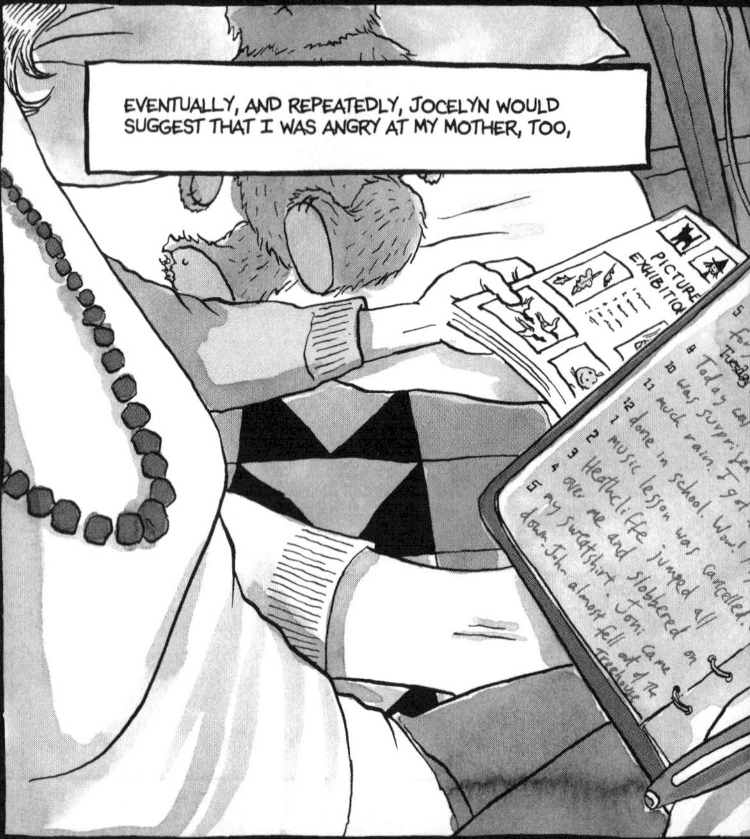
EVENTUALLY, AND REPEATEDLY, JOCELYN WOULD SUGGEST THAT I WAS ANGRY AT MY MOTHER, TOO,

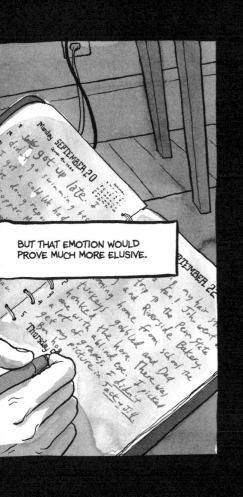

BUT THAT EMOTION WOULD
PROVE MUCH MORE ELUSIVE.

# 3 True and False Self

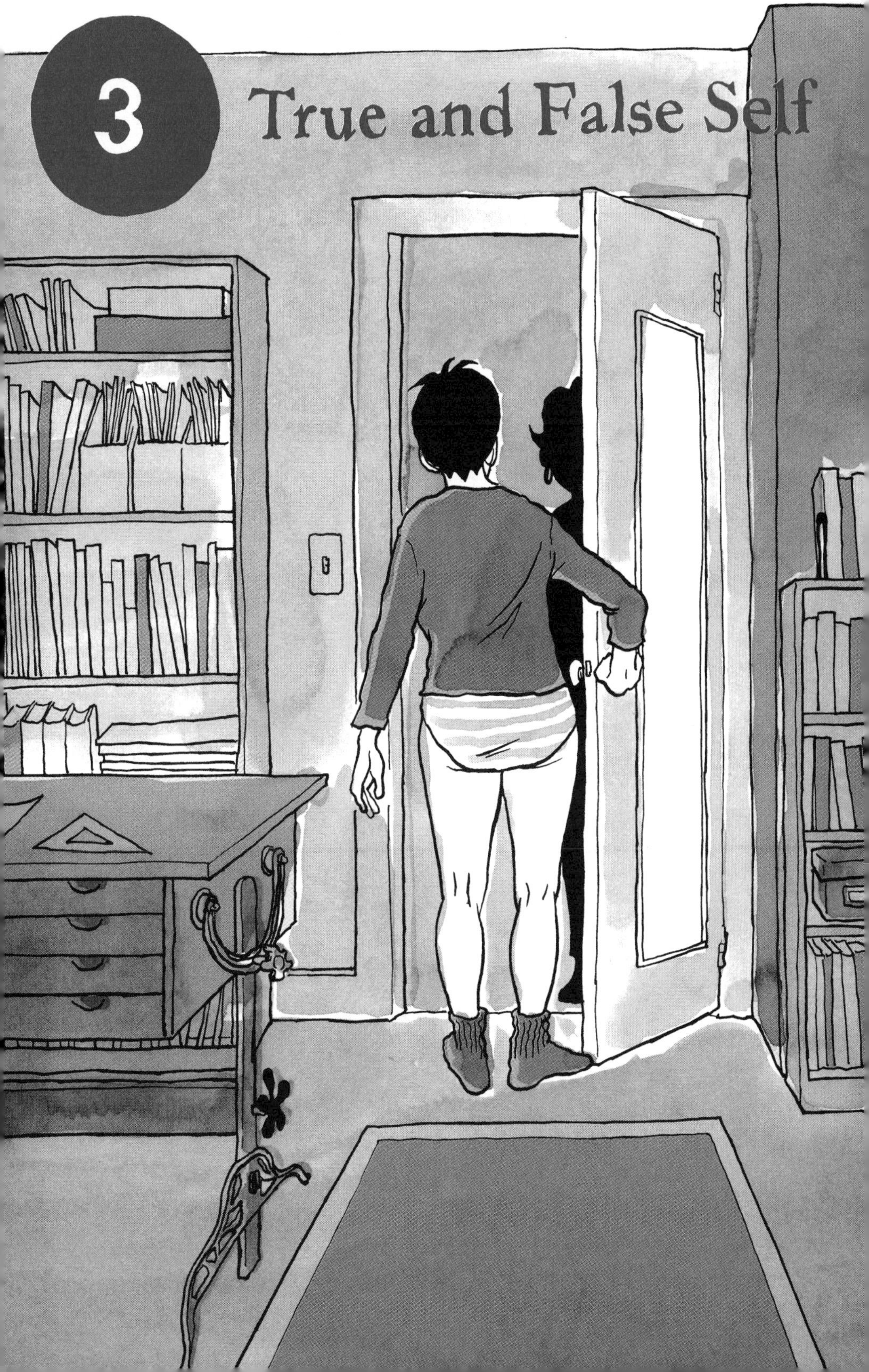

MY THERAPIST CAROL COMES TO MY OFFICE. IT'S NO BIG DEAL THAT I'M NOT WEARING PANTS. IT'S AS IF I'VE TAKEN THEM OFF TO THROW THEM IN THE LAUNDRY, OR IRON THEM.

SHE HAS ME LEAN ACROSS THE TABLE...

...THEN PROCEEDS TO GIVE ME A PERFECT MASSAGE. I DON'T SAY ANYTHING ABOUT MY STIFF NECK.

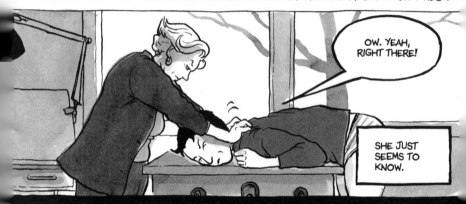

OW. YEAH, RIGHT THERE!

SHE JUST SEEMS TO KNOW.

SHE STROKES WITH ONE HAND WHILE HOLDING FIRMLY AND PUSHING IN THE OPPOSITE DIRECTION WITH THE OTHER. LIKE I PET MY CAT.

SHE FINISHES BRISKLY.

THERE YOU GO!

I MAKE SMALL TALK AS SHE PREPARES TO GO.

I'M GOING TO A BAR MITZVAH THIS AFTERNOON.

OH, I'LL TAKE THESE.

I'LL FIND SOME MATCHING MATERIAL TO PATCH THE TEAR.

OH, JEEZ. YOU DON'T HAVE TO...

...I MEAN...IT'S NOT NECESSARY TO MATCH THE COLOR EXACTLY.

TCH!

WELL... OKAY!

AS SHE LEAVES WITH MY PANTS, I FEEL AS SECURE AND HAPPY AS I EVER HAVE.

I HAD THE MENDING DREAM A MONTH AFTER THE SPIDERWEB DREAM. FOR THE PAST TWO NIGHTS, I HAD BEEN READING A BOOK BY JUNG. FIRST, THE SECTION ON REBIRTH.

THIS DESCRIBED VARIOUS PSYCHOLOGICAL EXPERIENCES OF RENEWAL AND TRANSFORMATION.

THEN ON THE NIGHT OF THE DREAM, I READ THE SECTION ON THE MOTHER ARCHETYPE.

LET'S FIX THAT HOLE IN YOUR JEANS. TAKE THEM OFF.

NO!

THIS HAS THREE BASIC ATTRIBUTES, JUNG SAYS. "GOODNESS, PASSION, AND DARKNESS."

YOU CAN PUT THEM RIGHT BACK ON. IT'LL ONLY TAKE A MINUTE.

IN MOST NEUROTIC PEOPLE, "DEFINITE CAUSES OF DISTURBANCES CAN BE FOUND IN THE PARENTS, ESPECIALLY IN THE MOTHER."

PICK OUT A PATCH THAT'S THE RIGHT SIZE AND COLOR.

BUT THE REAL ORIGIN LIES LESS WITH THE PERSONAL MOTHER THAN WITH THE MYTHIC ARCHETYPES THAT WE PROJECT ONTO HER.

IT'S IMPORTANT FOR THE ANALYST TO BE ABLE TO SORT OUT THE PROJECTIONS FROM THE REALITY, JUNG SAYS.

THERE. LIKE NEW!

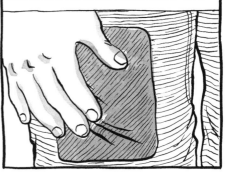

BUT THIS IS DONE MORE EASILY WITH ADULTS THAN WITH CHILDREN, BECAUSE ADULTS "ALMOST INVARIABLY TRANSFER THEIR FANTASIES TO THE PHYSICIAN DURING TREATMENT."

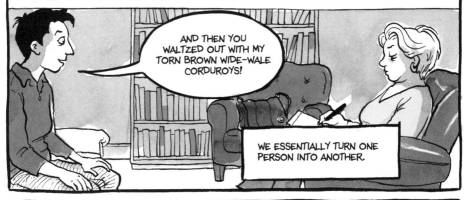

THE CONCEPT OF "TRANSFERENCE" HAS SO THOROUGHLY ENTERED OUR VERNACULAR THAT IT'S EASY TO OVERLOOK ITS ALCHEMICAL POWER.

AND THEN YOU WALTZED OUT WITH MY TORN BROWN WIDE-WALE CORDUROYS!

WE ESSENTIALLY TURN ONE PERSON INTO ANOTHER.

WINNICOTT, TOO, USES THE TELESCOPE OF THE TRANSFERENCE TO LOOK BACK IN TIME.

TRUE AND FALSE SELF (1960)          141

in the transference a phase (or phases) of serious regression to dependence.

My experiences have led me to recognize that dependent or deeply regressed patients can teach the analyst more about early infancy than can be learned from direct observation of infants, and more than can be learned from contact with mothers who are involved with i

with the normal and

relationship influenc

happens in the transference (in the regressed phases of certain of

THIS IS FROM "EGO DISTORTION IN TERMS OF TRUE AND FALSE SELF," PUBLISHED THE YEAR I WAS BORN.

THE PATCHING IN MY DREAM PERHAPS STANDS IN FOR AN EVEN EARLIER EXPERIENCE OF MATERNAL CARE AND RENEWAL. MY DISHABILLE. THE TABLE. THE BROWN PANTS...

I HAVE, IN FACT, BEEN TRYING TO HEAL MY MOTHER FOR AS LONG AS I CAN REMEMBER.

PAPA! PAPA!

PAPA ISN'T HERE! WHERE HAS HE GOT TO?

MY PARENTS SEEMED TO SPEND MY ENTIRE CHILDHOOD WATCHING A SERIES ON PUBLIC TELEVISION CALLED *THE FORSYTE SAGA.*

ACTUALLY, IT AIRED FOR 26 WEEKS DURING THE WINTER OF 1969–70, WHEN I WAS NINE.

I CAN'T SLEEP.

SIT DOWN AND WATCH THIS FOR A WHILE.

I'VE REALLY NO IDEA, JUNE.

WHERE'S DAD?

STILL AT THE FUNERAL HOME. SHHH.

BUT I WANT TO TELL HIM ABOUT THE WEDDING!

IT WAS BASED ON A SERIES OF NOVELS BY JOHN GALSWORTHY CRITIQUING VICTORIAN SOCIAL MORES.

BUT IN HER ARTICLE "MODERN FICTION," VIRGINIA WOOLF WOULD SUGGEST THAT GALSWORTHY'S WRITING EMBODIED THOSE VERY VALUES.

IT WAS UNUSUAL TO BE ALONE WITH MOM LIKE THIS. IT WOULD BE ANOTHER YEAR BEFORE SHE BEGAN HELPING ME WITH MY DIARY ENTRIES.

I'M NOT JEALOUS, IF THAT'S WHAT YOU MEAN.

THE PREVIOUS SPRING, BOTH HER PARENTS HAD DIED.

FIRST HER MOTHER, OF CANCER. THEN HER FATHER, OF A "BROKEN HEART." IN THE MONTHS FOLLOWING THEIR DEATHS, MOM FELL INTO A DEEP DEPRESSION.

Page 4—Tuesday, April 22, 1

Page 4—Thursday, May 29, 1969—The Expr

# Deaths and F

## Mrs. Fontana Die

## Kindergartner' a

Mrs. Andrew Fontana of 64 Susquehanna Ave., died at noon yesterday in the Lock Haven Hospital Extended Care Unit where she had been a patient since November. Her health had been failing over the past two years.

Mrs. Fontana was the former Rachel Victoria Rohe, daughter of George and Mary Carroll Rohe. She was born in the same house in which the Fontanas now live, and started to school in the first kindergarten at the present Lock Haven State College, from which she later graduated when the college was the Central State Normal.

Mrs. Fontana maintained a life-long interest in the college and its alumni affairs.

Before her marriage in 1929, she worked as a secretary for the Clark Printing and Manufacturing Co. where her father

I DIDN'T KNOW THIS THEN, OF COURSE.

# Funerals

## Andrew Fontana, 76, Dies 5

## Weeks after Wife's Death

Five weeks following the death of his wife, Rachel Rohe Fontana, Andrew Fontana, 75, died unexpectedly yesterday at his house, 64 Susquehanna Ave.

The retired Penn-Central Railroad employe and well-known baritone soloist of Lock Haven was found dead in bed of a heart attack, about noon. He had apparently turned off his alarm at 6:30 a.m., preparing to get up, when stricken.

Mr. Fontana was born Nov. 29, 1893 in Caioria, a parish district in southern Austria, in the Tyrol. His father, Candido, went first to South America to make his home and later the family came to the United States, in 1906, to live in Far-randsville.

Mr. Fontana worked for the Pennsylvania Railroad 56 years, retiring as a signal maintainer

Beech Creek; Miss Mary C., Boston, Mass; and three grand-children.

BUT NOW I SEE THAT IT EXPLAINS THE PAINFUL TENDERNESS I DEVELOPED TOWARD MOM AROUND THIS TIME. A TENDERNESS ALL THE MORE ACUTE FOR ITS HAVING NO OUTLET.

AND WHEN YOU CHANGE THIS MISTRESS FOR ANOTHER, AS YOU WILL, I DON'T WISH TO KNOW ANYTHING ABOUT HER EITHER.

84

MOM PETTED MY TWO YOUNGER BROTHERS AND COOED TO THEM, BUT SHE AND I NEVER TRAFFICKED IN THAT SORT OF THING.

DON'T GET ANY BIGGER!

I HAD TO FIGURE OUT OTHER WAYS OF EXPRESSING MY SOLICITUDE. ONE WAS TO GIVE HER A MORE RESPECTFUL TITLE. "MOMMY" HAD AN UNGRATEFUL, DEMANDING RING TO IT.

MOTHER, CAN I RIDE MY BIKE TO THE STORE?

ANOTHER WAS TO APOLOGIZE FREQUENTLY--BUT THIS HAD A SADLY COUNTERPRODUCTIVE EFFECT.

ALISON, SET THE TABLE.

I'M SORRY!

WHY?! WILL YOU STOP SAYING THAT?!

I'M SORRY!

ON THIS *FORSYTE SAGA* NIGHT, HOWEVER, I WAS ABOUT TO BE HANDED AN OPPORTUNITY TO TELL MY MOTHER EXACTLY HOW I FELT.

I THINK I CAN SLEEP NOW.

OKAY.

AND I WAS ABOUT TO BUNGLE IT.

ALISON?

THE QUESTION IS, FATHER, WHERE DO YOU STAND?

9:39

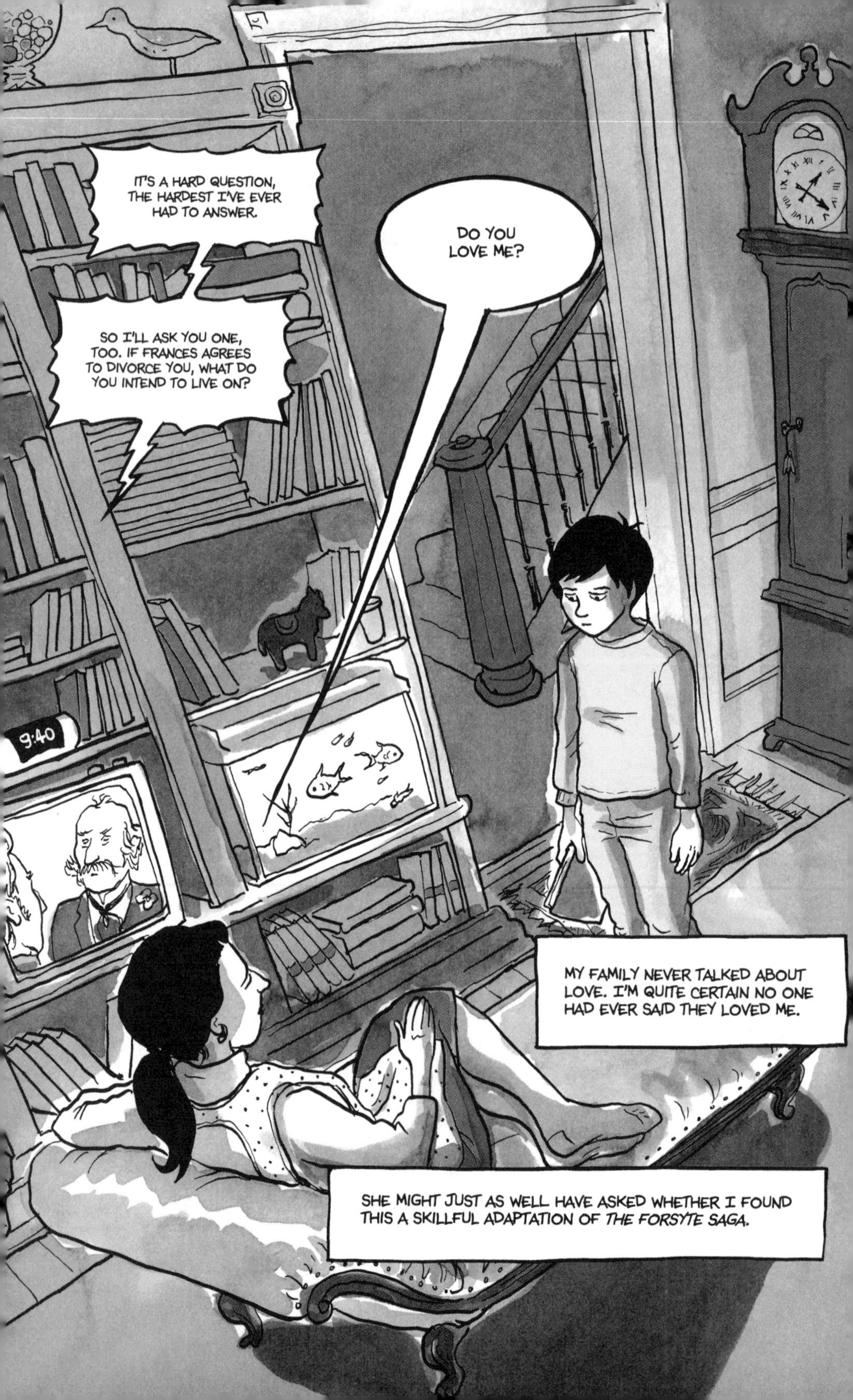
IT'S A HARD QUESTION, THE HARDEST I'VE EVER HAD TO ANSWER.
DO YOU LOVE ME?
SO I'LL ASK YOU ONE, TOO. IF FRANCES AGREES TO DIVORCE YOU, WHAT DO YOU INTEND TO LIVE ON?
9:40
MY FAMILY NEVER TALKED ABOUT LOVE. I'M QUITE CERTAIN NO ONE HAD EVER SAID THEY LOVED ME.
SHE MIGHT JUST AS WELL HAVE ASKED WHETHER I FOUND THIS A SKILLFUL ADAPTATION OF *THE FORSYTE SAGA*.

BUT INSTANTLY I KNEW THAT ALL I WANTED WAS TO ASSURE HER THAT I LOVED HER. I HAD TO BE CAREFUL HOW I REPLIED, THOUGH. TOO ENTHUSIASTIC, AND I'D SEEM DISINGENUOUS.

9:40

TOO SERIOUS, AND I'D SEEM GRUDGING.

YOU HAVE DUTIES, RESPONSIBILITIES!

TOO SLOW, AND I MIGHT MISS MY CHANCE FOREVER.

NOW I SEE THAT NO DEGREE OF SINCERITY OR ALACRITY ON MY PART WOULD HAVE SUFFICED.

YES.

IN *THE CHRONICLES OF NARNIA*, WHICH I DISCOVERED THAT WINTER, THE PEVENSIE CHILDREN HAD BEEN "SENT AWAY FROM LONDON DURING THE WAR BECAUSE OF THE AIR-RAIDS."

TO BE SENT AWAY FROM ONE'S PARENTS SEEMED LIKE THE WORST FATE IMAGINABLE. AT LEAST WORTH A BOOK OF ITS OWN.

The LION, the WITCH and the WARDROBE
a children's story
C.S. Lewis

BUT IT'S ONLY MENTIONED IN PASSING, IN THE FRAMING STORY.

I DON'T REMEMBER MY MOTHER'S PARENTS VERY WELL.

I WAS EIGHT WHEN THEY DIED. A FEW WEEKS AFTER NANA'S DEATH IN APRIL, AND A FEW WEEKS BEFORE GRANDPA FONTANA'S DEATH IN MAY, I MADE MY FIRST COMMUNION.

CATHOLIC DOCTRINE HAD AN INTERNAL LOGICAL CONSISTENCY THAT I FOUND CONSOLING.

SINGLE FILE. STEP LIVELY!

THERE WERE CLEAR PROCEDURES. IN ORDER TO RECEIVE COMMUNION, YOU HAD TO BE IN A "STATE OF GRACE," TO BE FREE OF SIN.

...AND AS SOON AS ONE PERSON COMES OUT, THE NEXT ONE GOES IN.

THE DAY BEFORE MY FIRST COMMUNION, I MADE MY FIRST CONFESSION.

shoont

THIS WAS PERHAPS NOT, STRICTLY SPEAKING, A MYSTICAL EXPERIENCE.

BLESS ME FATHER FOR I HAVE SINNED.

BUT AFTER TELLING THE PRIEST I'D YELLED AT MY BROTHERS AND HADN'T CLEANED MY ROOM, AFTER SAYING MY PENANCE AT THE ALTAR--I FELT AN INTOXICATING LIGHTNESS.

TO BE IN A STATE OF GRACE YOU ALSO HAD TO FAST FOR AN HOUR--TO BE EMPTY OF NOT JUST SIN BUT FOOD.

BODY OF CHRIST.

THE NEXT DAY, AS THE PAPERY WAFER MELTED ON MY TONGUE, I FELT COMPLETELY EMPTY, AND COMPLETELY GOOD.

IN OUR FAMILY ALBUM THERE WERE LOTS OF PHOTOS OF MY FATHER AS A CHILD, BUT ONLY ONE OF MOM--ON THE DAY OF HER FIRST COMMUNION.

SHE'S DARK, PALE, SHY. ALL THE THINGS I DISLIKED ABOUT MY OWN APPEARANCE.

WHEN MOM TALKED ABOUT HER CHILDHOOD, WHICH WAS NOT OFTEN, THE DEPRESSION AND THE WAR LOOMED LARGE. THEIR VICTORY GARDEN. THE AIRPLANE SILHOUETTES THEY HAD TO MEMORIZE.

MESSERSCHMITT!

DURING THE SPRING OF MY MOTHER'S FIRST COMMUNION, THE GERMANS WERE BLITZ-KRIEGING ACROSS EUROPE.

YES!

HAVE YOU PRACTICED YOUR CATECHISM TODAY?

IN ENGLAND, "OPERATION PIED PIPER" HAD RECENTLY EVACUATED HUNDREDS OF THOUSANDS OF CHILDREN AWAY FROM URBAN BOMBING TARGETS TO THE COUNTRYSIDE.

STRANGERS TOOK THE KIDS IN. SIBLINGS WERE OFTEN SEPARATED.

DONALD WINNICOTT WORKED AS A PSYCHIATRIC CONSULTANT TO THE EVACUATION PROGRAM, ADVISING THE STAFF OF HOSTELS FOR KIDS TOO TROUBLED TO BE PLACED WITH FAMILIES.

90

WINNICOTT WOULD LATER SAY THAT THESE CHILDREN WOULD HAVE BEEN BETTER OFF BOMBED THAN EVACUATED.

HELEN, KEEP AN EYE ON YOUR SISTER WHILE I GO NEXT DOOR.

OUT OF WINNICOTT'S WORK WITH THE EVACUEES CAME HIS IDEA THAT DELINQUENT BEHAVIOR WAS ACTUALLY A SIGN OF HEALTH...

...A WAY THAT THE CHILD IS ASKING FOR SOMETHING THAT HE OR SHE USED TO HAVE, AND STILL NEEDS.

FLYING FORTRESS!

THE OBVERSE OF THIS—THE IDEA THAT COMPLIANT BEHAVIOR IS UNHEALTHY—IS AT THE CORE OF WINNICOTT'S POSTWAR THINKING ABOUT THE FALSE SELF.

THE MOTHER WHO IS NOT "GOOD-ENOUGH" FAILS TO MEET THE INFANT'S "SPONTANEOUS GESTURE."

infant gesture; instead she substitutes her own gesture which is to be given sense by the compliance of the infant. This compliance on the part of the infant is the earliest stage of the False Self, and

COMPLIANCE IS WINNICOTT'S BÊTE NOIRE, SPONTANEITY HIS SUMMUM BONUM. HE DOESN'T REALLY DEFINE THE TRUE SELF, BUT IT "FEELS REAL." THE FALSE SELF, OF COURSE, FEELS FALSE.

At the earliest stage the True Self is the theoretical position from which come the spontaneous gesture and the personal idea. The spontaneous gesture is the True Self in action. Only the True Self can be creative and only the True Self can feel real. Whereas a True Self feels real, the existence of a False Self results in a

IF THE BABY'S GESTURE GOES UNMET, THE BABY LEARNS TO NOT RISK BEING SPONTANEOUS. A FALSE SELF DEVELOPS TO PROTECT THE TRUE SELF.

MARY, WATCH!

THERE'S A LITTLE BIT OF THE FALSE SELF IN NORMAL SOCIAL BEHAVIOR—WE LEARN TO BE POLITE AND TO MAKE COMPROMISES.

REMEMBER THAT LADY IN THE MOVIE WHO TORE OFF HER NECKLACE?

I'M GONNA PRETEND TO DO THAT!

BUT WINNICOTT IS MORE CONCERNED WITH THE "TRULY SPLIT-OFF COMPLIANT FALSE SELF." AS, FOR EXAMPLE, IN "THE CHILD WHO GROWS UP TO BE AN ACTOR."

yank

MY MOTHER DID GROW UP TO BE AN ACTOR.

WATCH ME AGAIN!

BUT NOT THE KIND THAT WINNICOTT DESCRIBES AS NEEDING TO BE APPLAUDED CONSTANTLY TO FEEL AS IF THEY EXIST.

SHE WAS THE QUIET, WATCHFUL KIND. THE KIND WHO BLENDS INTO THE BACKGROUND.

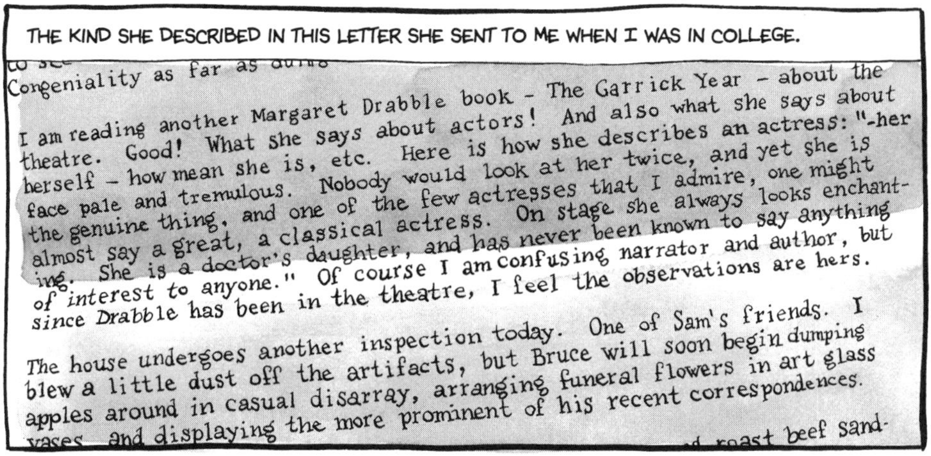
THE KIND SHE DESCRIBED IN THIS LETTER SHE SENT TO ME WHEN I WAS IN COLLEGE.

Congeniality as far as

I am reading another Margaret Drabble book - The Garrick Year - about the theatre. Good! What she says about actors! And also what she says about herself - how mean she is, etc. Here is how she describes an actress: "-her face pale and tremulous. Nobody would look at her twice, and yet she is the genuine thing, and one of the few actresses that I admire, one might almost say a great, a classical actress. On stage she always looks enchanting. She is a doctor's daughter, and has never been known to say anything of interest to anyone." Of course I am confusing narrator and author, but since Drabble has been in the theatre, I feel the observations are hers.

The house undergoes another inspection today. One of Sam's friends. I blew a little dust off the artifacts, but Bruce will soon begin dumping apples around in casual disarray, arranging funeral flowers in art glass vases and displaying the more prominent of his recent correspondences.

roast beef sand-

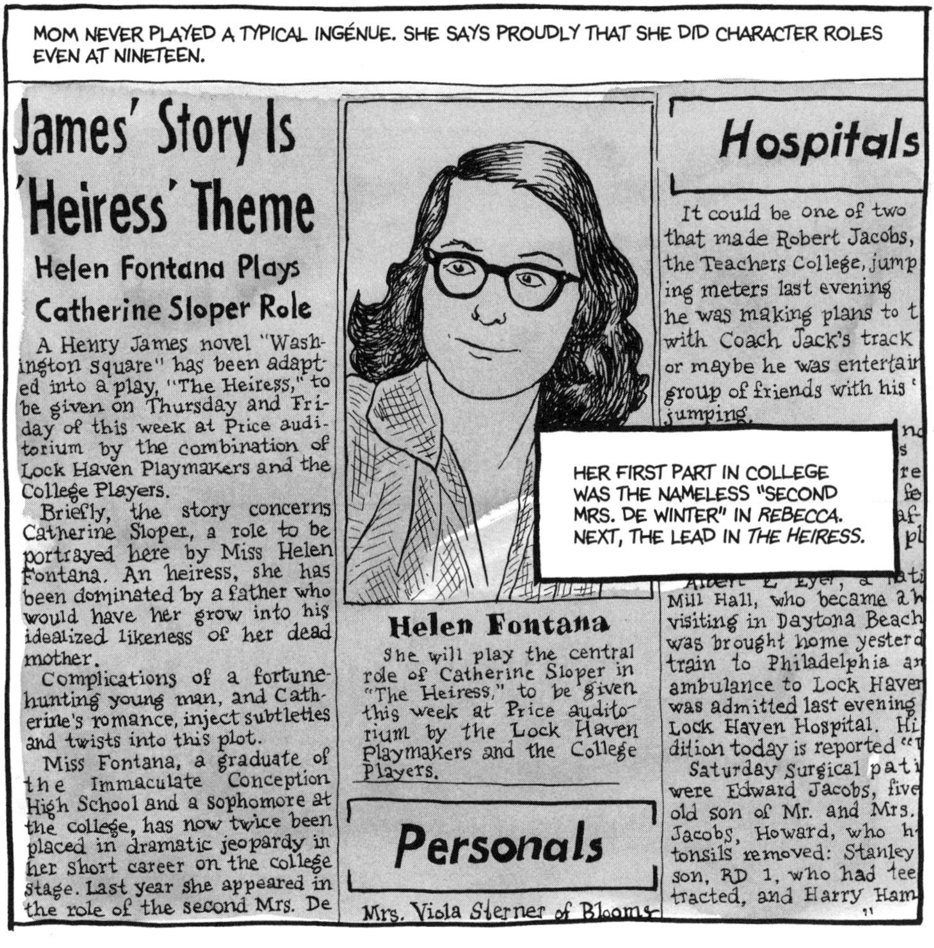
MOM NEVER PLAYED A TYPICAL INGÉNUE. SHE SAYS PROUDLY THAT SHE DID CHARACTER ROLES EVEN AT NINETEEN.
HER FIRST PART IN COLLEGE WAS THE NAMELESS "SECOND MRS. DE WINTER" IN *REBECCA*. NEXT, THE LEAD IN *THE HEIRESS*.

# James' Story Is 'Heiress' Theme

## Helen Fontana Plays Catherine Sloper Role

A Henry James novel "Washington square" has been adapted into a play, "The Heiress," to be given on Thursday and Friday of this week at Price auditorium by the combination of Lock Haven Playmakers and the College Players.

Briefly, the story concerns Catherine Sloper, a role to be portrayed here by Miss Helen Fontana. An heiress, she has been dominated by a father who would have her grow into his idealized likeness of her dead mother.

Complications of a fortune-hunting young man, and Catherine's romance, inject subtleties and twists into this plot.

Miss Fontana, a graduate of the Immaculate Conception High School and a sophomore at the college, has now twice been placed in dramatic jeopardy in her short career on the college stage. Last year she appeared in the role of the second Mrs. De

**Helen Fontana**

She will play the central role of Catherine Sloper in "The Heiress," to be given this week at Price auditorium by the Lock Haven Playmakers and the College Players.

## Personals

Mrs. Viola Sterner of Blooms-

## Hospitals

It could be one of two that made Robert Jacobs, the Teachers College, jumping meters last evening he was making plans to t with Coach Jack's track or maybe he was entertain group of friends with his ' jumping.

Mill Hall, who became a h visiting in Daytona Beach was brought home yesterd train to Philadelphia an ambulance to Lock Haven was admitted last evening Lock Haven Hospital. Hi dition today is reported "

Saturday Surgical pati were Edward Jacobs, five old son of Mr. and Mrs. Jacobs, Howard, who h tonsils removed: Stanley son, RD 1, who had tee tracted, and Harry Ham

MOM TOOK SOME TIME OFF FROM COLLEGE TO ACT. SHE APPRENTICED FOR A YEAR AT THE CLEVELAND PLAYHOUSE, WHERE SHE RAN PROPS, SEWED COSTUMES, AND PERFORMED.

SHE ALSO PALLED AROUND WITH DOM DELUISE. ONCE THEY WENT TO MIDNIGHT MASS TOGETHER BEFORE A CHRISTMAS PARTY.

YOU CAN START NOW, THE CATHO-LICS ARE HERE.

WHEN I WAS GROWING UP, SOMETIMES DOM DELUISE WOULD BE ON TELEVISION.

WHAT WAS HE LIKE?

HE WAS SO FUNNY! HE'D MAKE UP LINES ONSTAGE TO TRY AND CRACK YOU UP.

DOMINICK the GREAT

WHY DIDN'T YOU BECOME AN ACTRESS?

OH, I WANTED TO GET MARRIED AND HAVE KIDS.

AS A CHILD, WHEN I HEARD THE STORY OF MOM ACCIDENTALLY BREAKING HER TREASURED NECK-LACE, HOW I WISHED THAT I COULD FIX IT.

OR BETTER YET, GO BACK IN TIME AND WARN HER.

MOM RETURNED HOME FROM CLEVELAND AND FINISHED HER DEGREE AT THE TEACHERS COLLEGE DOWN THE STREET FROM HER PARENTS' HOUSE.

SHE FIRST MET MY FATHER THERE, IN A PRODUCTION OF *THE TAMING OF THE SHREW.*

AFTER GRADUATING, SHE SPENT TWO YEARS IN NEW YORK CITY, WORKING AS A SECRETARY.

THEN SHE MARRIED DAD, AND ELEVEN MONTHS LATER, I WAS BORN.

ONE OF THE REASONS WHY THE MOTHER MIGHT FAIL TO MEET THE INFANT'S SPONTANEOUS GESTURE, WINNICOTT WRITES, IS BECAUSE THE FATHER IS NOT PERFORMING HIS PART WELL ENOUGH.

the simplest case the man, supported by a social attitude which is itself a development from the man's natural function, deals with external reality for the woman, and so makes it safe and sensible for her to be temporarily in-turned, self-centred.

CAN'T YOU KEEP THAT BRAT QUIET?

95

MY FATHER HAD HIS OWN STRUGGLES.

HE HAD A CLOSED-CASKET FUNERAL, BUT MY BROTHERS AND I WERE ALLOWED IN, TOGETHER, TO SEE HIM.

MOM WENT ALONE.

More towards health: The False Self has as its main concern a search for conditions which will make it possible for the True Self to come into its own. If conditions cannot be found then

BUT IF THOSE CONDITIONS CAN'T BE FOUND, "THE CLINICAL RESULT IS SUICIDE."

When suicide is the only defence left against betrayal of the True Self, then it becomes the lot of the False Self to organize the suicide. This, of course, involves its own destruction, but at the same time eliminates the need for its continued existence, since its function is the protection of the True Self from insult.

DO YOU EVER FEEL ANGRY AT YOUR FATHER FOR COMMITTING SUICIDE?

UH...NO.

I DON'T THINK SO.

IN HIS TRUE AND FALSE SELF PAPER, WINNICOTT TALKS ABOUT PATIENTS WHO, IN THE TRANSFERENCE, EXPERIENCE "SERIOUS REGRESSION TO DEPENDENCE."

HERE THE ANALYST HAS A CHANCE TO "FEED" THE PATIENT THE THING THAT WAS MISSING THE FIRST TIME AROUND.

WHATEVER WAS HAPPENING BETWEEN ME AND JOCELYN HAPPENED WHETHER WE SPOKE OR NOT, WHETHER I LOOKED AT HER OR COULD NOT BRING MYSELF TO MEET HER TERRIBLE GAZE.

WHEN I TOLD MOM THAT I WAS THINKING ABOUT SEEING A THERAPIST, I WAS BRACED FOR A BOOTSTRAPS LECTURE.

IT'S LIKE THIS AWFUL, DEAD FEELING.

BUT SHE WAS SYMPATHETIC. SHE TOLD ME SHE HAD EXPERIENCED DEPRESSION, TOO, SEVERAL TIMES—THE WORST, AFTER HER PARENTS DIED.

DR. MALCOLM WAS FEEDING ME ANTI-DEPRESSANTS AND SLEEPING PILLS.

GOD. I HAD NO IDEA.

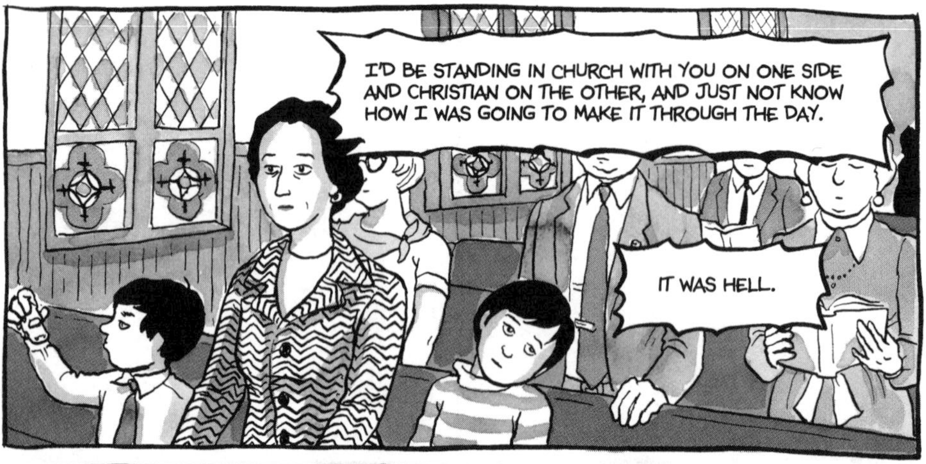
I'D BE STANDING IN CHURCH WITH YOU ON ONE SIDE AND CHRISTIAN ON THE OTHER, AND JUST NOT KNOW HOW I WAS GOING TO MAKE IT THROUGH THE DAY.
IT WAS HELL.

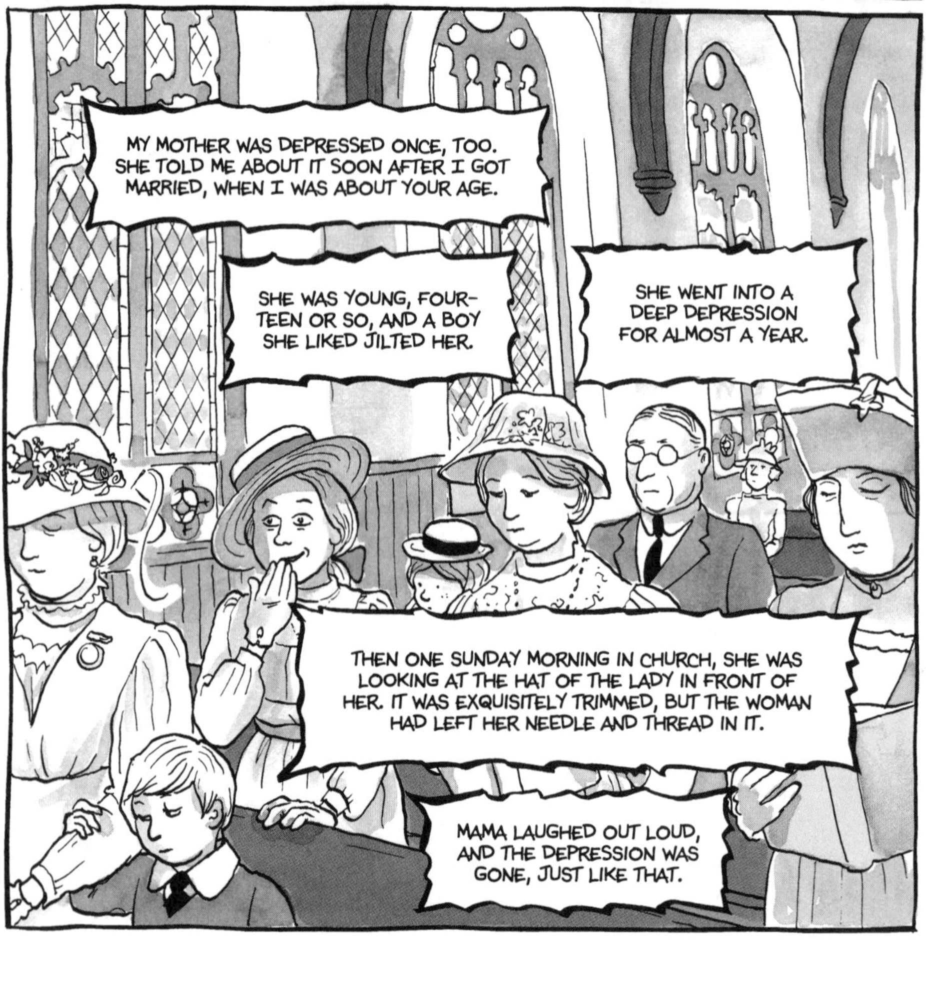
MY MOTHER WAS DEPRESSED ONCE, TOO. SHE TOLD ME ABOUT IT SOON AFTER I GOT MARRIED, WHEN I WAS ABOUT YOUR AGE.
SHE WAS YOUNG, FOUR-TEEN OR SO, AND A BOY SHE LIKED JILTED HER.
SHE WENT INTO A DEEP DEPRESSION FOR ALMOST A YEAR.
THEN ONE SUNDAY MORNING IN CHURCH, SHE WAS LOOKING AT THE HAT OF THE LADY IN FRONT OF HER. IT WAS EXQUISITELY TRIMMED, BUT THE WOMAN HAD LEFT HER NEEDLE AND THREAD IN IT.
MAMA LAUGHED OUT LOUD, AND THE DEPRESSION WAS GONE, JUST LIKE THAT.

DONALD WINNICOTT'S MOTHER SUFFERED FROM DEPRESSION, TOO. LATE IN LIFE HE WROTE A POEM ABOUT HER CALLED "THE TREE."

THE TREE IS A CROSS, AND WINNICOTT IS A CHRIST FIGURE.

"TO ENLIVEN HER WAS MY LIVING" READS ONE LINE.

MY DEPRESSION AT AGE TWENTY-SIX LASTED ONLY A FEW WEEKS. BUT AS A CHILD I USED TO EXPERIENCE OCCASIONAL FLEETING PANGS OF A TERRIBLE SADNESS.

THEY ALMOST ALWAYS HAPPENED IN CHURCH.

AS SOON AS I BECAME CONSCIOUS OF THE FEELING, IT WOULD DISSIPATE.

AS I GOT OLDER, I TRIED TO DESCRIBE IT TO MYSELF. THE BEST WORD I COULD COME UP WITH WAS "ORPHANED."

AS AN ADULT, I HAVE CONTINUED TO EXPERIENCE THESE BRIEF SPASMS OF MELANCHOLY --AND WORSE-- ON SOME OF THE RARE OCCASIONS I'VE ATTENDED CHURCH...

AND ALSO, SOMETIMES, AFTER SEX.

NOW DO YOU FEEL RELAXED?

AS I HAVE SAID, MY DEPRESSION LIFTED ALMOST THE MINUTE I BEGAN SEEING JOCELYN. BUT A RATHER ACUTE STATE OF ANXIETY PERSISTED FOR SOME MONTHS.

NOT REALLY.

THE ANXIETY WAS ONLY SLIGHTLY EASED BY MY NEW HABIT OF OBSERVING MY OWN EXPERIENCE THROUGH THE FILTER OF WHAT I THOUGHT JOCELYN WOULD THINK OF IT.

DO YOU HAVE THE SALOON AD DONE YET? I WANT TO RUN IT BY THEM.

I CONTINUED TO FUNCTION IN THE EXTERNAL WORLD, BUT MY LIFE THAT SUMMER WAS ALMOST COMPLETELY INTERNAL.

I WENT TO THERAPY.

I READ ABOUT THERAPY.

I WROTE ABOUT THERAPY.

100

AFTER FIVE MONTHS OF THIS, A STRANGE FEELING CAME OVER ME ONE DAY AT THE GYM.

I WASN'T ANXIOUS.

I DIDN'T MENTION IT TO ELOISE. BUT I SUGGESTED THAT WE GO OUT TO DINNER.

WE WENT TO A RESTAURANT WHERE ONLY A FEW WEEKS EARLIER I HAD BEEN UNABLE TO EAT BECAUSE OF THE STROBE EFFECT OF THE CEILING FAN AND THE FLUORESCENT LIGHTS.

SO I'M MOVING INTO BARRIE'S PLACE AT THE END OF THE MONTH.

AFTERWARD, WE RAN INTO SOME FRIENDS-- SUCH A PLEASANT BLAST OF NORMALCY THAT I RECOUNTED OUR CONVERSATION IN MY JOURNAL IN SOME DETAIL.

TYING THE OLE NOOSE, EH?

I DREAMED LAST NIGHT THAT SHE WANTED TO HAVE A SEXUAL EXPERIENCE WITH SOMEONE ELSE FIRST.

GRAD STUDENT

POET

ACTOR

HOW ODD! WHAT COULD IT POSSIBLY MEAN?

101

THE ACTOR WAS WEARING A T-SHIRT I HAD DESIGNED. THIS MAGNIFIED MY PLEASANT SENSE OF CONNECTION WITH THE OUTSIDE WORLD.

BUT MY ANXIETY FLARED UP AFTER A TRIP BACK EAST A FEW MONTHS LATER.

THE FRIEND I WAS STAYING WITH IN NEW YORK HAD THE STOMACH FLU, AND I WAS **TOTALLY PANICKED** I WAS GONNA CATCH IT AND THROW UP.

I GOT SO ANXIOUS THAT I ACTUALLY *FELT* SICK. WEAK AND NAUSEATED AND CLAUSTROPHOBIC.

I USED TO BE A SANE PERSON! WHAT'S HAPPENING TO ME?

WELL...I HAVE WHAT MIGHT SEEM LIKE AN ODD QUESTION. I'M NOT EVEN QUITE SURE HOW TO PUT IT, BUT...DO YOU BELIEVE IN GOD?

UHH...

LET ME REPHRASE THAT. CAN YOU DESCRIBE YOUR COSMOLOGY TO ME?

OH. OKAY.

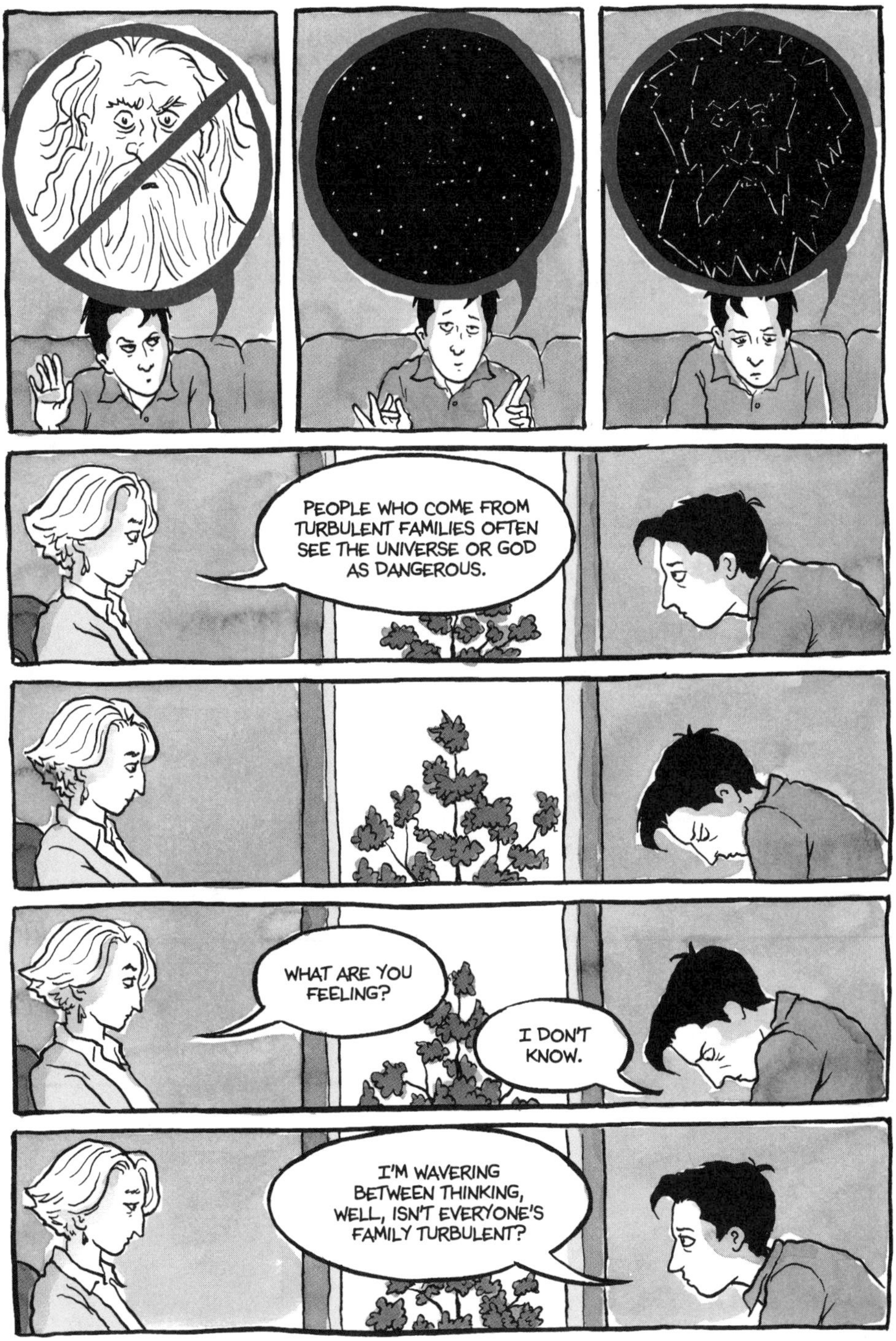
PEOPLE WHO COME FROM TURBULENT FAMILIES OFTEN SEE THE UNIVERSE OR GOD AS DANGEROUS.
WHAT ARE YOU FEELING?
I DON'T KNOW.
I'M WAVERING BETWEEN THINKING, WELL, ISN'T EVERYONE'S FAMILY TURBULENT?

...AND THINKING, OH MY GOD, MY FAMILY WAS SO FUCKED UP.

THE COSMOLOGY SESSION MARKED A DECIDED BREACH IN MY DEFENSES.

NOT LONG AFTER THAT, JOCELYN EXPERIENCED A FREAK ACCIDENT AT THE GROCERY STORE.

A **CASE** OF TIDE?!

ON YOUR **HEAD**?!

I FELT AN INCREASINGLY URGENT NEED TO CONFESS HOW DEPENDENT ON HER I HAD BECOME...

...BUT IT TOOK ME WEEKS TO GET UP THE NERVE.

...LIKE YOU'RE INSIDE MY HEAD LOOKING OUT WITH ME.

JUST BEFORE CHRISTMAS I CRIED QUITE FREELY FOR THE FIRST TIME IN JOCELYN'S PRESENCE.

AS I LEFT THAT DAY, SHE HUGGED ME. I HAD NEVER FULLY UNDERSTOOD THIS CUSTOM BEFORE.

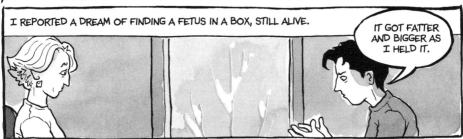

I REPORTED A DREAM OF FINDING A FETUS IN A BOX, STILL ALIVE.

IT GOT FATTER AND BIGGER AS I HELD IT.

I TOLD JOCELYN I HATED BEING JUST ANOTHER CLIENT. I LIVED FOR WEEKS ON HER REPLY.

I *LIKE* YOU.

WHAT'S THE WORST THAT COULD HAPPEN, SHE ASKED, IF I JUST LET MYSELF FEEL MY LOSS?

I WISH I COULD SAY THAT WITH THE ARRIVAL OF SPRING I WAS HEALED.

MY FAMILY WASN'T THAT BAD. I DON'T KNOW WHAT I'M COMPLAINING ABOUT.

BUT BEHIND EACH DISMANTLED FORTIFICATION LAY ANOTHER PERFECTLY INTACT ONE.

working with the patient on the basis of ego-science mechanisms. The patient's False Self can collaborate indefinitely with the analyst in the analysis of defences, being so to speak on the analyst's side in the game. This unrewarding work is only cut

YOU GET CLOSE, YOU MAKE A CONNECTION, THEN YOU DISCOUNT IT.

I KNOW. I'M RESISTING.

THE FALSE SELF, WINNICOTT SAYS, IS ALSO A PRODIGIOUS CONTORTIONIST.

living through imitation, and it may even be possible for the child to act a special role, that of the True Self *as it would be if it had had existence.*

I WANT TO DO THIS RIGHT! I WANT TO BE YOUR BEST CLIENT.

GOD. IT'S A GOOD THING MY CARTOONS GET ME A LITTLE ATTENTION, I'M SO DESPERATE FOR IT.

YET WHEN I GET IT, I FEEL SO UNWORTHY.

AND WOE BETIDE THE PERSON WITH THE "DOUBLE ABNORMALITY" OF A FALSE SELF AND "A FINE INTELLECT" THAT THEY FIND THEY CAN USE TO ESCAPE THEIR PAIN.

but are into intellect. A clinical picture results which is peculiar in that it very easily deceives. The world may observe academic success of a high degree, and may find it hard to believe in the very real distress of the individual concerned, who feels 'phoney' the more he or she is successful. When such individuals destroy

LIKE THIS SPEECH I HAVE TO GIVE AT U. PENN.

WHAT WERE THEY THINKING? I'M A **FRAUD**.

THE MORE YOU SUCCEED, THE MORE EMPTY YOU FEEL, THEREFORE THE MORE YOU MUST SUCCEED.

LET'S HAVE A DATE FRIDAY NIGHT.

THIS VICIOUS BUT HIGHLY FUNCTIONAL CIRCLE IS THE PLIGHT OF ALICE MILLER'S "GIFTED CHILD."

OH, BEEZE! I HAVE TO WRITE THAT SPEECH!

THE FALSE SELF, SHE SAYS, IS NOT AN OBSTACLE TO INTELLECTUAL GROWTH, "BUT IT IS ONE TO THE UNFOLDING OF AN AUTHENTIC EMOTIONAL LIFE."

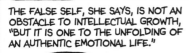

PLUS I HAVE TO MAKE THIS SLIDE SHOW FOR MY BOOK TOUR.

A FEW DAYS LATER, ELOISE TOLD ME SHE WAS ATTRACTED TO OUR FRIEND CHRIS, THE ACTOR.

IT'S NOT LIKE I WANT TO ACT ON IT.

MIDDLE OF THE NIGHT

I JUST WANTED TO TELL YOU.

NO, THAT'S GOOD. I'M GLAD YOU DID.

I'M GLAD WE CAN BE HONEST ABOUT STUFF LIKE THAT.

I CHANGED MY MIND, HOWEVER, ABOUT GOING OUT FRIDAY NIGHT.

HOPE AND GLORY
7 & 9:30

UPTOWN

ROCKY HORROR
SATURDAY AT MIDNIGHT

WE SAW A MOVIE ABOUT A BOY GROWING UP IN LONDON DURING THE BLITZ. EARLY ON, HIS MOTHER TAKES HIM AND HIS LITTLE SISTER TO A CHAOTIC TRAIN STATION TO BE EVACUATED.

PLEASE LEAVE YOUR CHILDREN AT THE BARRIER AND MAKE SURE THAT THEY CARRY THE CORRECT LABELS FOR THEIR DESTINATION.

SAY GOODBYE AND PASS THEM THROUGH!

EXIT

BUT THE MOTHER CAN'T BEAR IT, AND AT THE LAST MINUTE GRABS THE CHILDREN OFF THE TRAIN.

I WANT MY FAMILY!!

(BEFORE THERAPY, I NEVER CRIED AT MOVIES.)

IN A COMIC TWIST, SHE CHANGES HER MIND AGAIN...BUT IT'S TOO LATE. THE KIDS GET TO STAY AND EXPERIENCE THE TERRORS AND JOYS OF WARTIME LONDON FIRSTHAND.

ALICE MILLER WRITES THAT THE CHILD WHO SUPPRESSES HIS OWN FEELINGS IN ORDER TO ACCOMMODATE A PARENT HAS BEEN, IN A SENSE, ABANDONED.

sion of his own distress. Later, when these feelings of being deserted begin to emerge in the analysis of the adult, they are accompanied by such intensity of pain and despair that it is quite clear that these people could not have survived so much pain. That would only have been possible in an empathic, attentive environment, and this they lacked. The

SHE ALSO SAYS THAT THE MOTHER WHO REQUIRES ACCOMMODATION FROM HER CHILD IS JUST TRYING TO GET WHAT HER OWN MOTHER REFUSED HER.

I'VE DECIDED TO USE MOTHER/DAUGHTER MODELS FOR MY SHOW.

OH, THAT'S BRILLIANT!

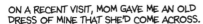

MOM IS PUTTING TOGETHER A FASHION SHOW FOR THE LIFELONG LEARNING INSTITUTE WITH COSTUMES FROM HER PERSONAL COLLECTION.

SHE'LL DRESS MODELS TO DEMONSTRATE THE EVOLUTION OF STYLE BY DECADE, FROM 1860 TO 1960.

ON A RECENT VISIT, MOM GAVE ME AN OLD DRESS OF MINE THAT SHE'D COME ACROSS.

I HAVE TO DECIDE HOW MANY DRESSES TO REPAIR. I HAVE A WORTH EVENING GOWN I COULD GET THOUSANDS FOR IF IT WERE IN GOOD SHAPE.

CIRCA 1967

WITH ITS MOD STRIPES, IT'S STRANGELY AU COURANT. JUST ABOVE THE HEM IS A TEAR THAT HAS BEEN MENDED.

JULY

...I'M USING NYLON NET TO FIX THE FRAYED SHOULDERS ON A PINK SILK GEORGETTE DRESS...

ON THE INSIDE, THERE'S AN IRON-ON PATCH AS FAMILIAR AS MY OWN HAND. THIS EVIDENCE OF MY MOTHER'S CARE IS WRENCHING.

JEEZ, MOM, THAT SOUNDS SO PAINSTAKING.

I KNOW. NO ONE WILL APPRECIATE IT. BUT THIS IS NOTHING, REALLY.

NOTHING LIKE THE SUMMER I DID COSTUMES FOR *THE SOUND OF MUSIC!*

I HAD TWO WEEKS TO OUTFIT FOUR-TEEN NUNS, FIVE NAZIS, SEVEN KIDS IN THREE CHANGES OF MATCHING CLOTHES, A WEDDING PARTY! DIRNDLS!...

INTERESTINGLY, IT WAS IMMEDIATELY AFTER WATCHING *THE SOUND OF MUSIC* ON TV IN 1987 THAT MY OWN DEPRESSION SET IN.

The summer I did costume
worked all day, didn't even
7 kids in three changes of
A wedding party!
Dirndls!
Lederhosen!|

I WAS UNABLE TO FALL ASLEEP THAT NIGHT AND STAYED UP WATCHING MTV, FEELING INCREASINGLY ANXIOUS AND FRIGHTENED.

WILD, WILD LIFE!

IN THE CONVERSATION I HAD WITH MOM A FEW DAYS LATER ABOUT HOW I WAS GOING TO START SEEING A THERAPIST, SHE TOLD ME AN INTERESTING STORY.

...THE FIRST TIME I WAS DEPRESSED WAS WHEN I WAS AT THE CLEVE-LAND PLAYHOUSE.

I'D BEEN UP FOR SEV-ERAL NIGHTS STRAIGHT SEWING COSTUMES FOR A SHOW. I WAS GOOD FRIENDS WITH ONE OF THE OTHER GIRLS.

SHE WAS A COUPLE YEARS OLDER THAN ME AND I RESPECTED HER A LOT.

BUT THEN SHE CONFIDED IN ME THAT SHE HAD A CRUSH ON ONE OF THE *ACTRESSES!*

I WAS JUST SO SHOCKED! AND WITH THE LACK OF SLEEP, IT THREW ME INTO A DEPRESSION FOR WEEKS.

I FELT SOME SHAME AT THIS GLIMPSE OF HOW THE NEWS OF MY OWN LESBIANISM MUST HAVE SHOCKED MY MOTHER.

WOW.

BUT THE WORST TIME WAS RIGHT AFTER MY PARENTS DIED. DR. MALCOLM WAS FEEDING ME ANTIDEPRESSANTS AND SLEEPING PILLS.

GOD. I HAD NO IDEA.

WHEN MOM TOLD ME THIS, I WAS THE SAME AGE SHE'D BEEN WHEN SHE WAS PREGNANT WITH ME.

I'D BE STANDING IN CHURCH ON SUNDAY WITH YOU ON ONE SIDE AND CHRISTIAN ON THE OTHER...

I REMEMBER THE FIRST TIME I SAW *THE SOUND OF MUSIC.* I WAS FOUR. NANA AND GRANDPA FONTANA TOOK ME.

YEARS LATER I LEARNED THAT MY GRANDFATHER, WHO HAD LEFT THE TYROL AS A BOY, HAD BEEN MOVED TO TEARS BY THE SONG "EDELWEISS."

BLESS MY HOME- LAND FOREVER. ♪

I HAD MY OWN PROFOUND RESPONSE TO THE MOVIE-- A STRANGE NEW FEELING THAT I CAN ONLY DESCRIBE AS EROTIC.

IT'S HARD TO SAY WHICH MARIA I DESIRED MORE--THE CHILD SHE WAS TO THE NUNS AT THE CONVENT.

THE LOVER SHE WAS TO CAPTAIN VON TRAPP.

OR THE ENLIVENING MOTHER SHE WAS TO THE REPRESSED CHILDREN, SEWING THEM PLAY CLOTHES FROM THE DRAPERIES.

I JUST KNEW THAT I WANTED HER.

IT WAS SIMILAR IN SOME WAYS TO HOW I FELT ABOUT JOCELYN. SOMETHING HAPPENED IN OUR FIRST SESSION THAT SHE WOULD LATER TELL ME HAD BEEN "A THERAPEUTIC NO-NO."

MY MOTHER DIED WHEN I WAS SEVENTEEN, AND I DIDN'T DEAL WITH IT UNTIL I WAS TWENTY-FIVE.

BUT IT WAS THIS CONFESSION, THIS GLIMPSE OF HER OWN PAIN, THAT INSTANTLY CEMENTED ME TO HER.

I RETURNED FROM THE SUCCESSFUL DELIVERY OF MY SPEECH AND THE SUCCESSFUL PRESENTATION OF MY SLIDE SHOW TO A SORDID PRIVATE FAILURE.

WHAT MOVIE?!

IN MY ABSENCE ELOISE HAD NOT ONLY GONE OUT WITH CHRIS, BUT—I GRADUALLY EXTRACTED—HAD KISSED HER.

SAMMY AND ROSIE GET LAID.

THE TEARFUL CONVERSATION THAT ENSUED TOOK A PERHAPS PREDICTABLE TURN.

BUT WHEN ELOISE BEGAN TO MAKE LOVE TO ME, I COULDN'T FEEL HER.

I LEAPT FROM THE BED.

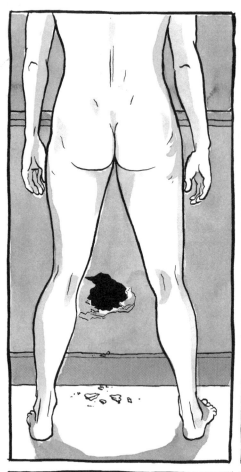

IT WAS A PERFECT KICK WITH THE BALL OF MY FOOT, LIKE I'D LEARNED IN KARATE.

JESUS.

I WAS LUCKY I HADN'T HIT A STUD.

I TOOK A PERVERSE PLEASURE IN THAT HOLE. I DON'T REMEMBER ANYONE EVER FIXING IT. THERE IT GAPED, AS LONG AS I LIVED IN THAT HOUSE.

ELOISE'S FULL CONFESSION A FEW DAYS LATER--AT CHRIS'S INSISTENCE, AS IT TURNED OUT--WAS ALMOST ANTICLIMACTIC.

WE DIDN'T JUST KISS.

Dave's GARAGE

THERE'S A NOTE IN MY DATEBOOK THAT I SLEPT WITH MY OLD TEDDY BEAR THAT NIGHT AND FOUND IT COMFORTING.

I'M MORE EMBARRASSED TO CONFESS THIS THAN TO CONFESS KICKING A HOLE IN THE WALL.

BUT MR. BEEZUM IS NOT SOME MASS-PRODUCED, BUTTON-EYED TOY. HIS FINELY CRAFTED GAZE EXPRESSES A SUBLIME AND INFINITE COMPASSION. IT ALWAYS CALMS ME TO LOOK AT HIM.

HE'S NOT ME, BUT HE'S NOT NOT-ME, EITHER.

THE PARENT WHO USES THE CHILD'S FALSE SELF FOR STRUCTURAL SUPPORT, ALICE MILLER SAYS, PREVENTS THE CHILD FROM BUILDING UP HER OWN STRUCTURE.

on his parents. He cannot rely on his own emotions, has not come to experience them through trial and error, has no sense of his own real needs, and is alienated from himself to the highest degree. Under these circumstances he cannot separate from his parents, and even as an adult he is still dependent on affirmation from his partner, from groups, or especially from his own children. The heirs of the par-

I WENT THROUGH A PHASE, AS A CHILD, OF RENOUNCING MR. BEEZUM. OF TAKING AN ALMOST SADISTIC PLEASURE IN LEAVING HIM OUTSIDE ON THE LAWN, EXPOSED TO THE ELEMENTS.

DURING THAT PERIOD, THE NEIGHBOR'S DOG PICKED HIM UP AND DRAGGED HIM BY THE FOOT.

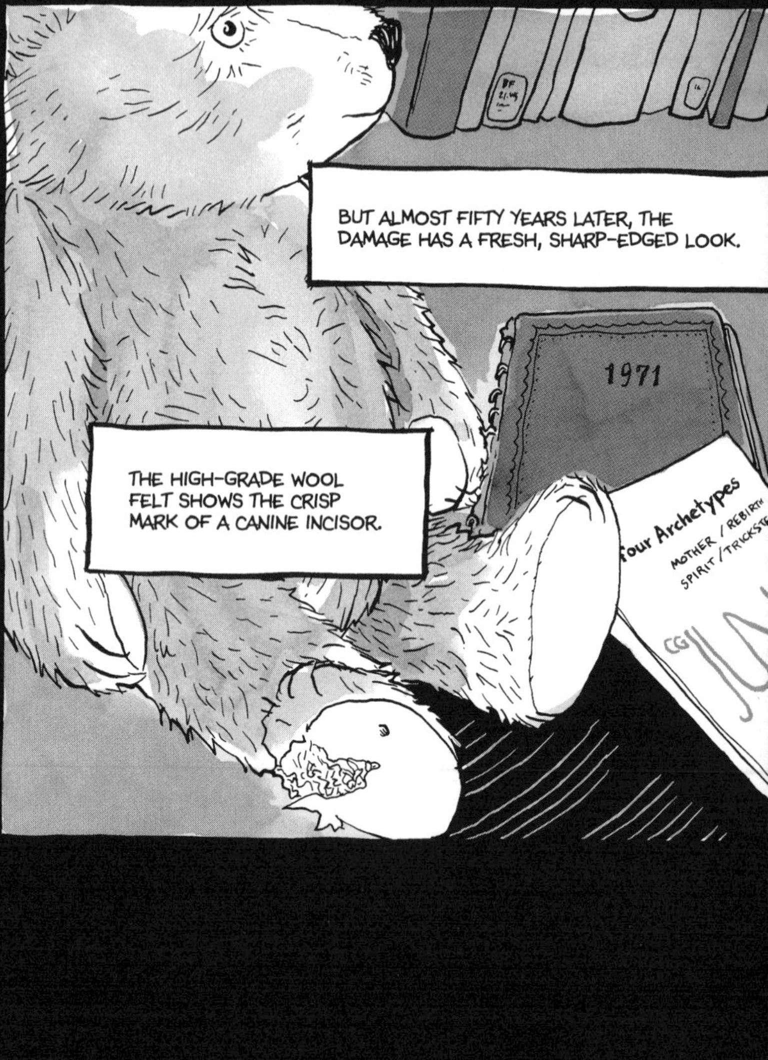
BUT ALMOST FIFTY YEARS LATER, THE DAMAGE HAS A FRESH, SHARP-EDGED LOOK.
1971
THE HIGH-GRADE WOOL FELT SHOWS THE CRISP MARK OF A CANINE INCISOR.

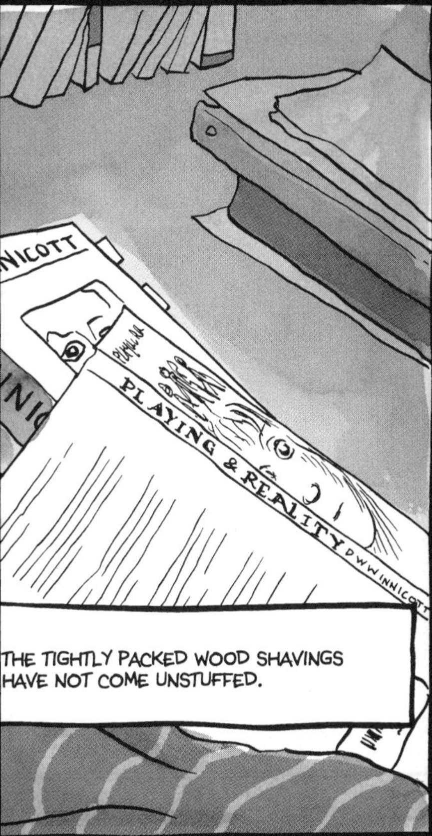

NICOTT
PLAYING & REALITY
DW WINNICOTT
THE TIGHTLY PACKED WOOD SHAVINGS HAVE NOT COME UNSTUFFED.

# 4 Mind

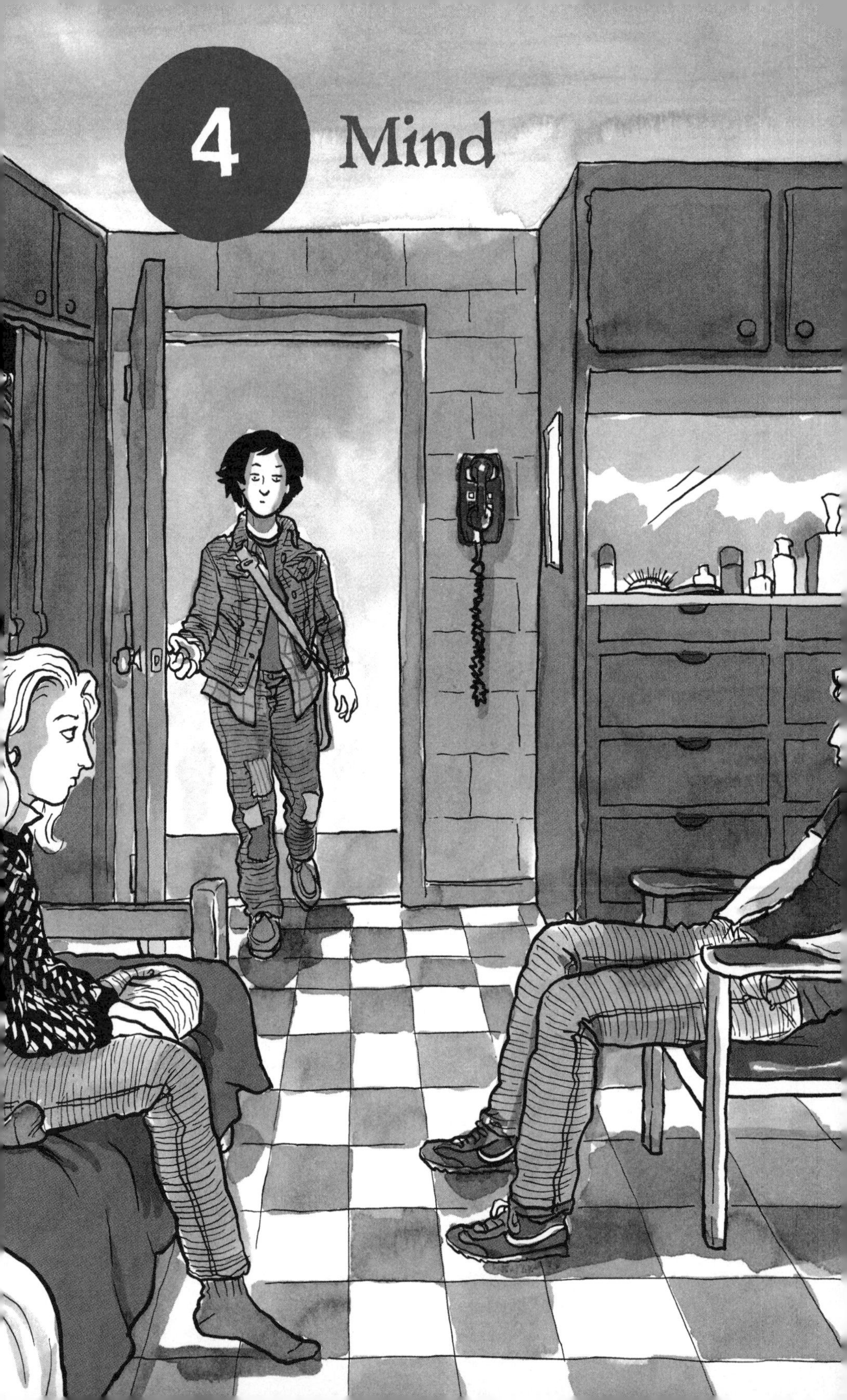

I'M BACK IN COLLEGE, AND THE MOMENT I ENTER MY DORM ROOM, I CAN TELL THAT SOMETHING BAD HAS HAPPENED.

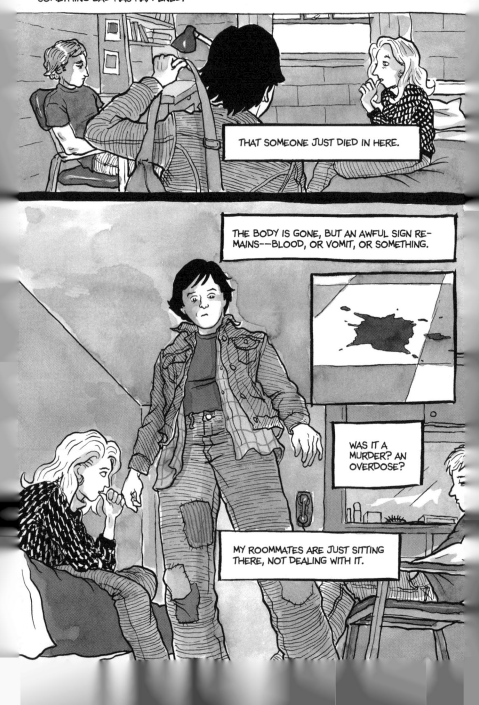

THAT SOMEONE JUST DIED IN HERE.

THE BODY IS GONE, BUT AN AWFUL SIGN RE-MAINS--BLOOD, OR VOMIT, OR SOMETHING.

WAS IT A MURDER? AN OVERDOSE?

MY ROOMMATES ARE JUST SITTING THERE, NOT DEALING WITH IT.

THERE'S A COMPLICATED INTRA-CAMPUS PHONE SYSTEM.

YOU HAVE TO PRESS A SEQUENCE OF FUNCTION KEYS BEFORE YOU PRESS THE EXTENSION FOR THE CAMPUS POLICE——18.

I MIX UP THE ORDER AND GET A WRONG NUMBER. I FEEL IMPOTENT AND CRAZED. THIS IS AN EMERGENCY!

THE BUTTONS ARE STICKY AND UNRE-SPONSIVE. I PUNCH THEM FURIOUSLY, OVER AND OVER AGAIN.

THE MOMENT I WOKE UP, I CONNECTED "4" AND "8" TO THE JEWISH SYMBOL *CHAI*.

I HAD LEARNED FROM AMY THAT IN HEBREW *CHAI* MEANS "LIVING," AND THAT THE NUMERO-LOGICAL SUM OF ITS LETTERS IS EIGHTEEN.

AND THAT THE NUMBER EIGHTEEN HAS THUS ATTAINED A MYSTICAL, OR AT ANY RATE SUPER-STITIOUS, ASSOCIATION WITH LIFE AND PROSPERITY.

I THINK THE DEAD PERSON IS YOUR FATHER.

YEAH...THAT WAS THE DORM ROOM I MOVED OUT OF JUST BEFORE HE DIED.

IT WAS APRIL 16, 2002. I HAD JUST PAID MY TAXES. THE PREVIOUS WEEK, THE PUBLISHER OF MY CARTOON BOOKS HAD FILED FOR CHAPTER 11. MY FINANCIAL SITUATION WAS GRIM.

...AND PUNCHING THE PHONE KEYS IS THE ACT OF WRITING. IT'S TOTALLY ABOUT THE DAD BOOK.

I HAVE TO GET IT DONE. SO I CAN SELL IT. SO I CAN AFFORD TO LIVE.

IT'S LIKE MY LIFE DEPENDS ON IT.

MMM. THE PHONE IS LITERALLY A LIFELINE.

BUT WHO'S THE AUTHORITY YOU'RE APPEALING TO?

UH...YOU?

ME? LIKE, MY OWN AUTHORIAL VOICE?

I DON'T KNOW. I JUST KNOW I HAVE TO GET IT DONE.

I TOLD MOM I WAS ALMOST READY TO SEND HER SOME CHAPTERS. SHE SAID SHE WAS NERVOUS.

THEN SHE ASKED IF I'D SEEN AN ARTICLE IN THE *TIMES* ABOUT SOME CARTOONIST WHO WENT TO THE SAME COLLEGE AS ME.

I CONTINUED TO BE DOGGED BY ENVY.

I HAD EXPERIENCED A PARTICULARLY BAD BOUT OF IT DURING A VISIT TO MOM THE PREVIOUS SUMMER.

HAVE YOU READ THAT LESBIAN COLUMNIST, NORAH VINCENT?

YES, AND SHE BUGS ME!

VINCENT WAS A LIBERTARIAN JOURNALIST BECOMING WELL-KNOWN AT THIS TIME IN PART FOR HER CRITIQUE OF LEFT-LEANING GAY AND LESBIAN ACTIVISTS.

I SAW HER ON SOME NEWS SHOW THE OTHER NIGHT. SHE'S SMART AND VERY ATTRACTIVE.

SHE IS SMART. THAT'S WHY SHE'S SO ANNOYING.

THEY WERE TALKING ABOUT ABORTION, AND SHE SAID FETUSES ARE MORE ENDANGERED THAN GAYS RIGHT NOW.

YEAH, GREAT. THE ONLY WAY GAY PEOPLE GET MAINSTREAM AIRTIME IS IF THEY'RE SPOUTING SOME CONSERVATIVE HORSESHIT.

I LIKED HER. SHE'S INDEPENDENT.

SHE'S AN OPPORTUNIST!

SHE'S *ENTERTAINMENT!* SHE WOULDN'T BE ON TV IF SHE WERE SAYING, Y'KNOW, PRO-CHOICE STUFF.

I ALWAYS HAVE TO THINK FOR A SECOND BEFORE I SAY "PRO-CHOICE" OR "PRO-LIFE." I GET THEM CONFUSED. ABORTION HAS ALWAYS BEEN A RATHER ABSTRACT CONCEPT FOR ME.

I'VE NEVER HAD TO THINK ABOUT BIRTH CONTROL, NEVER HAD A MOMENT'S ANXIETY OR EXCITEMENT THAT I MIGHT BE PREGNANT.

I HAD LONG SINCE GIVEN UP TRYING TO DEBATE ABORTION WITH MOM. NONE OF MY FEMINIST ARGUMENTS COULD SWAY HER.

124

MY CHILDHOOD, DESPITE THE WAR AND SOCIAL CHAOS UNFOLDING ON THE NIGHTLY NEWS, HAD BEEN SERENELY APOLITICAL. MY FAMILY DIDN'T DISCUSS CURRENT EVENTS.

THERE WAS SOMETHING EMBARRASSING, IT SEEMED, ABOUT THE OUTSIDE WORLD. I'D NEVER KNOWN ANYONE TO TAKE A STAND ABOUT ANYTHING.

SO IT WAS HIGHLY UNUSUAL WHEN MOM TOOK A BUS TO WASHINGTON TO PROTEST THE FOURTH ANNIVERSARY OF *ROE V. WADE*. I WAS SIXTEEN.

WASHINGTON, **D.C.?**

SHE DIDN'T SAY MUCH WHEN SHE GOT HOME LATE THAT NIGHT. BUT I WAS DEEPLY IMPRESSED BY HER QUIET, PRINCIPLED ACT.

NORAH VINCENT DOESN'T CARE ABOUT FETUSES!

WELL, I LIKED HER.

SHE WAS JUST SO **SMART!**

THE CONVERSATION RANKLED. I COULDN'T SLEEP AT ALL THAT NIGHT.

HEY, NORAH VINCENT! QUIT KICKING THAT SAND IN OUR FACES!

THE NEXT DAY, MOM SEARCHED WITH ME FOR MY FATHER'S OLD FRATERNITY SCRAPBOOK. I WANTED IT FOR MY WORK ON THE BOOK ABOUT HIM, BUT WE COULDN'T FIND IT ANYWHERE.

OH. HERE'S A BOX OF LETTERS DAD WROTE TO ME. DO YOU WANT THEM?

WELL, THANKS FOR HELPING ME. I KNOW YOU'RE UNEASY ABOUT THIS WHOLE THING.

?!

YES!

WAIT. WHAT IF I FIND STUFF I WANT TO USE? YOU SHOULDN'T GIVE THEM TO ME UNLESS YOU'RE OKAY WITH THAT.

TAKE THEM.

THE NEXT MORNING, MOM TOLD ME ABOUT THE TERRIBLE NIGHTMARE SHE'D JUST HAD.

I WAS LOOKING AND LOOKING FOR A BOOK ... AND THEN FINALLY I FOUND IT.

BUT JUST AS I DID, I WAS OVERCOME WITH FEAR AND STARTED SCREAMING! I WOKE MYSELF UP!

OH MY GOD!

I KNOW!

IT WAS MY BOOK!

I KNOW!

IT WAS VERY STRANGE TO READ MY FATHER'S LETTERS TO MY MOTHER.

IT'S WEIRD! HE'S ALWAYS CALLING YOU MY DARLING AND SAYING I LOVE YOU!

OH, HE WAS A DIFFERENT PERSON IN HIS LETTERS.

HE WASN'T LIKE THAT WHEN WE GOT TOGETHER.

I BROUGHT THE LETTERS HOME WITH ME AND BEGAN TYPING UP ONE OR TWO FIRST THING EVERY MORNING.

THIS WAS A PECULIAR PERFORMANCE IN WHICH I PLAYED BOTH MY MOTHER THE READER...

...AND MY FATHER THE WRITER.

THE LAST LETTERS ARE FROM WHEN THEY WERE LIVING IN WEST GERMANY, WHERE DAD WAS IN THE ARMY. HE WROTE TO MOM WHEN HE WAS AWAY ON FIELD ASSIGNMENT.

FRAU BECHDEL.

MIXED IN WITH THESE POST-MARRIAGE MISSIVES ARE FOUR POEMS, CLEARLY BY MOM. HER LIGHT, NEAT TYPING IS AS IDENTIFIABLE AS A SIGNATURE.

IF SHE WROTE THESE AT THE SAME TIME THAT DAD WROTE HIS FIELD LETTERS, IT WOULD HAVE BEEN JUST AFTER SHE FOUND OUT SHE WAS PREGNANT WITH ME.

THE POEMS ARE FORMAL IN STRUCTURE AND TONE. TWO ARE SONNETS, WHICH SCAN GRACEFULLY. BUT THERE'S AN ARM'S-LENGTH, SELF-CONSCIOUS QUALITY TO THEM.

AS FAR AS I KNOW, THESE WERE THE LAST POEMS SHE WOULD WRITE FOR THE NEXT FORTY YEARS.

ANYWAY, SHE'S NERVOUS ABOUT WHAT I'VE WRITTEN. AND SO AM I.

WHY ARE YOU NERVOUS?

WELL...I GUESS BECAUSE I'M KNOCKING ON HER PLEXIGLASS DOME. ALWAYS A TERRIFYING PROSPECT.

PLEXIGLASS DOME?

OH! THAT WAS A KIND OF SHORTHAND I HAD WITH MY FIRST THERAPIST.

FOR HOW MY MOM WOULD GO OFF DUTY AT NIGHT.

IT WAS SOMETIMES FRUSTRATING, STARTING FROM SCRATCH WITH A NEW THERAPIST, RETREADING GROUND I FELT I'D COVERED WITH JOCELYN A DECADE EARLIER.

YOU COULD SEE HER RIGHT THERE IN HER CHAIR, READING AND SMOKING. BUT YOU COULDN'T TALK TO HER. SHE WAS CLOCKED OUT.

IT WAS LIKE SHE HAD THIS INVISIBLE DOME OVER HER.

THIS PLEXI-GLASS DOME.

IT'S TRUE THAT I HAD MY OWN WAY OF CLOCKING OUT AS A CHILD, OF GETTING AWAY FROM THE PRESS OF OTHERS' NEEDS.

WHERE'S THE EXTENSION CORD?

I WOULD BUILD MYSELF AN "OFFICE."

I DON'T KNOW. DON'T BOTHER ME NOW.

I WOULD BARRICADE MYSELF OFF IN THE BACK OF A CLOSET OR A CORNER OF THE DINING ROOM AND WORK THERE AT MY DRAWINGS.

THE SENSATION OF BEING INVISIBLE, INVIOLABLE, WAS A KIND OF ECSTASY.

WINNICOTT TALKS ABOUT SOMETHING HE CALLS "GOING-ON-BEING."

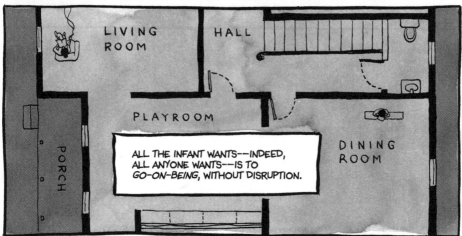

LIVING ROOM

HALL

PLAYROOM

PORCH

DINING ROOM

ALL THE INFANT WANTS—-INDEED, ALL ANYONE WANTS—-IS TO GO-ON-BEING, WITHOUT DISRUPTION.

THE "GOOD-ENOUGH MOTHER" MINIMIZES THE IMPINGEMENTS OF HUNGER, WETNESS, AND COLD. BUT SHE DOESN'T HAVE TO ADAPT ABSOLUTELY PERFECTLY TO THE BABY'S NEEDS.

tive care or an alive neglect. The mental activity of the infant turns a *good enough* environment into a perfect environment, that is to say, turns relative failure of adaptation into adaptive success. What releases the mother from her need to be near-perfect is the infant's understanding. In the ordinary course of

A HUNGRY INFANT, FOR EXAMPLE, CAN SOOTHE ITSELF FOR A BIT BY REMEMBERING OR IMAGINING THE EXPERIENCE OF BEING FED.

BUT IF FOR SOME REASON THE MOTHER IS PREOCCUPIED, THE BABY MIGHT HAVE TO RELY TOO MUCH ON ITS OWN CAPACITY FOR UNDERSTANDING.

WINNICOTT LAYS THESE IDEAS OUT IN A PAPER CALLED "MIND AND ITS RELATION TO THE PSYCHE-SOMA."

IN HIS LAPIDARY WAY, HE PACKS MUCH OF HIS THESIS INTO THE TITLE.

HUMANS ARE A HYPHENATED UNITY OF BODY AND PSYCHE, FROM WHICH "MIND" CAN BECOME SEPARATED.

IN THE PERFECT ENVIRONMENT OF MY OFFICES, ONE OF THE THINGS I WOULD DRAW WAS OTHER PERFECT ENVIRONMENTS.

ENCLOSED, IMPREGNABLE SPACES LIKE THIS BUG'S HOME UNDER A MOUND OF EARTH.

THE "KEEP OUT" SIGN, A HALLMARK OF THESE INTERIORS, BETRAYS A SEUSSIAN INFLUENCE.

INDEED, A SEARCH FOR ITS SOURCE YIELDS MORE THAN I'D EXPECTED.

*I love you s*

*...very cause me to repress. And so it... ...et your condition lovingly. My soul ...doesn't seem possib... ...world ...Well I love yo... ...baby. ...very night. Don't let...*

HERE'S THE
KEEP OUT SIGN.

HERE ALSO IS MY MOTHER'S
PLEXIGLASS DOME.

...to it
...amount
Count.
...halfway between Reno and Rome,
...ove a machine in a plexiglass dome,
Which listens and looks into everyone's home.
...sees a new sleeper go flop,
...new Biggel Ball drop.
...three balls as the...
...e know who

HERE, IN FACT, IS A PICTURE
OF ME IN MY OFFICE.

Vilseck
24 Feb. 60

...I seldom do -- seems like
...n the message run
...but...

...ny the colonel took me
...a coup de maitre and I

...is and London. I've looked
...the only paperback worth
...id back. There are at least
...shock. Send me a blank as
...ty in check. I'll send them
...s some fine Shubert, a
...Bach, Oistrac selections,
...Sibelius, well they are

...ine, bu...
...i...

KEEP OUT

5 OCT 1958 326
ARMY AIR APO
POSTAL SERVICE
US 7

VIA AIR MAIL

THE US ARMY
A KEY TO PEACE

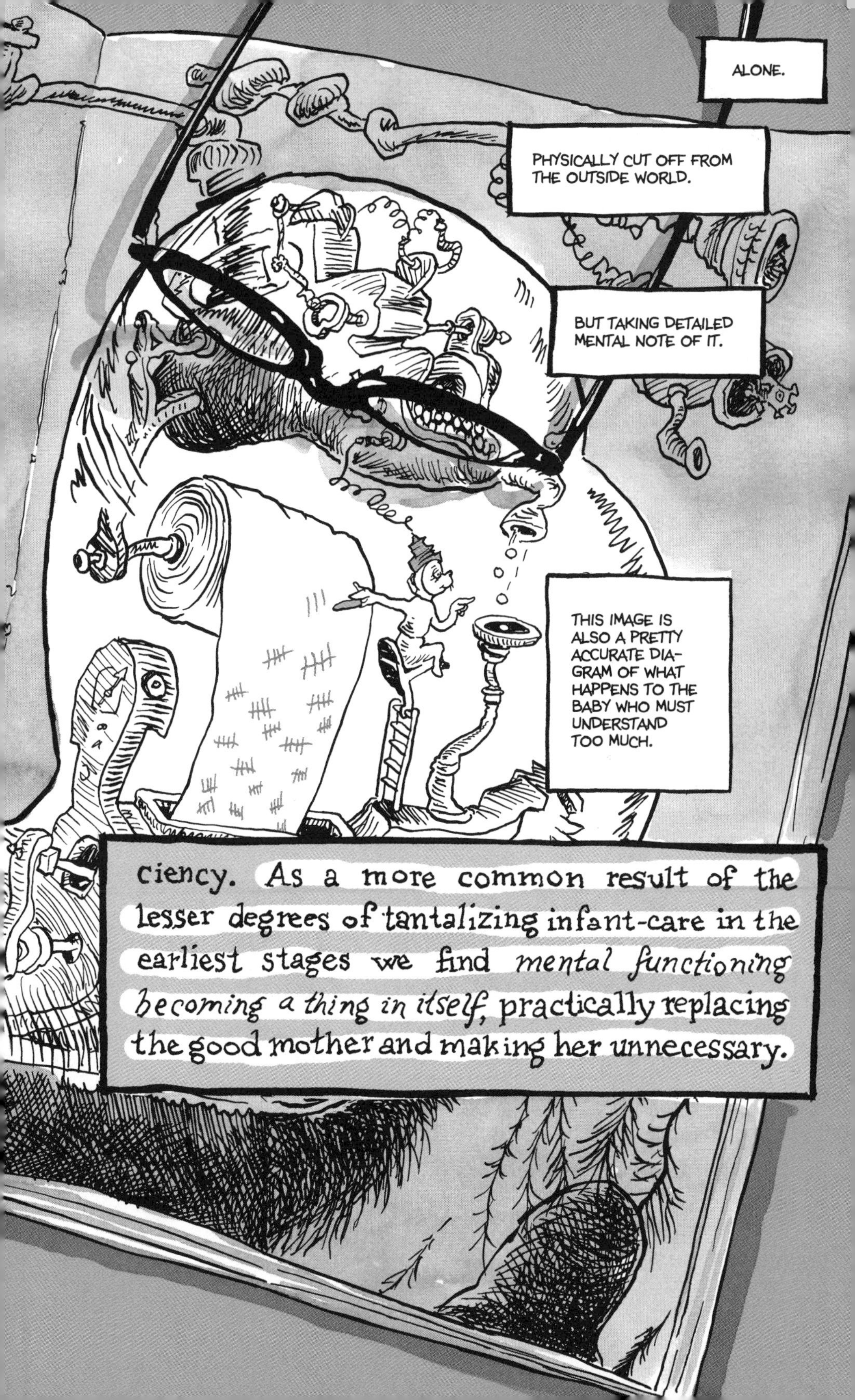
ALONE.
PHYSICALLY CUT OFF FROM THE OUTSIDE WORLD.
BUT TAKING DETAILED MENTAL NOTE OF IT.
THIS IMAGE IS ALSO A PRETTY ACCURATE DIAGRAM OF WHAT HAPPENS TO THE BABY WHO MUST UNDERSTAND TOO MUCH.
ciency. As a more common result of the lesser degrees of tantalizing infant-care in the earliest stages we find *mental functioning becoming a thing in itself*, practically replacing the good mother and making her unnecessary.

INSTEAD OF DEPENDING ON THE MOTHER, THE BABY LEARNS TO DEPEND ON HIS OR HER OWN MIND. IT'S A DENIAL OF DEPENDENCE, A FANTASY OF SELF-SUFFICIENCY.

THE CLEVER CONCEIT OF *THE SLEEP BOOK* ENTRANCED ME AS A CHILD.

IT'S A BEDTIME STORY ABOUT CREATURES GOING TO SLEEP—INCLUDING, AS IT TURNS OUT, ME.

I'M READY!

I'M READY TOO! COME COOFY ME!

THE DESPERATION WITH WHICH MY BROTHERS AND I DEMANDED TO BE KISSED GOOD NIGHT AND TUCKED IN, OR "COOFIED," UNNERVED ME EVEN AT THE TIME.

GETTING COOFIED WAS EVERYTHING, AND IT WAS NEVER ENOUGH.

ME FIRST!

WE WOULD SAY OUR PRAYERS FOR MOM. NOT THE ONE THAT ENDS, "AND IF I DIE BEFORE I WAKE, I PRAY THE LORD MY SOUL TO TAKE," THOUGH OF COURSE THIS IS EXACTLY THE PROBLEM WITH SLEEP...

OUR FATHER, WHO ART IN HEAVEN...

...IT'S LIKE DEATH.

THEN PERHAPS MOM WOULD TELL US A STORY. VIRGINIA WOOLF, IN HER UNPUBLISHED MEMOIR, *A SKETCH OF THE PAST*, RECALLS HER MEMORIES OF THE NURSERY SHE SHARED WITH HER BROTHER.

fire. I was very anxious to see that the fire was low, because it frightened me if it burnt after we went to bed. I dreaded that little flickering flame on the walls; but Adrian liked it; and to make a compromise, Nurse folded a towel over the fender; but I could not

A LITTLE FURTHER ON, SHE TRIES HARD TO DESCRIBE WHAT SHE CAN REMEMBER ABOUT HER MOTHER.

like all children, I lay awake sometimes and longed for her to come. Then she told me to think of all the lovely things I could imagine. Rainbows and bells... But besides these minute separate details,

NEAR THE END OF THE FIRST PART OF *TO THE LIGHTHOUSE*, WOOLF COMBINES THESE MEMORIES IN THE SCENE WHERE MRS. RAMSAY PUTS CAM AND JAMES TO SLEEP.

CAM IS AFRAID OF THE SHADOWS CAST BY A BOAR'S SKULL NAILED TO THE NURSERY WALL.

"Well then," said Mrs. Ramsay, "we will cover it up," and they all watched her go to the chest of drawers, and open the little drawers quickly one after another, and not seeing anything that would do, she quickly took her own shawl off and wound it round the skull, round and round and round, and then she came back to Cam and laid her head almost flat on the pillow beside Cam's and said how lovely it looked now; how the fairies would love it; it was like a bird's nest; it was like a beautiful mountain such as she had seen abroad, with valleys and flowers and bells ringing and birds singing and little goats and antelopes and . . . She could see the

THE TOWEL OVER THE FENDER BECOMES THE SHAWL OVER THE SKULL--AN ELEGANT FORESHADOWING OF MRS. RAMSAY'S DEATH.

THIS IS FICTION.

OR, MORE BROADLY SPEAKING, ART.

BUT OF COURSE WOOLF IS ALSO WRITING ABOUT HER ACTUAL MOTHER'S DEATH. SHE DIED FROM RHEUMATIC FEVER AND EXHAUSTION.

ON TOP OF MANAGING EIGHT KIDS AND A DIFFICULT HUSBAND, SHE ALSO DID CHAR-ITABLE WORK WITH THE SICK AND THE POOR.

WHICH IS TO SAY, EVEN BEFORE SHE DIED, THERE WAS NOT MUCH OF HER TO GO AROUND.

YOU'RE TOO OLD TO BE KISSED GOOD NIGHT ANY-MORE.

WHEN MOM ABRUPTLY STOPPED KISSING ME GOOD NIGHT, I FELT ALMOST AS IF SHE'D SLAPPED ME.

GOOD NIGHT.

BUT I WAS STOIC. I BETRAYED NO REACTION.

GOOD NIGHT.

IF SEVEN WAS TOO OLD, IT WAS TOO OLD.

SLEEP IS LIKE DEATH, BUT IT'S ALSO LIKE BEING IN THE WOMB.

OUR WARM BED SURROUNDS US. WE CURL UP, LAPSE INTO UNCONSCIOUSNESS.

ANOTHER LOOK AT DR. SEUSS'S PLEXIGLASS DOME, AND IT RESEMBLES NOTHING SO MUCH AS A PREGNANT UTERUS.

THE WOMB IS AN ENVIRONMENT THAT ADAPTS ABSOLUTELY. NOTHING IMPINGES BECAUSE THERE'S NO OUTSIDE OR INSIDE.

NO SEPARATION.

AND IF THERE'S NO SEPARATION, THEN PROPERLY SPEAKING, THERE'S NO RELATION, EITHER.

AS THEY SAY, ALL IS ONE.

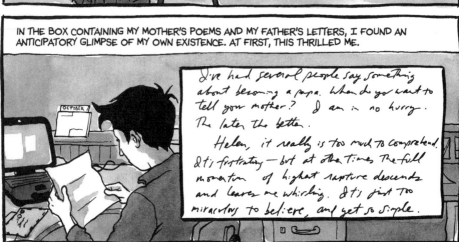

IN THE BOX CONTAINING MY MOTHER'S POEMS AND MY FATHER'S LETTERS, I FOUND AN ANTICIPATORY GLIMPSE OF MY OWN EXISTENCE. AT FIRST, THIS THRILLED ME.

I've had several people say something about becoming a papa. When do you want to tell your mother? I am in no hurry. The later the better.

Helen, it really is too much to comprehend. It's frustrating — but at other times the full momentum of highest rapture descends and leaves me whirling. It's just too miraculous to believe, and yet so simple.

138

BUT AS I CONTINUED TO READ THE UNDATED LETTERS, LOOKING FOR CLUES TO THEIR CHRONO-LOGICAL ORDER, A MORE COMPLICATED PICTURE EMERGED OF DAD'S REACTION TO THE PREGNANCY.

*Do you know how saintly you are? How brilliant! Kind, good, honest? That I love you so much I am almost unaware of it?*

HERE HIS HANDWRITING IS EVEN MORE OF A SCRAWL THAN USUAL.

*My daily trials with The Army cause me to repress. And so it was that I refused to treat your condition lovingly. My soul should rot in hell! It doesn't seem possible that I could stoop to such crassness. Well I love you — and our baby. I will be better. I will question my soul every night. Don't let me forget!*

I REMEMBERED WHAT MOM HAD TOLD ME.

OH, HE WAS A DIFFERENT PERSON IN HIS LETTERS.

IN THIS ONE, HIS PRAISE OF MOM IS EVEN MORE EXCESSIVE THAN HIS SELF-ABASEMENT.

"MY SOUL SHOULD ROT IN HELL"?

BUT I DIDN'T THINK TO PRESS MOM FOR MORE INFORMATION UNTIL YEARS LATER, AFTER I'D PUBLISHED THE BOOK ABOUT DAD.

SO HOW DID HE TAKE THE NEWS THAT YOU WERE PREGNANT?

WELL, HE WAS CERTAINLY NOT HAPPY.

I THINK...I THINK HE LAUGHED AT ME, THIS INAPPROPRIATE LAUGHTER.

WHY WOULD HE *LAUGH* AT YOU?

139

I KNOW! IT WASN'T "THAT'S TOO BAD" OR "OH, THAT'S GREAT," BUT LAUGHTER. OR MAYBE HE GAVE ME THE SILENT TREATMENT.

A BABY WOULD COMPLICATE MY PARENTS' PLAN TO TRAVEL AROUND EUROPE WHEN DAD'S HITCH IN THE ARMY WAS UP.

I WANTED TO GET ON A PLANE AND COME HOME.

WERE THEY USING SOME KIND OF BIRTH CONTROL? I DON'T KNOW. THE FDA WOULD APPROVE THE PILL LATER THAT YEAR, SIX MONTHS AFTER I WAS CONCEIVED.

I WALKED OUT, WALKED AROUND THE TOWN FOR ABOUT A DAY.

JOH. BUHL

MY MOTHER DID NOT TELL ME, DID NOT SUGGEST IN ANY WAY, THAT MY FATHER HAD PROPOSED AN ABORTION.

BUT I CAN'T HELP SUSPECTING THIS WAS THE "CRASSNESS" HE "STOOPED TO." APPARENTLY HE TOOK THE NEWS OF MOM'S PREGNANCIES WITH MY BROTHERS JUST AS BADLY.

AT SOME POINT MOST OF US WONDER:

HOW MUCH OF ME IS ME?

ME.

ME.

STILL ME.

ME!

in the overgrowth of the mental function re-active to erratic mothering, we see that there can develop an opposition between the mind and the psyche-soma, since in reaction to this abnormal environmental state the thinking of

because the psyche of the individual gets 'seduced' away into this mind from the intimate relationship which the psyche originally had with the soma. The result is a mind-psyche, which is pathological.

THIS "MIND-PSYCHE" THAT TAKES OVER AND REPLACES THE MOTHER IS A VERSION OF THE COMPLIANT FALSE SELF.

I'M IN MY BRAIN.

I FOUND THAT I COULD SOOTHE MYSELF TO SLEEP WITH A FANTASY. I WOULD CONJURE UP ONE OR ANOTHER OF THE NICE STUDENT TEACHERS AT SCHOOL.

SHE WOULD BE STANDING OVER THE BED WATCHING ME SLEEP. SHE WOULD SEE HOW INNOCENT I LOOKED AND FEEL A PANG OF TENDERNESS.

IT WAS AN ELABORATE CONSTRUCT.

I COULD CONCOCT ANY NUMBER OF FANTASIES. I MAY HAVE LOOKED LIKE I WAS SPONTANEOUSLY FLINGING MYSELF ON THE LAWN.

BUT IN FACT, I WAS IMAGINING MY MOTHER WATCHING ME LIKE A MOTHER IN A DETERGENT COMMERCIAL, SIGHING WITH LOVING EXASPERATION AT THE GRASS STAINS THAT WOULD REQUIRE HER CARE.

I COULD SEE HER AT THE KITCHEN SINK. BUT I KNEW SHE WASN'T LOOKING AT ME.

I EXPENDED SO MUCH EFFORT ON MY SCENARIOS THAT I FAILED TO NOTICE WHEN MY MOTHER ACTUALLY WAS WATCHING ME.

ALISON? WE'RE EATING!

ONE DAY, AT WORK IN ONE OF MY OFFICES, I HAD A STRANGE IDEA.

OR PERHAPS THE STRANGE SENSATION CAME FIRST, A FEELING THAT WAS SORT OF LIKE THE URGE TO PEE.

TO BE ON THE SAFE SIDE, I TOOK MY PEN AND PAPER INTO THE BATHROOM.

THE BATHROOM ALSO OFFERED PRIVACY, AND SOMEHOW I KNEW THAT NO ONE ELSE SHOULD SEE THIS DRAWING.

ALISON!

I'M IN THE BATHROOM!

TO MY GREAT RELIEF, I CAN'T REPRODUCE IT HERE BECAUSE MY MOTHER THREW IT OUT. IT DEPICTS A DOCTOR EXAMINING A LITTLE GIRL.

EXAMINING, IN PARTICULAR, HER GENITALIA. NO--*CLEANING* HER GENITALIA. I REMEMBER WRITING A CAPTION: "DOCTOR CLEANING A LITTLE GIRL'S TEE-TEE PLACE."

I WAS AMAZED EVEN AT THE TIME BY MY ABIILITY TO IMAGINE SUCH AN UNIMAGINABLE SCENARIO.

IN FACT, THAT WAS PART OF MY EXCITE-MENT--REALIZING THE APPARENTLY UNLIM-ITED POTENTIAL OF MY OWN MIND TO INVENT.

IN THIS GYNECOLOGICAL FANTASY, I WAS BOTH THE POWERFUL MALE SUBJECT AND THE VULNERABLE FEMALE OBJECT, THOUGH I WOULD NOT HAVE ADMITTED THE LATTER.

ON MY WAY TO THE DINNER TABLE, I HID THE DRAWING, INGENIOUSLY, IN PLAIN SIGHT--IN THE STYROFOAM ICE CHEST WHERE I COLLECTED ALL MY DRAWINGS.

LIVER?!!

DID MOM RIFLE THROUGH MY ICE CHEST WHILE I WAS GETTING READY FOR BED?

IF SHE DID, SHE DIDN'T SAY ANYTHING TO ME. MAYBE SHE WANTED TO CONSULT DR. SPOCK FIRST, TO FIND OUT HOW TO HANDLE IT.

I'M READY!

IT OCCURS TO ME NOW THAT PERHAPS THIS IS WHY SHE STOPPED KISSING ME GOOD NIGHT.

YOU'RE TOO OLD TO BE KISSED GOOD NIGHT ANYMORE.

UNTIL NOW, THE MEMORIES HAVE BEEN SEPARATE: THE TIME MOM STOPPED KISSING ME, THE TIME MOM FOUND THE DIRTY PICTURE.

THE NEXT DAY, AFTER SCHOOL...

ALISON! I WANT TO TALK TO YOU ABOUT A DRAWING I FOUND.

PERHAPS I FAILED TO LINK THE EVENTS BECAUSE AN ENTIRE DAY--AN ETERNITY AT AGE SEVEN--HAD ELAPSED BETWEEN THEM.

ALISON!

144

YOU CAN'T HIDE FOREVER!

THE DOSAGE YOU INSISTED ON WAS TOO POWERFUL, BARNABAS!

WELL, BEAVER, I'M GLAD YOU DECIDED TO TELL US THE TRUTH.

EVENTUALLY I CREPT OUT FROM BEHIND THE DOOR AND PUT ON MY PLAY CLOTHES.

YOU ARE MY WIFE!

GOODBYE, CITY LIFE!

MOM SEEMED TO CONSIDER MY LENGTHY SELF-EXILE PENANCE ENOUGH. THERE WAS NO FURTHER MENTION OF THE DRAWING.

EVER.

GOD, I CAN'T BELIEVE I TOLD YOU THAT.

I'M STILL, LIKE, FROZEN WITH SHAME ABOUT IT.

WHAT A LITTLE PERVERT.

I DON'T THINK YOUR FAMILY WAS A VERY SAFE PLACE TO BE A LITTLE GIRL.

WITH JOCELYN, I BEGAN TO FEEL MORE REAL.

BUT AFTER FOUR YEARS I STOPPED SEEING HER RATHER ABRUPTLY.

AT AGE THIRTY, I GOT INVOLVED WITH SOMEONE WHO LIVED IN VERMONT, AND DECIDED TO MOVE THERE.

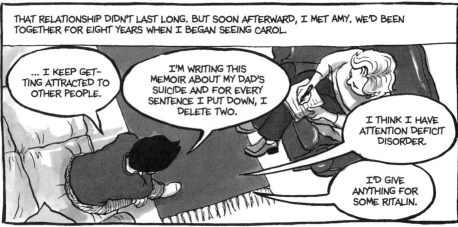

THAT RELATIONSHIP DIDN'T LAST LONG. BUT SOON AFTERWARD, I MET AMY. WE'D BEEN TOGETHER FOR EIGHT YEARS WHEN I BEGAN SEEING CAROL.

... I KEEP GETTING ATTRACTED TO OTHER PEOPLE.

I'M WRITING THIS MEMOIR ABOUT MY DAD'S SUICIDE AND FOR EVERY SENTENCE I PUT DOWN, I DELETE TWO.

I THINK I HAVE ATTENTION DEFICIT DISORDER.

I'D GIVE ANYTHING FOR SOME RITALIN.

I'D WORKED WITH A FEW OTHER THERAPISTS IN THE PRECEDING YEARS, BUT CAROL HAD MORE CREDENTIALS THAN ANY OF THEM, EVEN JOCELYN.

...AND I RECENTLY STARTED TRAINING TO BE A PSYCHO-ANALYST.

HUH.

AFTER EXACTLY FOUR SESSIONS WITH CAROL, I HAD OCCASION TO RETURN TO MINNESOTA FOR THE FIRST TIME SINCE I'D LEFT A DECADE EARLIER. I'D BEEN INVITED TO SPEAK AT THE UNIVERSITY.

I WOULD BE STAYING WITH MY EX, ELOISE, AND CHRIS, THE WOMAN SHE HAD LEFT ME FOR, IN MY OLD NEIGHBORHOOD.

THEY'D BEEN TOGETHER FOR THIRTEEN YEARS AT THAT POINT. THE THREE OF US HAD LONG SINCE GOTTEN OVER THE AFFAIR/BREAKUP AND NOW ENJOYED A WARM RAPPORT.

HOW'S THE ANXIETY?

THE USUAL. YOU?

MANAGING IT.

WHILE I WAS IN TOWN, IT OCCURRED TO ME TO TRY TO SCHEDULE A VISIT WITH JOCELYN.

THE TEN YEARS COLLAPSED, AS IF I'D NEVER LEFT. SHE LOOKED EXACTLY THE SAME.

OH, COME ON. MY HAIR'S GONE COMPLETELY GRAY!

OH.

IN AN ODD COINCIDENCE, SHE'D JUST BEEN CULLING OLD FILES, AND WHEN SHE GOT TO MINE HAD READ THE ENTIRE THING.

I COULDN'T HAVE PREPARED LIKE THAT ON SUCH SHORT NOTICE, BUT NOW EVERYTHING'S FRESH IN MY MIND!

I WANTED TO EVALUATE THE WORK I DID WITH YOU. I FEEL LIKE MY UNDERSTANDING OF THE HUMAN PSYCHE HAS GOTTEN MUCH DEEPER OVER THE YEARS.

IN FACT, I RECENTLY BEGAN TRAINING IN PSYCHOANALYSIS.

IT WAS, OF COURSE, INTERESTING TIMING THAT I SHOULD REVISIT MY OLD THERAPIST JUST AS I WAS BEGINNING WORK WITH A NEW ONE.

!

I HAD SOME NEED TO FORGE A LINK BETWEEN THEM.

ISN'T IT WILD THAT YOU'RE BOTH IN TRAINING TO BE PSYCHO-ANALYSTS?

YES, IT IS.

OR TO PIT THEM AGAINST ONE ANOTHER.

IN FACT, ALL ALONG I'VE BEEN PITTING MYSELF AGAINST EACH OF THEM IN TURN. WHAT I REALLY WANT IS TO CURE MYSELF. TO BE MY OWN ANALYST.

THE PARTICULAR "GIFTED CHILD" ALICE MILLER IS TALKING ABOUT IS THE PSYCHOANALYST.

"EVERY ONE" OF THE PSYCHOANALYTIC TRAINEES SHE HAS SUPERVISED HAS THE SAME HISTORY:

NINE O'CLOCK! TIME TO GET READY FOR BED!

AN INSECURE PARENT WHO DID NOT APPEAR TO BE INSECURE, BUT WHO DEPENDED ON THE CHILD BEHAVING IN A PARTICULAR WAY.

MEDICAL CENTER'S ON NEXT!

IT'S SUMMER!

AND AN "AMAZING ABILITY" ON THE PART OF THE CHILD TO PERCEIVE THIS AND TAKE ON THE ASSIGNED ROLE.

This role secured "love" for the child—that is, his parents' narcissistic cathexis. He could sense that he was needed and this, he felt, guaranteed him a measure of existential

**"love"**

THESE ARE THE PEOPLE WHO TEND TO GROW UP TO ANALYZE OTHER PEOPLE.

PSYCHOANALYTIC INSIGHT, MILLER SEEMS TO SUGGEST, IS ITSELF A PATHOLOGICAL SYMPTOM.

Wednesday JUNE 16

9
10
11
12
1
2
3
4

Dad & Mother got a new kingsize bed! I got their bed! Mother cut her finger. I put Bactine & a band aid on it. The mattress came in a big box. We made a tent out of it. I got some Crackerjacks.

AND SURELY WINNICOTT WAS THINKING OF HIMSELF WHEN, IN THE PSYCHE-SOMA PAPER, HE MADE THIS OBSERVATION ABOUT THE PERSON WHOSE PSYCHE HAS BEEN "SEDUCED" INTO THEIR MIND:

identification with the dependent individual. Clinically one may see such a person develop into one who is a *marvellously good mother to others* for a limited period; in fact a person who has developed along these lines may have almost magical *healing properties* because of an extreme capacity to make active adaptation

HE GIVES AN ILLUSTRATION OF HIS WORK WITH A FORTY-SEVEN-YEAR-OLD WOMAN WHO "FELT COMPLETELY DISSATISFIED, AS IF ALWAYS AIMING TO FIND HERSELF AND NEVER SUCCEEDING."

I THINK YOUR DIARY WAS A WAY TO DISTANCE YOURSELF.

YOUR ROLE IN THE FAMILY WAS TO ABSORB PEOPLE'S EMOTIONS. YOU TOOK IN TOO MUCH.

YOU *KNEW* TOO MUCH.

THE WOMAN HAD ALREADY BEEN ANALYZED, TO NO AVAIL. WINNICOTT COULD SEE THAT SHE "MUST MAKE A VERY SEVERE REGRESSION OR ELSE GIVE UP THE STRUGGLE."

SHE KEPT A DETAILED DIARY OF HER ANALYSIS WITH WINNICOTT, BUT AT THE CLIMAX OF THEIR WORK, SHE STOPPED WRITING IN IT.

could perceive that has not been at least in- dicated in this diary. The meaning of the diary now became clear— it was a projection of her mental apparatus, and not a picture of the true self, which, in fact, had never lived till, at the bottom of the regression, there came a new chance for the true self to start.

THE WOMAN WAS NOW ABLE TO FEEL SOME- THING SHE DESCRIBED AS A "NOT-KNOWING."

AND THE WAY YOUR MOTHER ENCOURAGED THE DIARY- WRITING MAKES HER COMPLICIT.

"ACCEPTANCE OF NOT-KNOWING," WINNICOTT WRITES, "PRODUCED TREMENDOUS RELIEF."

BUT...MY DIARY SAVED ME!

151

IT TOOK SEVERAL YEARS BEFORE I COULD BEGIN TO UNDERSTAND CAROL'S DIAGNOSIS.

WHY *CAN'T* MY LIFE AND MY WORK BE THE SAME THING?

MY WORK IS *ABOUT* MY LIFE!

OY, VEY.

THE THING IS, YOU RELATE TO YOUR OWN MIND LIKE IT'S AN OBJECT...

...LIKE IT'S AN INTERNALIZED PARENT OR LOVER.

BEING ATTACHED TO YOUR WORK, YOUR MIND, THE WAY YOU WOULD BE TO ANOTHER PERSON--THAT CUTS YOU OFF FROM THE WORLD.

WAIT, I GOTTA WRITE THIS DOWN!

THE IRONY OF THE FACT THAT I'M WRITING A BOOK ABOUT ALL THIS IS NOT LOST ON ME. YET I DON'T SEEM TO HAVE A CHOICE.

IN HER 1928 DIARY, VIRGINIA WOOLF MAKES A SECOND MENTION OF HOW WRITING *TO THE LIGHTHOUSE* RELEASED HER FROM HER PARENTS' THRALL.

*Wednesday 28 November*

1928

Father's birthday. He would have been 1832 96, yes, today; & could have been 96, like other people one has known; but mercifully was not. His life would have entirely ended mine. What would have happened? No writing, no books;—inconceivable. I used to think of him & mother daily; but writing The Lighthouse, laid them in my mind. And now he comes back sometimes, but differently. (I believe this to be true—that I was obsessed by them both, unhealthily; & writing of them was a necessary act.) He comes back now more as a contemporary. I must read him some day. I wonder if I can feel again, I hear his voice, I know this

ONCE, WHEN I WAS AROUND FIVE, MOM HAD A BAD MIGRAINE. DAD WAS TAKING US KIDS AWAY SOMEWHERE TO GIVE HER A BREAK.

BUT I NEED MY RAT FINK!

WELL, HURRY UP. AND BE *QUIET.*

SOB!

THIS GLIMPSE OF MY MOTHER'S PRIVATE AGONY ONLY CONFIRMED WHAT I ALREADY KNEW.

ohhhhhh.

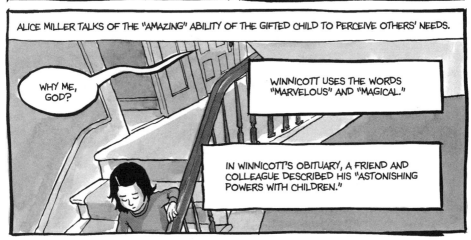
ALICE MILLER TALKS OF THE "AMAZING" ABILITY OF THE GIFTED CHILD TO PERCEIVE OTHERS' NEEDS.

WHY ME, GOD?

WINNICOTT USES THE WORDS "MARVELOUS" AND "MAGICAL."

IN WINNICOTT'S OBITUARY, A FRIEND AND COLLEAGUE DESCRIBED HIS "ASTONISHING POWERS WITH CHILDREN."

A GLIMPSE OF HIM AT WORK IS VISIBLE IN *THE PIGGLE*, A PUBLISHED CASE HISTORY OF HIS ANALYSIS OF A LITTLE GIRL. IN THEIR FIRST CONSULTATION, THE GIRL IS TWO YEARS AND FOUR MONTHS OLD.

HERE'S ANOTHER ONE.

AND HERE'S ANOTHER ONE!

AT FIRST IT SEEMS ABSURD THAT WINNICOTT IS BOTHERING TO WRITE DOWN, IN DETAIL, THE NONSENSE OF A TODDLER.

BUT THEN YOU SEE THAT SHE'S EXPLAINING HER PROBLEM QUITE COHERENTLY.

AND ANOTHER ONE.

ANOTHER BABY.

"THIS WAS EVIDENTLY THE CORRECT THING TO SAY," WINNICOTT NOTES, SINCE THE GIRL BEGAN GIVING HIM AN ACCOUNT OF THE TIME HER LITTLE SISTER WAS BORN.

I WAS A BABY. I WAS IN A COT. I WAS ASLEEP.

THE GIRL, "GABRIELLE," HAD BEEN LISTLESS AND SAD SINCE THE BIRTH OF THIS SECOND BABY EIGHT MONTHS EARLIER.

SHE WAS ALSO HAVING REGULAR NIGHTMARES ABOUT SOMETHING CALLED A "BABACAR."

THIS MYSTIFIED HER PARENTS. A MONTH AFTER HER FIRST VISIT WITH WINNICOTT, THE GIRL ASKED TO SEE HIM AGAIN.

WHAT'S THIS?

DO YOU KNOW ABOUT THE BABACAR?

NO. WHAT IS IT?

TELL ME ABOUT THE BABACAR.

WAS IT YOUR CAR? IS IT THE BABY'S CAR?

THE GIRL WAS SILENT.

"I THEN INTERPRETED," WINNICOTT WRITES. "I TOOK A RISK."

IT'S THE MOTHER'S INSIDE WHERE THE BABY IS BORN FROM.

YES, THE BLACK INSIDE.

BY MY CALCULATIONS, I'M EXACTLY A YEAR OLDER THAN GABRIELLE. WINNICOTT SAW HER INFREQUENTLY UNTIL SHE WAS FIVE.

SHE PLAYED OUT THE MYSTERIES OF SEX, BIRTH, LOVE, HATE, DEATH, THE SELF, THE OTHER, AND WHETHER GOD EXISTS.

WINNICOTT PLAYED, TOO.

I'M CURIOUS WHETHER "GABRIELLE" MIGHT HAVE WRITTEN ABOUT HER ANALYSIS WITH WINNICOTT.

BUT I CAN'T FIND ANYTHING. MAYBE HIS TREATMENT WAS SO EFFECTIVE SHE DIDN'T *NEED* TO WRITE ABOUT IT.

SHE'S PROBABLY JUST OFF LIVING HER LIFE SOMEWHERE.

SHE WAS THIRTEEN WHEN *THE PIGGLE* WAS PUBLISHED. HER PARENTS SAY IN AN AFTERWORD THAT SHE'S "UNSELF-CONSCIOUS...SPONTANEOUS...VERY MUCH PART OF A GROUP...AT SCHOOL."

AT THIRTEEN, I WAS SO PARALYZED WITH SELF-CONSCIOUSNESS THAT SOMETIMES I'D GET HOME FROM SCHOOL AND REALIZE I HADN'T SPOKEN OUT LOUD ALL DAY.

LATER, I WOULD BLAME MY SOCIAL AWKWARDNESS ON MY HOMOSEXUALITY.

BUT NOW I SPECULATE THAT BEING A LESBIAN ACTUALLY SAVED ME. WHEN I CAME OUT TO MOM IN COLLEGE, SHE RESPONDED WITH A LETTER. THE ENDING PRETTY MUCH SUMS IT UP.

Couldn't you just get on with your work? You are young, you have talent, you have a <u>mind</u>. The rest, whatever it is, can wait.

Love, Muth

IF IT WEREN'T FOR THE UNCONVENTIONALITY OF MY DESIRES, MY MIND MIGHT NEVER HAVE BEEN FORCED TO RECKON WITH MY BODY.

156

A COUPLE MONTHS AFTER RECEIVING MOM'S LETTER, AND A FEW WEEKS BEFORE MY FATHER DIED, I CALLED HOME.

HI, MOM. I JUST WANTED TO SEE IF MY GRADES CAME YET.

WHERE HAVE YOU BEEN?! I'VE BEEN CALLING AND CALLING YOU!

WH-WHAT?

MOM NEVER CALLED ME UNLESS SOMETHING WAS WRONG.

LAST NIGHT I LET THE PHONE RING AT LEAST TWENTY TIMES!

BUT I WAS HERE ALL NIGHT!

SHE HAD ASKED DAD FOR A DIVORCE. I KNEW SHE'D BEEN CONSIDERING THIS.

SEVERAL MONTHS EARLIER SHE TOLD ME HOW BAD THINGS HAD GOTTEN, AND I HAD ENCOURAGED HER TO LEAVE.

EVEN SO, I WAS STUNNED.

BEFORE HANGING UP, WE DETER- MINED THAT SHE'D BEEN CALLING MY OLD NUMBER, THE DORM ROOM I'D LEFT THE MONTH BEFORE.

I WASN'T THERE WHEN SHE HAD NEEDED ME.

THE PHONE RINGING IN THE EMPTY ROOM. I COULDN'T GET IT OUT OF MY HEAD.

IIINNNGGGDRRRIIINI

ONE RING REVERBERATING INTO ANOTHER.

AND ANOTHER.

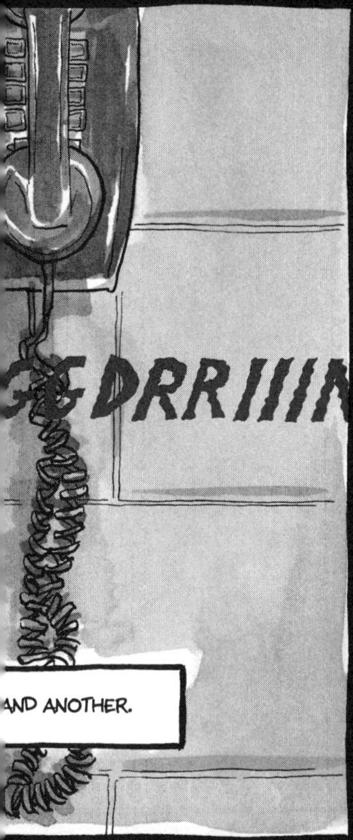
DRRIIIN
AND ANOTHER.

# 5 Hate

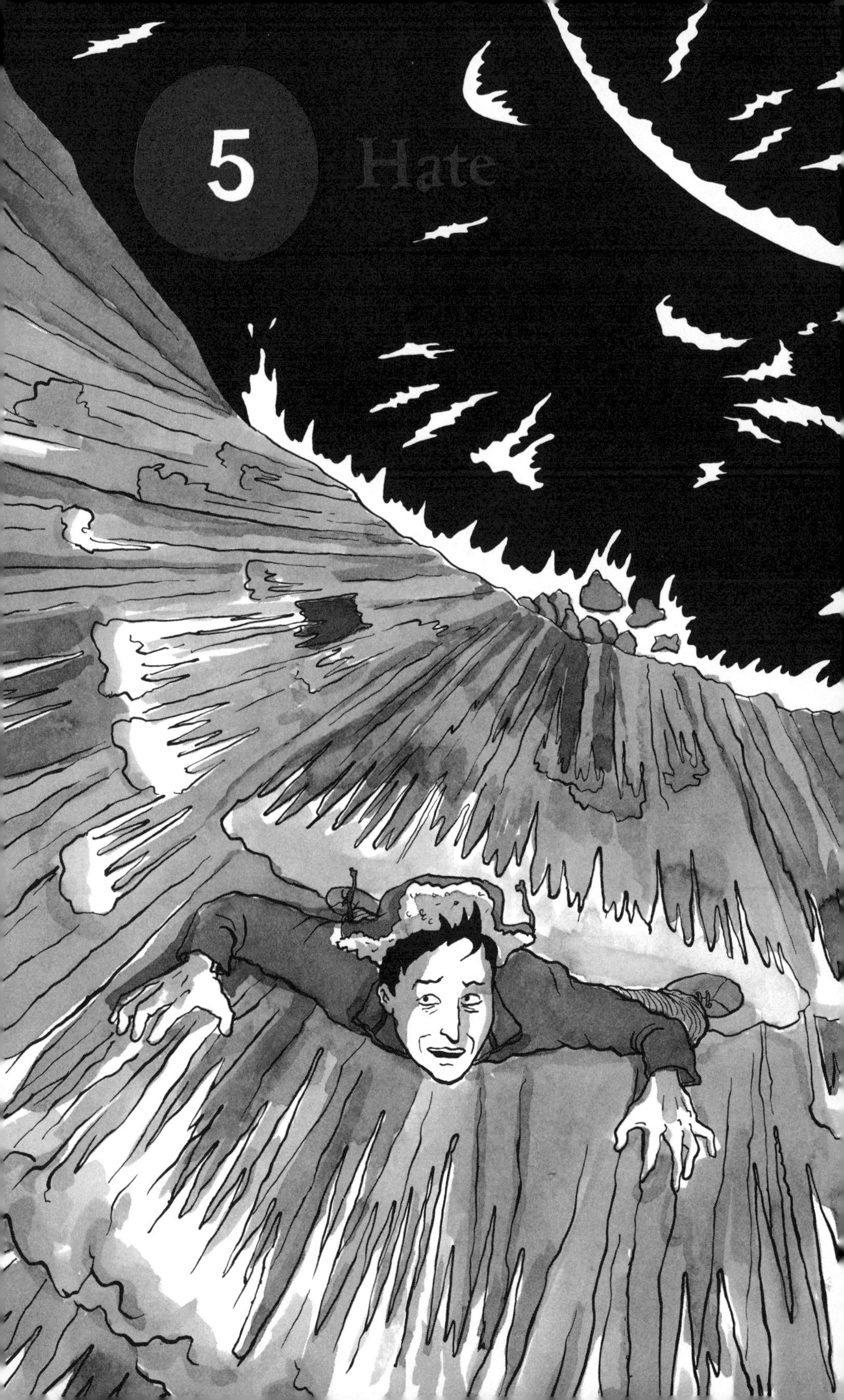

I'M CLINGING TO A PRECIPICE OF ICE.

SOMEHOW, I HAVE TO HAUL MYSELF UP OVER THE TOP. THAT'S THE ONLY WAY THE RESCUE HELICOPTER CAN GET TO ME.

I CAN'T TELL HOW FAR IT FALLS AWAY BELOW ME.

I MANAGE TO DIG OUT A LITTLE SQUARE HOLE AND WEDGE MY ARM INTO IT. NOW I CAN TWIST AROUND AND ASSESS MATTERS.

THE DISTANCE TO THE WATER IS DIZZYING. I SPIT, AND A LONG MOMENT LATER IT HITS THE SURFACE.

APPARENTLY I'M ON AN ISLAND. I CAN SEE THE LIGHTS OF THE MAINLAND.

THEN THE DREAM FAST-FORWARDS AND I'M SAFE AT THE TOP.

I'M ASTONISHED TO REALIZE THAT THE CLIFF HAD IN FACT BEEN MERELY MY CHILDHOOD HOME, COVERED IN ICE.

NOW IT'S MELTED. IT'S A BEAUTIFUL SPRING MORNING.

I'D BEEN HANGING FROM THE EDGE OF THE ROOF. EVEN IF I HAD LOST MY GRIP, I WOULDN'T HAVE FALLEN FAR.

I TRY TO SHOW A NEIGHBOR, THEN MY FATHER, HOW PERILOUS IT HAD BEEN, HOW AMAZING THAT I MANAGED TO SAVE MYSELF.

BUT IN THIS THAWED, MILD CLIMATE, IT'S IMPOSSIBLE TO CONVEY THE EXTREMITY OF MY SITUATION.

ON THE LAST MONDAY IN APRIL 2002, I SENT THE PARTIALLY COMPLETED DAD BOOK TO MOM.

EXPRESS, TO MINIMIZE THE PERIOD OF SUSPENSE.

Flump

FedEx

BUT I WOULDN'T HEAR FROM HER THE NEXT DAY, OR THE ONE AFTER THAT.

I HAD MADE TWO COPIES OF THE MANUSCRIPT. ONE FOR MOM, AND ONE FOR ME TO REFER TO WHEN I TALKED TO HER. I PUT MY COPY IN A RE-USED FOLDER.

THEN I NOTICED IT'S THE FOLDER I TOOK NOTES ON IN OUR "REACTION FORMATION" SESSION A COUPLE MONTHS AGO!

REMEMBER? I WAS TALKING ABOUT MY AWFUL, GNAWING ENVY OF OTHER PEOPLE'S SUCCESS?

I REMEMBER!

YOU SAID I'D REVERSED MY OWN AGGRESSION, TURNED IT ON MYSELF. AND I FELT THIS IMMEDIATE RELIEF!

I WONDER IF WRITING THE BOOK IS A WAY OF DIRECTING MY AGGRESSION OUT INSTEAD OF IN? AND THAT'S WHY I PUT IT IN THIS PARTICULAR FOLDER?

THAT WOULD BE A VERY FREUDIAN FREUDIAN SLIP!

LATE ON THE THIRD DAY AFTER I'D SENT THE PACKAGE...

WHAT'S WRONG?!

hnnnn

E-MAIL FROM MOM.

OH, GOD. WHAT'D SHE SAY?

SHE SAID AT FIRST SHE COULDN'T READ IT, COULDN'T FIGURE IT OUT. SHE THOUGHT THERE'D BE MORE TEXT AND NOT SO MANY DRAWINGS.

SHE SAID MY BROTHER WAS THERE KNOCKING OUT A WALL OF HER GARAGE WITH A CONCRETE CUTTER, AND SHE FELT LIKE, "CHRISTIAN IS WRECKING MY GARAGE, ALISON IS WRECKING MY LIFE."

SHE SAID SHE FELT THE DREAD SHE USED TO FEEL WITH DAD, OF EXPOSURE AND SCANDAL.

DON'T PET ME! I DON'T DESERVE TO BE TOUCHED!

165

THE CRAZY THING IS I WAS HOPING SHE'D SAY SOMETHING ABOUT THE WRITING. YOU KNOW? THAT I'D IMPRESS HER!

WHAT WAS I *THINKING*?

I DON'T DESERVE TO LIVE.

OH, WAIT. SHE SENT A P.S. A LITTLE LATER.

SHE ACTUALLY SAYS SOME NICE STUFF HERE!

"THE SECTION ON DAD AS MAGICIAN/MANIAC IS PRICELESS."

PLUS SHE LIKED THE CHAPTER ABOUT HER ACT-ING IN SUMMER STOCK.

"THE ONLY THING YOU COULD HAVE SAID BESIDES THAT I WAS BEAUTI-FUL WAS THAT I WAS ALSO THIN."

SHE CAN'T BE TOO MAD IF SHE CAN JOKE. ARE YOU GONNA CALL HER?

NO. SHE'S BUSY WITH A DEAD-LINE.

SINCE HER RETIREMENT FROM TEACHING, MOM HAD BEEN WRITING ARTICLES, REVIEWS, AND A COLUMN FOR THE LOCAL PAPER.

SHE SAID SHE'LL TRY TO TALK TO ME THIS WEEKEND.

AT BEDTIME, I TURNED TO THAT ENDLESSLY CONSOLING ODE TO SENSITIVE CHILDREN EVERYWHERE.

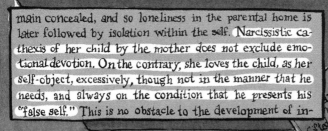

main concealed, and so loneliness in the parental home is later followed by isolation within the self. Narcissistic cathexis of her child by the mother does not exclude emotional devotion. On the contrary, she loves the child, as her self-object, excessively, though not in the manner that he needs, and always on the condition that he presents his "false self." This is no obstacle to the development of in-

THAT NIGHT I HAD THE DREAM.

THIS IMAGE OF MY CHILDHOOD AS AN EMOTIONAL DEEP FREEZE WAS THE OPPOSITE, I'M CERTAIN, OF THE PSYCHOLOGICAL ATMOSPHERE MY PARENTS THOUGHT THEY WERE PROVIDING.

LITTLE BOYS LIKE THEIR MOTHER BEST. THAT'S CALLED THE OEDIPUS COMPLEX.

IN CONTRAST TO THEIR OWN REPRESSIVE, WORKING-CLASS CHILDHOODS, MOM AND DAD WOULD LAVISH MY BROTHERS AND ME WITH THE FRUITS OF THEIR HARD-EARNED LIBERAL EDUCATIONS.

GIRLS LIKE THEIR FATHER BEST. THAT'S AN ELECTRA COMPLEX.

DO THEY HAVE TO?

THEY JUST DO.

OUR HOUSE WAS FILLED WITH BOOKS. MANY OF OUR TOYS WERE EDUCATIONAL ONES. ONCE A CATALOG ARRIVED FROM CREATIVE PLAYTHINGS WITH AN ANATOMICALLY CORRECT BOY DOLL IN IT.

HA! MAYBE IT'S A WAY TO WORK OUT PENIS ENVY.

I VIVIDLY RECALL MY MOTHER'S RESPONSE TO THIS.

OH, PLEASE. PENIS ENVY!

WHO'D WANT ONE OF THOSE THINGS DANGLING BETWEEN THEIR LEGS?

SHE SCANDALIZED US FURTHER BY PERFORMING A SILLY WALK.

THE IDEA OF PENIS ENVY, OF COURSE, CAN BE SEEN AS A REACTION FORMATION, A DEFENSE AGAINST WHAT FEMINISTS WOULD LATER CALL "WOMB ENVY." ENVY OF THE POWER TO GIVE BIRTH.

THAT'S WHERE YOUR FORESKIN WAS ATTACHED. WHEN YOU WERE A BABY, THE DOCTOR CUT IT OFF.

DID IT HURT?

NO, YOU DIDN'T EVEN NOTICE.

MY YOUNGER BROTHERS' PENISES, SCROTUMS, AND ABSENT FORESKINS WERE INTERESTING ENOUGH. BUT WHAT I REALLY ENVIED WERE ALL THESE WORDS.

WHAT'S MINE CALLED?

YOUR TEE-TEE PLACE?

IS THAT THE REAL NAME?

NO. I'LL FIND OUT WHAT IT IS AND TELL YOU LATER.

I SUPPOSE THE REASON I REMEMBER THIS EXCHANGE IS THAT IT WAS SO ODD.

WHY WOULD MY MOTHER--WHO SUPPOSEDLY HAD THIS SAME APPARATUS--HAVE TO GET BACK TO ME ABOUT WHAT IT WAS CALLED?

WHEN SHE REPORTED IN NEXT EVENING, I UNDERSTOOD WHY THE TERM WAS NOT IN COMMON USAGE.

VAGINA.

WAS IT HER TONE? THE SUSPICIOUS DELAY? OR COULD A WORD ACTUALLY CONVEY DISTASTE FOR ITS OWN MEANING?

WHERE DID WORDS COME FROM, ANYWAY?

WHEN I GOT TO COLLEGE, I FOUND A LOT OF WOMEN ASKING AND ANSWERING THAT VERY QUESTION.

ADRIENNE RICH WAS NOT ASSIGNED READING FOR ANY OF MY CLASSES. MY NEW LESBIAN FRIENDS HAD TURNED ME ON TO HER.

SHE WAS APPARENTLY A RESPECTED POET OF MY MOTHER'S GENERATION, BUT SHE'D RECENTLY COME OUT AS A LESBIAN. A RADICAL ONE. AND A REALLY SMART ONE.

The specter of this kind of male judgment, along with the misnaming and thwarting of her needs by a culture controlled by males, has created problems for the woman writer: problems of contact with herself, problems of language and style, problems of energy and survival.

In rereading Virginia Woolf's *A Room of One's Own* (1929) for the first time in some years, I was astonished at the sense of effort, of pains taken, of dogged tentativeness, in the tone of that essay. And I recognized that tone. I had heard it often enough, in myself and other women. It is the tone of a woman almost in touch with anger, who is determined not to appear angry ... is willing to be calm, detached, and even charming in a ...

RICH UNDERSTANDS WOOLF'S "DETACHMENT" BECAUSE SHE ONCE PRACTICED IT, TOO, SHE SAYS, IMITATING THE DISTANCE AND FORMALISM OF THE MALE POETS SHE ADMIRED.

BUT NOW SHE WAS KIND OF GOING FOR BROKE.

"...YOUR STRONG TONGUE AND SLENDER FINGERS REACHING WHERE I HAD BEEN WAITING YEARS FOR YOU IN MY ROSE-WET CAVE..."

THE ESSAY IN WHICH RICH CITES *A ROOM OF ONE'S OWN* COVERS SOME OF THE SAME GROUND AS WOOLF'S BOOK. LIKE, FOR EXAMPLE, THE WOMAN WRITER'S PECULIAR CHALLENGE TO CEASE BEING AN OBJECT AND START BEING A SUBJECT.

"words' masculine persuasive force" of literature she comes up against something that negates everything she is about; she meets the image of Woman in books written by men. She finds a terror and a dream, she finds a beautiful pale face, she finds La Belle Dame Sans Merci, she finds Juliet or Tess or Salomé, but precisely what she does not find is that absorbed, drudging, puzzled, sometimes inspired creature, herself, who sits at a desk trying to put words together.

Tud
Ta
Tud
Tud

ONE OF THE POEMS MY MOTHER WAS WRITING THAT WINTER IN GERMANY, SEVEN MONTHS OR SO BEFORE I WAS BORN, IS CALLED "LA BELLE DAME."

LA BELLE DAME

The Beautiful Lady with Compassion
Wraps about her r...

IT COPIES THE FORM OF THE KEATS BALLAD. BUT MOM'S POEM IS ABOUT THE WOMAN HERSELF, NOT THE KNIGHT'S FANTASY OF HER.

WHAT ELSE DID MY MOTHER WRITE? WHERE ARE *HER* LETTERS?

NOW I'M READING THIS FICTIONAL VERSION OF PLATH'S LIFE, CALLED *WINTERING*.

AND ALSO HELEN VENDLER'S BOOK ABOUT POETS' LAST WORKS, INCLUDING PLATH'S.

YOU CAN SEE WHY TED HUGHES HAD TO LEAVE. HER POSSESSIVENESS, HER DEMANDS...

PLUS SHE EXHAUSTED HERSELF MAKING CURTAINS AND GINGER-BREAD. WHY DID SHE WASTE HER TIME DOING ALL THAT STUFF?

WELL, I DID IT, TOO...I THOUGHT IT WAS IMPORTANT. I REMEMBER FEELING VERY ANGRY AT BETTY FRIEDAN.

**WHAT?!** WHY?

WELL...SHE HATED HOUSEWORK AND WANTED WOMEN TO BE INDEPENDENT. BUT THEN SHE'D HIRE OTHER WOMEN TO DO HER HOUSEWORK.

BY THE TIME *THE FEMININE MYSTIQUE* WAS PUBLISHED IN 1963, MOM WAS STUCK AT HOME WITH TWO SMALL CHILDREN. I GUESS I WOULD HAVE BEEN PRETTY ANGRY, TOO.

HEY, MOM...IN MY BOOK, I SAY THAT I'VE NEVER READ PLATH AND YOU'VE NEVER READ WOOLF. THAT'S TRUE, RIGHT?

WELL, I'VE READ *A ROOM OF ONE'S OWN*. BUT NONE OF HER NOVELS.

OF COURSE SHE'S READ *A ROOM OF ONE'S OWN*.

PROBABLY IN THE SEVENTIES. CERTAINLY NOT IN COLLEGE IN THE FIFTIES.

172

WOOLF'S BIOGRAPHER HERMIONE LEE REPORTS THAT EVEN IN THE MID-SIXTIES, WOOLF "WASN'T READ" IN THE ACADEMY, WAS CONSIDERED "A MINOR MODERNIST."

IT WAS MY FATHER, NOT MY MOTHER, WHO WENT TO GRAD SCHOOL. WHEN HE STARTED AT PENN STATE, MOM WAS LIVING IN THE VILLAGE AND WORKING AS A SECRETARY.

IN DAD'S LETTERS TO HER AT THAT TIME, HE ENLISTS HER AID WITH HIS COURSEWORK.

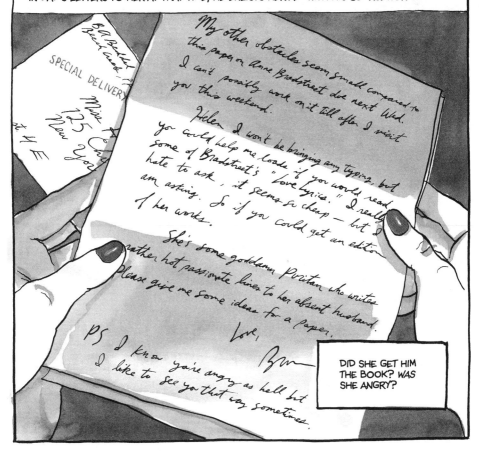

DID SHE GET HIM THE BOOK? WAS SHE ANGRY?

173

IN "HATE IN THE COUNTERTRANSFERENCE," HE LISTS JUST "SOME OF THE REASONS WHY A MOTHER HATES HER BABY."

A. The baby is not her own (mental) conception.
B. The baby is not the one of childhood play, father's child, brother's child, etc.
C. The baby is not magically produced.
D. The baby is a danger to her body in pregnancy and at birth.
E. The baby is an interference with her private life, a ch... tion.
F. To a greater or... feels that her o... baby, so that he... placate her mo...

(WINNICOTT'S USE OF THE PRONOUN "HE" HERE, TO DENOTE THE BABY, IS AN ABERRATION...

G. The baby hurts her nipples even by suckling, which is at first a chewing activity.
H. He is ruthless, treats her as scum, an unpaid servant, a slave.
I. She has to love him, excretions and all, at any rate at the beginning, till he has doubts about himself.
J. He tries to hurt her, periodically bites her, all in love.
K. He shows disillusionment about her.
L. His excited love is cupboard love, so that having got what he wants he throws her...
M. The baby... be protect... must unfol... needs his r... tailed study...

...ONE OF HIS ECCENTRICITIES WAS HIS REVOLUTIONARY USE OF "HE OR SHE," "HIS OR HER," DECADES BEFORE ANYONE ELSE DID IT...

not be anxious when holding him, etc.
N. At first he does not know at all what she does or what she sacrifices for him. Especially he canno...
O. He is suspicious,... and makes her de... well with his aunt...

...THIS ALONE MAKES ME LOVE HIM.)

P. After an awful morning with him she goes out, and he smiles at a stranger, who says: "Isn't he sweet!"
Q. If she fails him at the start she knows he will pay her out for ever.
R. He excites her but frustrates—she mustn't eat him or trade in sex with him.

THE MOTHER LOVES THE BABY, TOO. BUT THIS IS THE POINT. HATE IS A PART OF LOVE.

WINNICOTT USES THE MOTHER'S HATE AS AN ANALOGY FOR THE ANALYST'S HATE OF THE BURDENSOME PATIENT.

HOW DO YOU PRONOUNCE E-R-S-A-T-Z?

COUNTERTRANSFERENCE––THE ANALYST'S UNCONSCIOUS REACTION TO THE PATIENT'S TRANSFERENCE––WAS SEEN BY FREUD AS AN OBSTACLE.

IN WINNICOTT'S HANDS IT BECOMES MORE OF A TOOL.

THE ANALYST CAN'T HELP THE PATIENT "UNLESS THE ANALYST'S OWN HATE IS EXTREMELY WELL SORTED-OUT AND CONSCIOUS."

IN MY TEENAGE YEARS, MY MOTHER AND I FOUGHT A LOT.

ER-**ZATZ.**

YOU CAN ALSO SAY IT **ER**-ZATZ.

WINNICOTT GIVES A CASE ILLUSTRATION FROM HIS WORK WITH EVACUATED CHILDREN.

WHY IN THE HELL DID YOU ASK IF YOU KNEW?

ONE DAY A NINE-YEAR-OLD BOY ARRIVED AT THE HOSTEL "NOT BECAUSE OF BOMBS BUT BECAUSE OF TRUANCY."

I *DIDN'T* KNOW!

HE'D BEEN RUNNING AWAY FROM HOME SINCE HE WAS SIX AND SOON RAN AWAY FROM THE CHILDREN'S HOSTEL, TOO.

THE DICTIONARY HAS TWO DIFFERENT WAYS. I MEANT HOW DO *YOU* PRONOUNCE IT, NOT JUST HOW IS IT PRONOUNCED.

WINNICOTT WAS "NOT VERY SURPRISED" WHEN THE BOY TURNED UP ONE DAY AT A POLICE STATION CLOSE TO WINNICOTT'S HOME. HE AND HIS WIFE ALICE TOOK THE CHILD IN FOR THREE MONTHS.

WHY DO YOU PERSIST IN PERSECUTING ME?

I JUST ASKED YOU HOW TO PRONOUNCE A STUPID **WORD!**

"THREE MONTHS OF HELL," WINNICOTT ADDS.

IT IS PERHAPS WORTH MENTIONING HERE THAT WINNICOTT NEVER HAD CHILDREN OF HIS OWN.

WHY DO **YOU** PERSIST IN ACCUSING ME OF INTENTIONALLY **PERSECUTING** YOU!?

SOON, THE BOY'S SYMPTOM "TURNED AROUND." INSTEAD OF RUNNING AWAY, HE WOULD HAVE TANTRUMS INSIDE THE HOUSE.

PUT THAT CAN AWAY! I'M GETTING SUPPER.

I'M HUNGRY.

WINNICOTT WOULD MANAGE THESE FITS BY PICKING THE CHILD UP, "WITHOUT ANGER OR BLAME," AND PUTTING HIM OUTSIDE THE FRONT DOOR.

YOU ARE **DELIBERATELY PROVOKING ME!**

WINNICOTT EXPLAINED TO THE BOY THAT WHEN HE CALMED DOWN, HE COULD RING THE BELL AND THEY WOULD LET HIM BACK IN.

YOU ARE **PSYCHOTIC!**

THE IMPORTANT PART OF THIS PROCESS, WINNICOTT SAYS, IS THAT EACH TIME, JUST AS HE PUT THE BOY OUTSIDE, HE TOLD HIM SOMETHING:

WHAT JUST HAPPENED HAS MADE ME HATE YOU.

Did I hit him? The answer is no, I never hit. But I should have had to have done so if I had not known all about my hate and if I had not let him know about it too. At crises I

GET OUT OF MY SIGHT. GET **OUT OF THIS KITCHEN!** I **DON'T** WANT TO **SEE** YOU!

FRUIT COCKTAIL

I WOULD LEAVE FOR COLLEGE SIX WEEKS AFTER THIS INCIDENT.

I KNOW NOW THAT CHILDREN AND PARENTS ENGINEER THESE SORTS OF CONFLICTS TO MAKE THEIR PARTING MORE BEARABLE.

AND IT WAS NO ACCIDENT THAT OUR FIGHT HAD BEEN ABOUT A WORD.

LANGUAGE WAS OUR FIELD OF CONTEST, AND HOWEVER UNCONSCIOUSLY, I HAD INDEED BEEN PROVOKING MY MOTHER.

—50—

"torment" her! I mean she always has some profound psychological reason for why I do what I do, like she's my stupid analyst or something. She gets me so angry!

AFTER COLLEGE I WENT, LIKE MY MOTHER, TO NEW YORK CITY. BY THE END OF MY FIRST YEAR THERE, I WAS STARTING TO GET MY BEARINGS.

SMIRNOFF
The sign of good taste

47–50 Streets
Rockefeller Center
Station

AT MY MENIAL OFFICE JOB I HAD AN ABUNDANCE OF FREE TIME, PRIVACY, AND TYPING PAPER. I BEGAN TO FILL THE LONG AFTERNOONS BY WRITING MY "MEMOIRS."

ACTUALLY, THIS BOUT OF WRITING BEGAN JUST AFTER A VISIT FROM MOM. I HAD TAKEN HER ONE DAY TO THE BOOKSTORE NEAR MY OFFICE.

WISE MEN FISH HERE
GOTHAM BOOK MART

OH, YES, THIS HAS BEEN HERE FOREVER. IT'S A REAL LANDMARK.

I WAS PROUD TO SHOW MOM A POEM A FRIEND OF MINE HAD JUST PUBLISHED.

REMEMBER ELLEN, FROM MY FRESHMAN YEAR?

WHAT DID I SEE IN HER FACE?

the Iowa Review

BACK AT WORK, I STARTED WRITING ABOUT THE TIME I TRIED TO GET GRASS STAINS ON MY PANTS IN A BID FOR MOM'S ATTENTION.

the grass stain____ of my childlike

I am already well-entrenched in the vicious circle of pretending to be artless.

Elite

I LABORED OVER THE PIECE FOR A WEEK, TYPED IT UP NEATLY, AND SENT IT OFF TO TWO LITERARY JOURNALS.

A REPLY FROM THE MORE PRESTIGIOUS ONE ARRIVED WITH SURPRISING RAPIDITY.

I WAS ASTONISHED BY THE SIGNATURE ON THE REJECTION LETTER.

at a rather superficial level. Even for yourself, I think it would be useful to go back and ask yourself some real questions as to the meaning of each incident, and its context.

I hope this is helpful. Don't be put off, or discouraged. Writing is a very long, demanding training, more hard work than luck. Strength to you.

           In sisterhood,

           Adrienne Rich

I MUST HAVE KNOWN SHE WAS ONE OF THE EDITORS, BUT SOMEHOW I HADN'T IMAGINED HER ACTUALLY READING MY SUBMISSION, LET ALONE RESPONDING PERSONALLY TO IT.

I cringe at my arrogance. Actually, cringing at my arrogance is just another, more rarified, level of arrogance.

SHE WAS RIGHT. I HAD NOT DONE THE HARD WORK.

I FELT ANOTHER WAVE OF SHAME SIX MONTHS LATER, WHEN MY UNREVISED STORY WAS PUBLISHED BY THE LESSER JOURNAL.

I HAD SET WRITING ASIDE BY THEN AND TURNED MY EFFORTS TO DRAWING A SERIES OF CARTOONS TO ENTERTAIN MY FRIENDS.

WITHIN THE YEAR I HAD BEGUN PUBLISHING THESE AT THE FEMINIST NEWSPAPER WHERE I VOLUNTEERED. I MET AN AGENT THERE WHO ENCOURAGED ME TO PUT TOGETHER A BOOK.

DO YOU HAVE MORE OF THESE?

YEAH, I HAVE A BUNCH.

WoMANEWS

I HADN'T BOTHERED TO TELL MOM ABOUT PUBLISHING THE STORY IN THE JOURNAL. BUT A BOOK WOULD BE SURE TO IMPRESS HER.

REALLY? THAT'S FANTASTIC!

MY TRIUMPH WAS SHORT-LIVED.

BUT I HAVE TO TELL YOU, THEY'LL BE CARTOONS ABOUT LESBIANS.

ISN'T THAT A RATHER NARROW SCOPE?

UH...

I MEAN, WON'T IT LIMIT WHAT YOU CAN DO NEXT?

I DON'T CARE!

YOU'RE NOT GOING TO USE YOUR REAL NAME, ARE YOU?

COULDN'T YOU USE ONE OF YOUR FUNNY NAMES?

THAT WOULD DEFEAT THE PURPOSE!

I WOULD LOVE TO SEE YOUR NAME ON A BOOK, BUT NOT ON A BOOK OF LESBIAN CARTOONS.

THIS KNOCKED THE WIND OUT OF ME.

WELL...DON'T WORRY. I HAVEN'T EVEN WRITTEN IT YET.

I UNDERSTOOD THAT SHE WAS UPSET MORE ABOUT MY FATHER'S HOMOSEXUALITY THAN MINE.

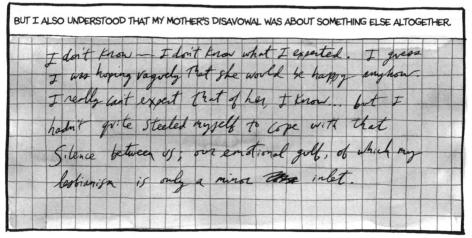

BUT I ALSO UNDERSTOOD THAT MY MOTHER'S DISAVOWAL WAS ABOUT SOMETHING ELSE ALTOGETHER.

I don't know — I don't know what I expected. I guess I was hoping vaguely that she would be happy anyhow. I really can't expect that of her, I know... but I hadn't quite steeled myself to cope with that silence between us; our emotional gulf, of which my lesbianism is only a minor inlet.

IT WAS THE WEEKEND AFTER THAT CONVER-SATION WITH MOM THAT I FIRST MET ELOISE.

CUANDO

PRINTS

St. Mark's Women's Health Collective BENEFIT

SHE'D RECENTLY BEEN FIRED FROM HER JOB.

SO YOU JUST DRIFT UP AND DOWN THE EASTERN SEABOARD DOING CIVIL DISOBEDIENCE?

PRETTY MUCH. I'VE BEEN HANG-ING OUT UP AT THE PEACE CAMP.

THE SENECA WOMEN'S PEACE ENCAMPMENT WAS AN ONGOING FEMINIST ANTIWAR PROTEST AT AN ARMY BASE UPSTATE.

LAST WEEK WAS "ZUKES NOT NUKES." WE STORMED THE FENCE AND STUCK ZUCCHINIS THROUGH THE CHAIN LINK.

AFTER OUR FIRST DINNER DATE, ELOISE HAD TO LEAVE FOR A DEMONSTRATION UPTOWN.

WE'RE GONNA WEAVE A WEB AROUND THE ARMORY.

JEEZ

S     way

ON OUR SECOND DATE, SHE KISSED ME IN A BAR. I INVITED HER HOME. WE JUST CAUGHT THE F TRAIN, WHICH SEEMED LIKE A GOOD OMEN.

1015

W4

IT WAS. I BEGAN SEEING HER EVERY WEEK OR TWO, BETWEEN HER STINTS AT THE PEACE CAMP AND HER RELOCATION TO WESTERN MASSACHUSETTS.

I LIKED THE BUILT-IN DISTANCE OF THIS ARRANGEMENT.

IN BETWEEN HER VISITS, THE ROUTINE OF MY LIFE CONTINUED UNDISTURBED.

I EVEN TOOK ANOTHER STAB AT WRITING. MY FOCUS NOW WAS THE TIME MY MOTHER STOPPED KISSING ME GOOD NIGHT.

RATATAT TAT TAT

I DON'T REMEMBER SENDING THIS TO MY MOTHER, BUT I DID. IN A COVER LETTER, I WROTE, "DO YOU REMEMBER THIS?"

I TOLD HER I HAD TRIED TO AVOID A RESENTFUL OR MORALISTIC TONE, AND ASKED, "TELL ME IF YOU THINK IT WORKS."

184

THE NEXT DAY, ELOISE ARRIVED FOR THE WEEKEND. THE SCOPE OF HER POLITICAL RESISTANCE WAS EXPANDING.

I WANT TO GO TO NICARAGUA.

ON MONDAY, SHE HAD TO GO BACK TO MASSACHUSETTS. AT THAT POINT WE'D SPENT A TOTAL OF SIX NIGHTS TOGETHER. BUT WE COULDN'T BEAR TO PART. I CALLED MY BOSS.

...REALLY ACHY AND FEVERISH...YEAH. I'M NOT SURE IF I'LL BE IN TOMORROW EITHER.

I SPENT THE NEXT FOUR DAYS IN AMHERST. ONE MELLOW SEPTEMBER AFTERNOON, ELOISE AND I WENT TO THE WOMEN'S BOOKSTORE. I COULDN'T RESIST FLAUNTING MY PUBLISHED STORY.

ELOISE, CHECK THIS OUT.

WOW!

I REFRAINED FROM MENTIONING THAT ADRIENNE RICH HAD REJECTED IT.

CURIOUSLY, HOWEVER, WE WERE ABOUT TO ATTEND A LECTURE SHE WAS GIVING THAT VERY EVENING.

SO WHAT'S THIS TALK ABOUT?

NICARAGUA. SHE JUST GOT BACK.

I COULDN'T QUITE UNDERSTAND THIS CRAZE TO GO TO A PLACE WHERE GUERRILLA WAR WAS STILL UNFOLDING IN THE AFTERMATH OF THE SANDINISTA REVOLUTION.

185

RICH'S TALK WAS FRAMED BY HER EXPERIENCE IN NICARAGUA, BUT I WAS MORE INTERESTED IN THE MIDDLE SECTION, THE STORY OF HER EVOLUTION AS A POET.

...I NATURALLY ABSORBED IDEAS ABOUT WOMEN, SEXUALITY, POWER FROM THE SUBJECTIVITY OF MALE POETS...

THE DISSONANCE BETWEEN THESE IMAGES AND THE DAILY EVENTS OF MY OWN LIFE DEMANDED A CONSTANT FOOTWORK OF IMAGINATION...

...A KIND OF PERPETUAL TRANSLATION, AND AN UNCONSCIOUS FRAGMENTATION OF IDENTITY: WOMAN FROM POET.

I TOOK FRENZIED NOTES.

RE-READING THESE NOW, I REALIZE THAT THE LECTURE I HEARD THAT NIGHT WAS PUBLISHED LATER AS THE ESSAY "BLOOD, BREAD, AND POETRY."

MY TRANSCRIPTION IS FAIRLY DETAILED. I LOVE THIS LINE...

"The moment when a feeling enters the body is political."

...BUT RICH SEEMS TO HAVE RECONSIDERED IT. I CAN'T FIND IT IN THE PUBLISHED VERSION.

...AS SOON AS I PUBLISHED—IN 1963—A BOOK OF POEMS WHICH WAS INFORMED BY ANY CONSCIOUS SEXUAL POLITICS...

...I WAS TOLD, IN PRINT, THAT THIS WORK WAS "BITTER," "PERSONAL" THAT I HAD SACRIFICED THE SWEETLY FLOWING MEASURES OF MY EARLIER BOOKS FOR A RAGGED LINE AND A COARSENED VOICE.

A ROOM OF ONE'S OWN, OF COURSE, BEGAN AS A LECTURE TO WOMEN STUDENTS AT CAMBRIDGE IN 1928. WOOLF READ FROM HER NOTES, ALMOST INAUDIBLY, IN A DARKENED DINING HALL.

...IF EVER A HUMAN BEING GOT HIS WORK EXPRESSED COMPLETELY, IT WAS SHAKESPEARE.

IF EVER A MIND WAS INCANDES-CENT, UNIMPEDED, I THOUGHT, TURNING AGAIN TO THE BOOKCASE, IT WAS SHAKESPEARE'S MIND.

THAT ONE WOULD FIND ANY WOMAN IN THAT STATE OF MIND IN THE SIXTEENTH CENTURY WAS OBVIOUSLY IMPOSSIBLE.

ONE HAS ONLY TO THINK OF THE ELIZABETHAN TOMBSTONES WITH ALL THOSE CHILDREN KNEELING WITH CLASPED HANDS...

...AND THEIR EARLY DEATHS; AND TO SEE THEIR HOUSES WITH THEIR DARK, CRAMPED ROOMS TO REALIZE...

...THAT NO WOMAN COULD HAVE WRIT-TEN POETRY THEN.

187

ADRIENNE RICH'S TALK GOT ELOISE EVEN MORE FIRED UP ABOUT GOING TO NICARAGUA.

I COULD NEVER GO. I COULD NEVER EVEN DO CIVIL DISOBEDIENCE!

YES, YOU COULD. ANYONE CAN. THAT'S THE POINT.

I ADMIRED AND ENVIED ELOISE'S APTITUDE FOR NONCOMPLIANCE, WHICH I NOW SEE WAS VERY WINNICOTTIAN.

I'M TOO MUCH OF A WIMP.

"THE MOMENT WHEN A FEELING ENTERS THE BODY IS POLITICAL."

IT WAS ONLY MY LESBIANISM, AND MY DETERMINATION NOT TO HIDE IT, THAT SAVED ME FROM BEING COMPLIANT TO THE CORE.

ONCE WINNICOTT'S ANALYST JAMES STRACHEY WAS TRYING TO FIGURE OUT HOW TO TAKE SOME TIME OFF FROM HIS PRACTICE. HIS WIFE, ALIX, JOKES IN A LETTER, "PERHAPS MR. W. WILL DIE OR FUCK HIS WIFE ALL OF A SUDDEN."

WHETHER IT WAS BECAUSE OF DONALD'S INHIBITIONS OR HIS WIFE ALICE'S EMOTIONAL DISTURBANCE, THE WINNICOTTS DID NOT HAVE SEX.

DURING THE WAR, WINNICOTT TOOK THE TRAIN DOWN TO OXFORDSHIRE ONCE A WEEK TO CONSULT WITH THE STAFF AT THE HOSTELS FOR EVACUATED CHILDREN.

PART OF CLARE'S JOB WAS TO MAINTAIN A LINK BETWEEN THE KIDS AND THEIR PARENTS. SHE'D GO UP TO LONDON REGULARLY AND WORK HARD TO TRACK PEOPLE DOWN.

HAVE YOU SEEN MY MUM, MISS?

HERE HE MET A SOCIAL WORKER NAMED CLARE BRITTON.

SHE'D CONVEY MESSAGES, GIFTS. SOMETIMES SHE'D FIND THAT A PARENT HAD BEEN KILLED.

CLARE ALSO BECAME THE LINK BETWEEN WINNICOTT AND THE STAFF, WHO LIKED HIM WELL ENOUGH BUT WERE FRUSTRATED BECAUSE HE WOULDN'T TELL THEM WHAT TO DO.

WE'LL JUST TELL HIM WHAT WE'VE DONE, AND SEE WHAT HE SAYS, AND LEARN IN THAT WAY.

AROUND THE TIME WINNICOTT MET CLARE, HE SENT A DRAFT OF A PAPER HE WAS WORKING ON TO MELANIE KLEIN. I DON'T HAVE ROOM HERE TO FULLY EXPLAIN WINNICOTT'S COMPLICATED PROFESSIONAL RELATIONSHIP WITH KLEIN, THAT OTHER, SLIGHTLY EARLIER PIONEER OF THE INFANT PSYCHE.

SHE SUPERVISED HIM FOR FIVE YEARS. HE ANALYZED HER SON.

HE'D BEEN STRONGLY INFLUENCED BY HER IDEAS, PARTICULARLY ABOUT THE NEWBORN'S AGGRESSION.

KLEIN TOOK A WHILE TO RESPOND TO WINNICOTT'S PAPER. WHEN SHE FINALLY DID, SHE APOLOGIZED FOR HAVING "CUT THE PAPER ABOUT," BUT EXPLAINED THAT IT HAD BEEN "NECESSARY."

SHE TELLS HIM HIS WORK IS EXCELLENT, THEN PROCEEDS TO EVISCERATE IT, INSERTING HER OWN IDEAS HERE AND THERE.

CLARE BRITTON WAS INTERESTED IN ANALYSIS AND EAGER TO TALK WITH DONALD ABOUT HIS IDEAS.

GOOD NIGHT, DR. WINNICOTT. HAVE YOU MISSED YOUR TRAIN?

A PROFOUND COLLABORATION BEGAN BETWEEN THEM THAT WOULD SHAPE THE REST OF BOTH THEIR CAREERS. EVENTUALLY CLARE WOULD BECOME AN ANALYST HERSELF.

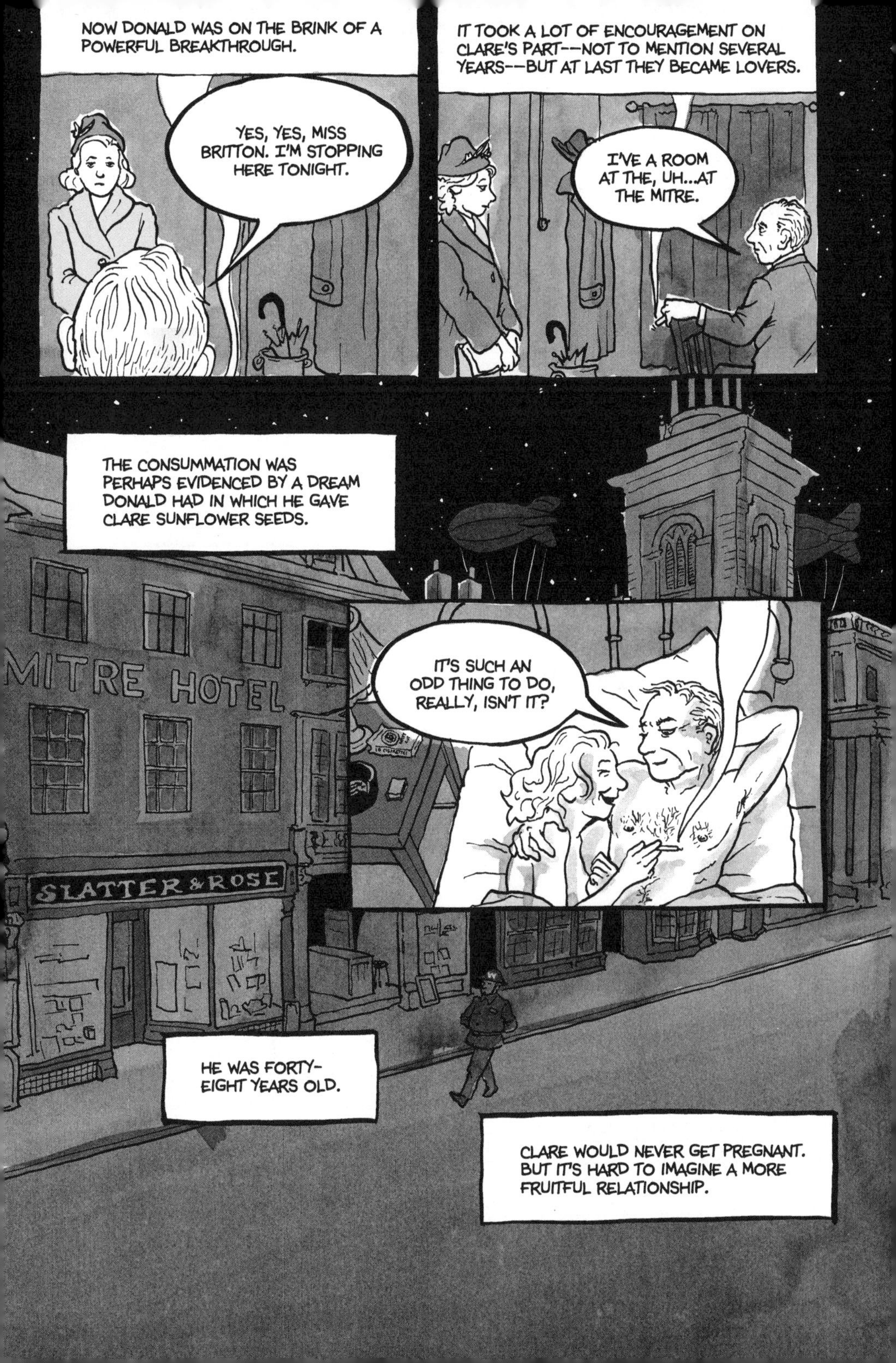

NOW DONALD WAS ON THE BRINK OF A POWERFUL BREAKTHROUGH.
YES, YES, MISS BRITTON. I'M STOPPING HERE TONIGHT.
IT TOOK A LOT OF ENCOURAGEMENT ON CLARE'S PART--NOT TO MENTION SEVERAL YEARS--BUT AT LAST THEY BECAME LOVERS.
I'VE A ROOM AT THE, UH...AT THE MITRE.
THE CONSUMMATION WAS PERHAPS EVIDENCED BY A DREAM DONALD HAD IN WHICH HE GAVE CLARE SUNFLOWER SEEDS.
MITRE HOTEL
IT'S SUCH AN ODD THING TO DO, REALLY, ISN'T IT?
SLATTER & ROSE
HE WAS FORTY-EIGHT YEARS OLD.
CLARE WOULD NEVER GET PREGNANT. BUT IT'S HARD TO IMAGINE A MORE FRUITFUL RELATIONSHIP.

THERE'S A NEW CONFIDENCE IN WINNICOTT'S POSTWAR WORK. HIS PERSONAL VOICE INFUSES HIS THEORETICAL WRITING.

HE STAYED WITH ALICE AND KEPT HIS AFFAIR WITH CLARE SECRET. BUT A SERIES OF HEART ATTACKS FINALLY CONVINCED HIM THAT THIS DOUBLE LIFE WAS KILLING HIM.

AFTER DONALD'S FORBIDDING FATHER DIED IN 1949, HE AT LAST MANAGED TO SEPARATE FROM ALICE.

IT'S NO GOOD. WE'RE HURTING ONE ANOTHER.

SOON AFTER THIS, HE WROTE HIS SEMINAL WORK, THE TRANSITIONAL OBJECT PAPER. HE AND CLARE GOT MARRIED.

AND AT LAST, HE STOOD UP TO MELANIE KLEIN, WHO HAD CONTINUED TO DENY THAT WINNICOTT HAD ANY CONTRIBUTIONS TO MAKE TO PSYCHOANALYSIS.

I DON'T GET IT. WHAT'LL YOU DO THERE?

TRAVEL AROUND. LEARN SPANISH. HELP WITH THE COFFEE HARVEST.

PERHAPS SHE WAS ENVIOUS OF HER PROTÉGÉ'S INCREASING POWERS.

PERHAPS HE WAS MAKING AN OEDIPAL REVOLT AGAINST HIS PSYCHOANALYTIC MOTHER.

BUT WINNICOTT REFUSED, IN A RESPECTFUL YET FORTHRIGHT LETTER, TO CONTRIBUTE THE TRANSITIONAL OBJECT PAPER TO A BOOK HONORING KLEIN ON HER SEVENTIETH BIRTHDAY.

ELOISE LEFT FOR NICARAGUA IN DECEMBER.

IN FEBRUARY, FIVE MONTHS AFTER I HAD SENT IT, MOM RETURNED MY "MEMOIR FRAGMENT."

Alison J. Bechdel
174 Prospect Park West
Brooklyn, NY 11215
Basement

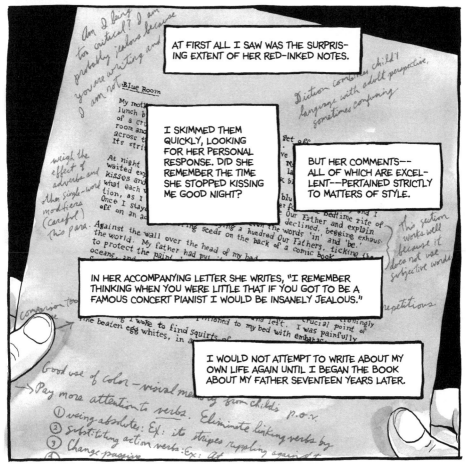

AT FIRST ALL I SAW WAS THE SURPRISING EXTENT OF HER RED-INKED NOTES.

I SKIMMED THEM QUICKLY, LOOKING FOR HER PERSONAL RESPONSE. DID SHE REMEMBER THE TIME SHE STOPPED KISSING ME GOOD NIGHT?

BUT HER COMMENTS—ALL OF WHICH ARE EXCELLENT—PERTAINED STRICTLY TO MATTERS OF STYLE.

IN HER ACCOMPANYING LETTER SHE WRITES, "I REMEMBER THINKING WHEN YOU WERE LITTLE THAT IF YOU GOT TO BE A FAMOUS CONCERT PIANIST I WOULD BE INSANELY JEALOUS."

I WOULD NOT ATTEMPT TO WRITE ABOUT MY OWN LIFE AGAIN UNTIL I BEGAN THE BOOK ABOUT MY FATHER SEVENTEEN YEARS LATER.

193

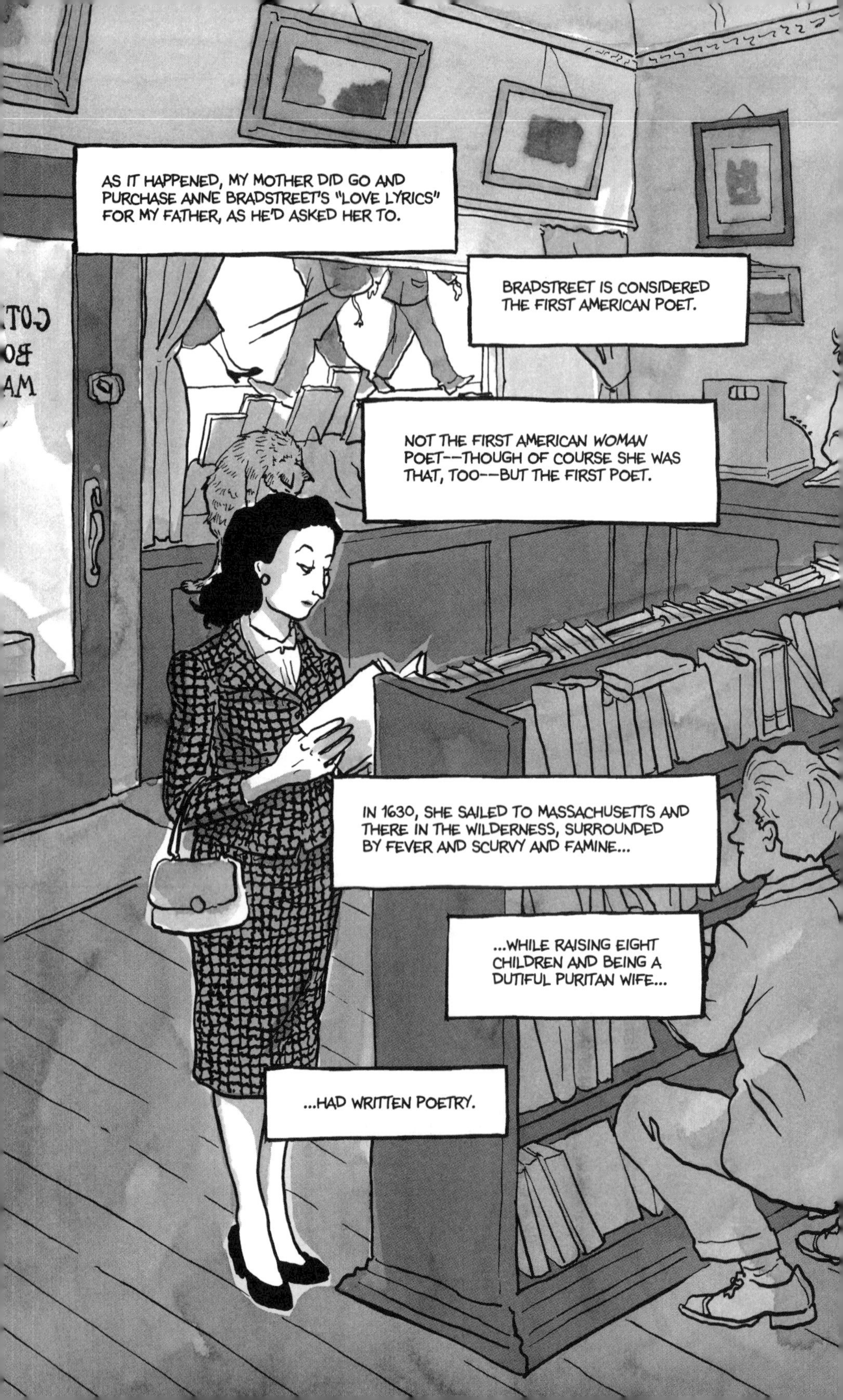

AS IT HAPPENED, MY MOTHER DID GO AND PURCHASE ANNE BRADSTREET'S "LOVE LYRICS" FOR MY FATHER, AS HE'D ASKED HER TO.
BRADSTREET IS CONSIDERED THE FIRST AMERICAN POET.
NOT THE FIRST AMERICAN *WOMAN* POET--THOUGH OF COURSE SHE WAS THAT, TOO--BUT THE FIRST POET.
IN 1630, SHE SAILED TO MASSACHUSETTS AND THERE IN THE WILDERNESS, SURROUNDED BY FEVER AND SCURVY AND FAMINE...
...WHILE RAISING EIGHT CHILDREN AND BEING A DUTIFUL PURITAN WIFE...
...HAD WRITTEN POETRY.

MY FATHER WROTE HIS PAPER ON ANNE BRADSTREET, APPARENTLY WITHOUT MOM'S HELP.

> I was up till 2 doing that Bradstreet paper. Just one week late. Oh, I'm sending the book back to ya today.

BUT IN HIS NEXT LETTER HE ANNOUNCES THAT HE'S QUITTING SCHOOL.

> My Bradstreet paper was a scanty 8 pages. Another guy's was 50 goddamn pages long. When I quit I'm going to demand my carbon copy back which is on display with the others. It was disgusting compared to them. One other was shorter, but good. Called the Draft Board to see when I might get in. Christ. I

IN HIS RAMBLING ELEVEN-PAGE LETTER, HE MENTIONS IN PASSING A TIME THAT MOM HAD VISITED HIS GRADUATE CLASSES WITH HIM.

THIS VIVID GLIMPSE OF MY FATHER'S SHAME IS AS SEARING FOR ME AS THE TIME, ONE MORNING WHEN I WAS NINE OR TEN, THAT I SAW HIM NAKED.

BOTH MY PARENTS WOULD EVENTUALLY GET MASTER'S DEGREES IN ENGLISH EDUCATION--LESS DEMANDING THAN A DEGREE IN ENGLISH--TO ADVANCE THEIR CAREERS AS HIGH SCHOOL TEACHERS.

IT'S INTERESTING THAT ANNE BRADSTREET HAD BEEN MY FATHER'S WATERLOO. I DECIDED I SHOULD READ SOME OF HER STUFF.

I FOUND A COLLECTION PUBLISHED IN 1967.

HUH!

The Works of
~ne Bradstreet

Edited by
Jeannine Hensley

Foreword by
Adrienne Rich

ADRIENNE RICH SAYS BRADSTREET'S EARLY POEMS ARE PEDESTRIAN, LISTLESS, AND IMPERSONAL, AND THAT IF SHE'D CONTINUED LIKE THAT, "ANNE BRADSTREET WOULD SURVIVE IN THE CATALOGUES OF WOMEN'S ARCHIVES, A SOCIAL CURIOSITY OR AT BEST A LITERARY FOSSIL."

BUT WHAT HAPPENED, RICH SAYS, IS THAT BRADSTREET'S SKILL IMPROVED. HER SUBJECT MATTER BECAME MORE INTIMATE.

OH, DID YOU SEE LOUISE RAFKIN'S *MODERN LOVE* COLUMN IN THE *TIMES* YESTERDAY?

NO! I'LL HAVE TO GO READ IT!

SHE SPECULATES THAT THIS WAS DUE IN PART TO THE FACT THAT BRADSTREET'S FAMILY SURPRISED HER BY PUBLISHING A SMALL EDITION OF HER EARLY VERSE.

WELL, DON'T READ IT TOO CLOSELY.

IT SOUNDS A LOT LIKE YOUR PROJECT. I'LL LET YOU GO. I HAVE TO GET BACK TO MY PUZZLE.

"SOME TENSION OF SELF-DISTRUST" WAS RELAXED BY THE PUBLICATION AND PRAISE.

I'M STARTLED TO DISCOVER THAT RICH'S BRADSTREET ESSAY HAD BEEN UNDER MY NOSE ALL ALONG. IT'S REPRINTED IN THE BOOK I'VE HAD SINCE COLLEGE.

HERE RICH HAS ADDED AN INTRO-DUCTORY NOTE WRITTEN A DECADE LATER IN WHICH SHE TAKES HER-SELF TO TASK FOR THE SCHOLARLY DETACHMENT OF HER 1966 ESSAY.

SHE REGRETS HER CONDESCENDING REMARKS ABOUT "WOMEN'S ARCHIVES." SHE CONFESSES THAT SHE HAD IN FACT FELT A POWERFUL PERSONAL IDENTIFICATION WITH BRADSTREET.

tion of the works of Anne Bradstreet, edited by Jeannine Hensley (1967).
Reading and writing about Bradstreet, I began to feel that furtive, almost guilty spark of identification so often kindled in me, in those days, by the life of another woman writer. There were real parallels between her life and mine. Like her, I had learned to read and write in my father's library; like her, I had known the ambiguities of patronizing compliments from male critics; like her, I suffered from chronic lameness; but above all, she was one of the few women writers I knew anything about who had also been a mother. The tension between creative work and motherhood had occupied a decade of my life, although it is barely visible in the essay I wrote in 1966. This essay, in fact, shows the limitations of a point of view which took

I WAS VISITING MOM AT THE TIME I HAD JUST BEGUN TO RESEARCH WINNICOTT IN EARNEST. I HADN'T YET TOLD HER THAT MY BOOK ABOUT HIM WOULD ALSO BE A BOOK ABOUT HER.

HE WRITES ABOUT THE MOTHER-INFANT BOND, THE INCREDIBLE STUFF THAT GOES ON IN THERE.

I JUST FIND HIM REALLY FASCINATING. I THINK YOU'D LIKE HIM.

197

I HAD FOUND A PASSAGE THAT I THOUGHT WOULD STRIKE A CHORD WITH HER.

LISTEN TO THIS.

"AT THE CENTER OF EACH PERSON IS AN INCOMMUNICADO ELEMENT, AND THIS IS SACRED AND MOST WORTHY OF PRESERVATION."

THAT'S GOOD. SOME THINGS ARE PRIVATE.

I JUST READ THESE POEMS IN HERE THAT WERE SO ANNOYING. THEY'RE TOO PERSONAL!

LIKE THIS CONFESSIONAL ONE BY MAXINE KUMIN, ALL ABOUT HER REGRET.

WHO CARES ABOUT THE FELLOWSHIP SHE DIDN'T PURSUE WHEN SHE WAS TWENTY BECAUSE SHE GOT MARRIED INSTEAD? IT'S TOO SPECIFIC.

UM...I DUNNO... CAN'T YOU BE MORE UNIVERSAL BY BEING SPECIFIC?

EVERYONE REGRETS SOMETHING, RIGHT?

I REGRET THAT I WASN'T HELEN VENDLER.

Fap

HELEN VENDLER IS A PROFESSOR AT HARVARD AND A DISTINGUISHED POETRY CRITIC.

I COULD HAVE DONE THAT.

I COULD HAVE GONE ON AFTER I GOT MY MASTER'S.

SHE'S KNOWN FOR "CLOSE READING." SHE'S OF THE SAME GENERATION AS MY MOTHER AND ADRIENNE RICH.

SHE'S GOOD AT EXPLAINING NOT JUST WHAT POEMS SAY, BUT HOW, FORMALLY, THEY SAY IT. SHE SHARES MY MOTHER'S DEEP ADMIRATION FOR WALLACE STEVENS.

I JUST DON'T KNOW WHY EVERYONE HAS TO WRITE ABOUT THEMSELVES.

I SUSPECTED WE WERE NO LONGER DISCUSSING MAXINE KUMIN.

MY MEMOIR ABOUT MY FATHER HAD BEEN PUBLISHED SIX MONTHS BEFORE THIS CONVERSATION.

MOM HAD TOLD ME THAT SHE FELT I'D BETRAYED HER BY REVEALING THINGS IN THE BOOK THAT SHE'D TOLD ME IN CONFIDENCE.

I'D THOUGHT I HAD HER TACIT PERMISSION TO TELL THE STORY, BUT IN FACT I NEVER ASKED FOR IT AND SHE NEVER GAVE IT TO ME. OUR TRUCE IS A FRAGILE ONE.

THE SELF HAS NO PLACE IN GOOD WRITING.

YET HERE I AM, MAKING ANOTHER INCURSION.

IN A 1966 TALK TO TEACHERS CALLED "THE CHILD IN THE FAMILY GROUP," WINNICOTT DESCRIBES THE "CONFLICTS OF LOYALTY WHICH ARE INHERENT IN CHILD DEVELOP-MENT."

*The Child in the Family Group* 141

encounter with disloyalty, is somewhat understated. The family leads on to all manner of groupings, groupings that get wider and wider until they reach the size of the local society and society in general.

The reality of the world in which the children eventually must live as adults is one in which every loyalty involves something of an opposite nature which might be called a disloyalty, and the child who has had the chance to reach to all these things in the course of growth is in the best position to take a place in such a world.

Eventually, if one goes back, one can see that these dis-

THE CHILD MUST BE ABLE TO MOVE AWAY FROM THE MOTHER AND COME BACK TO HER--AGAIN AND AGAIN--IN ORDER TO COMPLETE THE PROCESS OF SEPARATION.

UHH...

flip

WINNICOTT GIVES THE EXAMPLE OF A PATIENT WHO REMEMBERS WANDERING OFF ON HER OWN AT THE BEACH AT AGE TWO OR SO.

THE CHILD LOOKS AT SHELLS FOR A BIT, THEN BECOMES FRIGHTENED. SHE HAS FORGOTTEN HER MOTHER, WHICH MEANS THAT PERHAPS HER MOTHER HAS FORGOTTEN HER.

YEAH, BUT DON'T YOU THINK THAT...

EXPLAINING MYSELF TO MOM REQUIRED ENORMOUS EFFORT. I WAS SWIMMING AGAINST A RIP TIDE.

... THAT IF YOU WRITE MINUTELY AND RIGOROUSLY ENOUGH ABOUT YOUR OWN LIFE...

...YOU CAN, YOU KNOW, TRANSCEND YOUR PARTICULAR SELF?

WINNICOTT'S PATIENT RECALLS RUSHING BACK TO HER MOTHER IN A PANIC. THE MOTHER PICKS HER UP, BUT THEN PUTS HER DOWN AGAIN, JUST A MOMENT TOO S

Eventually, if one goes back, one can see that these dis-loyalties, as I am calling them, are an essential feature of living, and they stem from the fact that it is disloyal to everything that is not oneself if one is to be oneself. The most aggressive and therefore the most dangerous words in the languages of the world are to be found in the assertion I AM. It has to be admitted, however, that only those who have reached a stage at which they can make this assertion are really qualified as adult members of society.

THE WOMAN NOW REALIZES THAT SHE'S BEEN WAITING ALL HER LIFE FOR "THE NEXT STAGE...I WOULD HAVE THROWN MY ARMS ROUND HER NECK AND BURST INTO A FLOOD OF TEARS..."

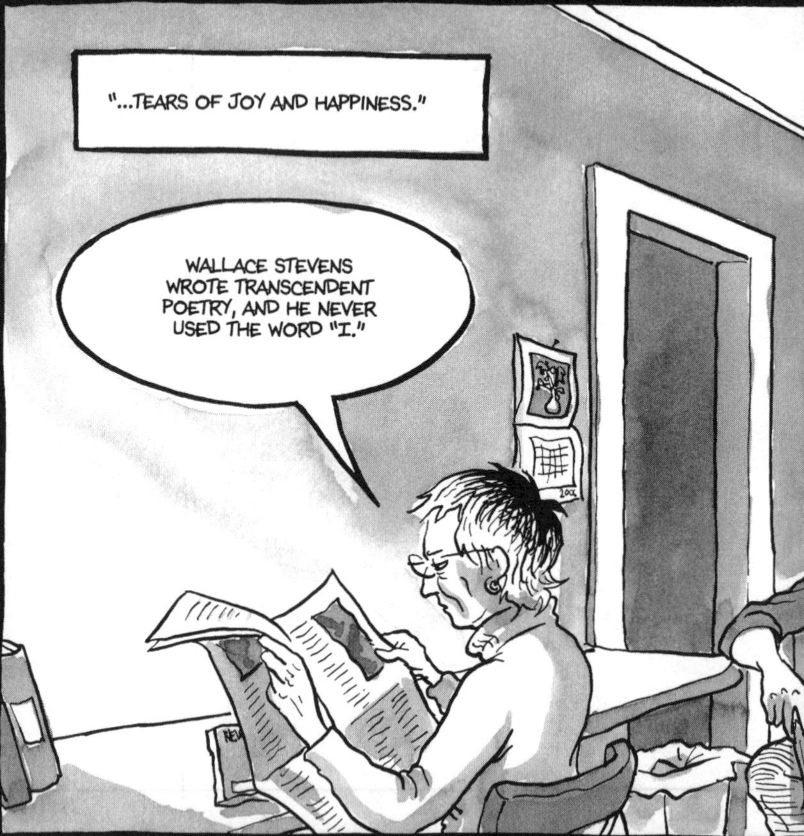
"...TEARS OF JOY AND HAPPINESS."
WALLACE STEVENS WROTE TRANSCENDENT POETRY, AND HE NEVER USED THE WORD "I."

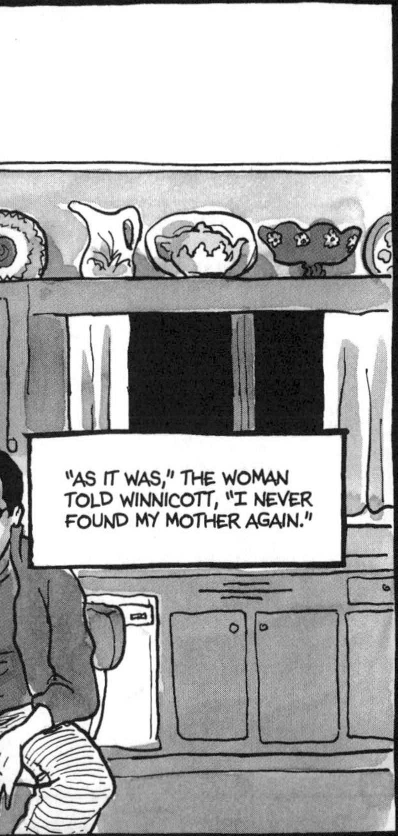
"AS IT WAS," THE WOMAN TOLD WINNICOTT, "I NEVER FOUND MY MOTHER AGAIN."

# 6 Mirror

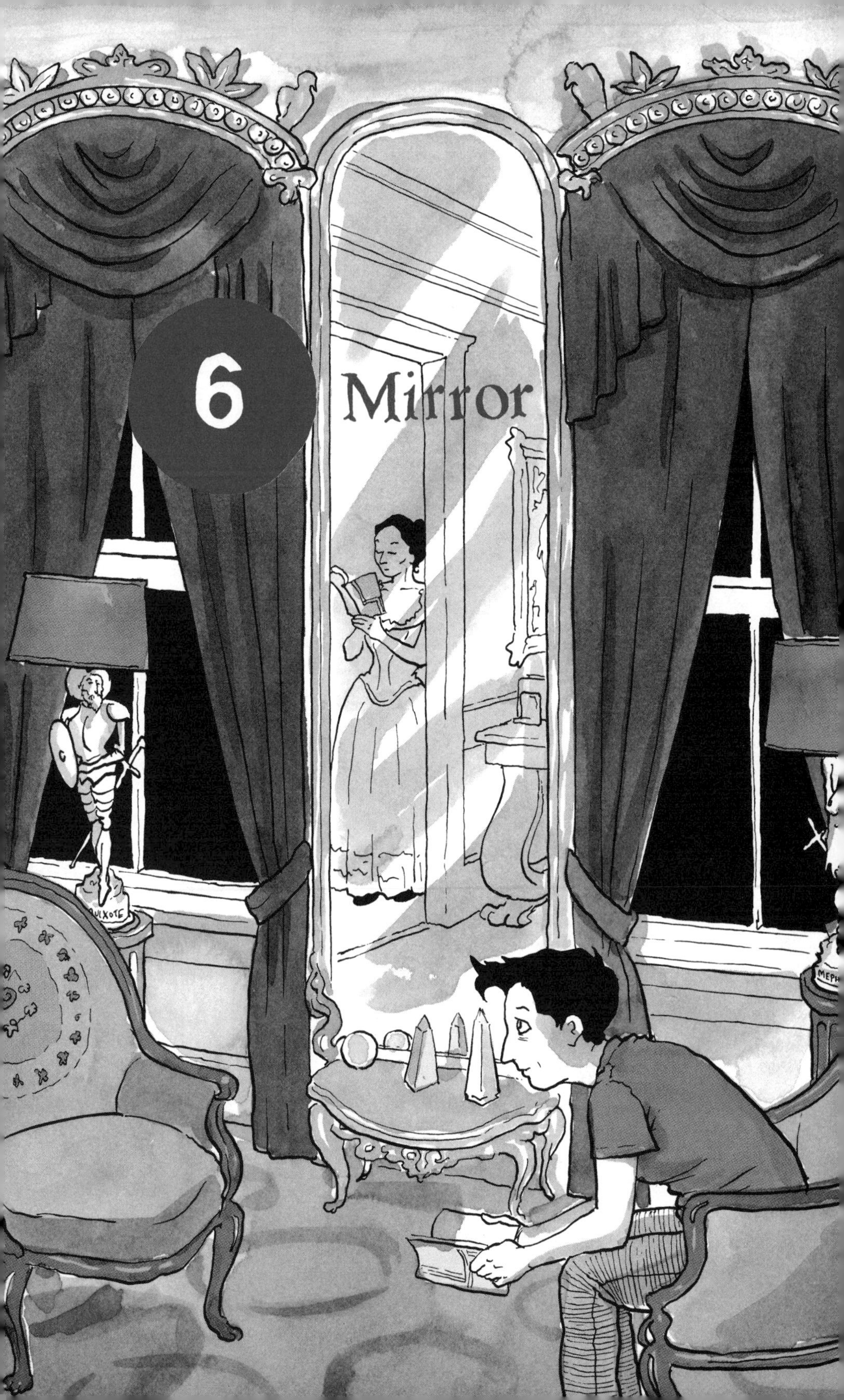

I'M IN THE LIBRARY OF MY CHILDHOOD HOME, WATCHING MOM REHEARSE FOR A PLAY. HER ENTRY THROUGH THE DOORWAY IS THE EQUIVALENT OF COMING ONSTAGE.

MOM'S PART IS A SMALL CHARACTER ROLE WHERE SHE SWEEPS IN, SAYS SOMETHING CUTTINGLY FUNNY, AND SWEEPS OUT AGAIN.

SHE'S WEARING ORNATE AND REVEALING PERIOD UNDERGARMENTS.

I WONDER IF THIS IS HER COSTUME, OR IF SHE'LL BE WEARING A DRESS OVER IT.

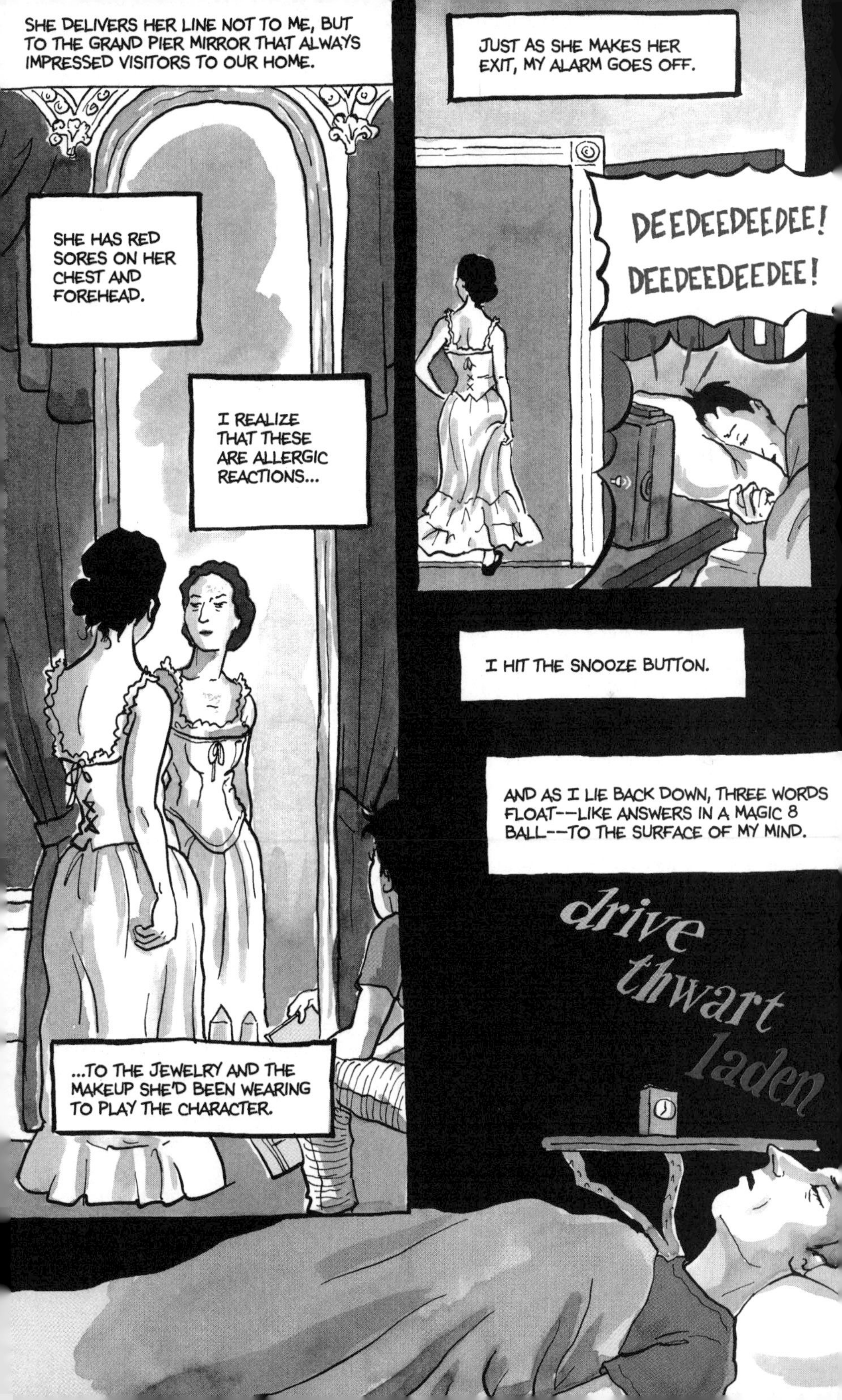
SHE DELIVERS HER LINE NOT TO ME, BUT TO THE GRAND PIER MIRROR THAT ALWAYS IMPRESSED VISITORS TO OUR HOME.
SHE HAS RED SORES ON HER CHEST AND FOREHEAD.
I REALIZE THAT THESE ARE ALLERGIC REACTIONS...
...TO THE JEWELRY AND THE MAKEUP SHE'D BEEN WEARING TO PLAY THE CHARACTER.
JUST AS SHE MAKES HER EXIT, MY ALARM GOES OFF.
DEEDEEDEEDEE! DEEDEEDEEDEE!
I HIT THE SNOOZE BUTTON.
AND AS I LIE BACK DOWN, THREE WORDS FLOAT--LIKE ANSWERS IN A MAGIC 8 BALL--TO THE SURFACE OF MY MIND.
drive
thwart
laden

I HAD THIS DREAM WHILE I WAS WAITING TO TALK TO MOM ABOUT MY MANUSCRIPT. SHE SAID SHE WOULD TRY TO CALL OVER THE WEEKEND, BUT BY MONDAY I HADN'T HEARD FROM HER.

I WAS A WRECK.

I WOKE IN A PANIC THAT NIGHT AND TURNED TO MY OLD STANDBY.

MILLER KEPT TALKING ABOUT "CATHECTED OBJECTS" AND "CATHEXIS." I WASN'T SURE WHAT THIS MEANT EVEN AFTER LOOKING IT UP. "CONCENTRATION OF EMOTIONAL ENERGY" SEEMED SO VAGUE.

With two exceptions, the mothers of all my patients had a narcissistic disturbance, were extremely insecure, and often suffered from depression. The child, an only one or often the first-born, was the narcissistically cathected object. What these mothers had once failed to find in their own mothers they were able to find in their children: someone at their disposal who can be used as an echo, who can be controlled, is completely centered on them, will never desert them, and offers full attention and admiration.

LATER THAT MORNING I HAD THE DREAM.

"LADEN" SEEMED LIKE A JOKE ABOUT THE OVERLADEN CONTENT OF THE DREAM ITSELF. BUT WHOSE DRIVE HAD BEEN THWARTED?

AND BY WHOM?

FIVE YEARS LATER, I WAS AT A BOOK SIGNING FOR THE PAPERBACK EDITION OF THE MEMOIR ABOUT MY FATHER.

I HAVE SOMETHING TO GIVE YOU.

A MAN PRESENTED ME WITH AN ASTONISHING PHOTOGRAPH.

OH MY GOD!

I WAS IN *THE MISER* WITH YOUR MOM ONE SUMMER.

SHE PLAYED THE MATCHMAKER.

THAT'S ME, THE GOOFY KID IN THE BACK.

MY MOTHER IN HER PRIME.

GOD, I DON'T REMEMBER THIS PLAY...I WONDER IF IT WAS AFTER I LEFT HOME?

WHEN I CONSULT MY JOURNAL, I SEE THAT IT WAS THE SUMMER BEFORE I LEFT HOME, WHEN MOM AND I WERE FIGHTING A LOT. I WAS VOLUNTEERING AS AN USHER AT THE PLAYHOUSE THAT SEASON.

*Mom opened in 'The Miser' last night, as Frosine the matchmaker. She was great. The*

NOW I REMEMBER THAT IT WAS IN *THE MISER* THAT MOM, WHO IS QUITE CLAUSTROPHOBIC, HAD TO WAIT TO MAKE AN ENTRANCE FROM A SMALL, ENCLOSED SPACE.

ON TOP OF THAT, HER COSTUME REQUIRED A CORSET. AS SHE LISTENED FOR HER CUE ONE HOT NIGHT, SHE FELT HERSELF BLACKING OUT.

...HE MUST HAVE SOMEWHERE A LARGE STORE OF FURNITURE..

BUT THROUGH SHEER FORCE OF WILL, SHE DID NOT.

AHH! FRO-SINE!

WHAT BRINGS YOU HERE?

THE SAME THAT BRINGS ME EVERYWHERE ELSE; TO FETCH AND CARRY, TO RENDER MYSELF SERVICEABLE...

I HAVE MORE DISTINCT MEMORIES OF THE OTHER PLAY MOM WAS IN THAT SUMMER. THE THEATER ALWAYS ENDED THE SEASON WITH A BIG MUSICAL THAT RAN FOR TWO WEEKS.

Mom was great in 'A Little Night Music'! That is a fantastic play! it's hypnotic! It's enchanting! It's addictive! It's neat. I could watch it 190 times. Ma was Madame Leonora Armfeldt. She had to sing a solo! It was called 'Liasons'. She really did it great. She's wonnerful. She's my Mum! YUP. Anyhow. I'm packing to leave in ONE WEEK! Packing to leave forever!

(I WAS GOING TO COLLEGE A YEAR EARLY, A PLAN THAT HAD FALLEN INTO PLACE RATHER SUDDENLY.)

MADAME ARMFELDT IS A RETIRED COURTESAN.

SHE HAS TAKEN OVER THE CARE OF HER GRAND-DAUGHTER, FREDRIKA, BORN OUT OF WEDLOCK TO HER DAUGHTER, DESIRÉE.

IF YOU CHEATED A LITTLE, IT WOULD COME OUT.

SOLITAIRE IS THE ONLY THING IN LIFE THAT DEMANDS AB-SOLUTE HONESTY.

DESIRÉE IS A ONCE-FAMOUS ACTRESS NOW TOURING THE PROVINCES. SHE SENDS LETTERS ENCLOSING HER REVIEWS TO FREDRIKA, WHO ADULATES HER.

...ORDINARY MOTHERS, LIKE ORDINARY WIVES,

FRY THE EGGS AND DRY THE SHEETS AND TRY TO DEAL WITH FACTS.

MINE **ACTS!**

I WAS ADMIRING MY MOTHER'S ACTING IN A PLAY IN WHICH A DAUGHTER ADMIRES HER MOTHER'S ACTING--A PARALLEL THAT WAS LOST ON ME AT THE TIME.

LIAISONS!

WHAT'S HAPPENED TO THEM?

MOM HAD BEEN TERRIFIED ABOUT HER SOLO.

LI-AI-SONS...

THESE NOTES ARE **IMPOSSIBLE!**

IF YOU'RE SO SCARED, WHY ARE YOU DOING IT?

I JUST HAVE TO.

I COULD NOT HAVE BEEN MORE IN AWE IF SHE WERE MARCHING INTO COMBAT.

AT SIXTEEN, I THOUGHT I UNDERSTOOD SONDHEIM'S MUSICAL WELL ENOUGH.

TAKE MY DAUGHTER, I TAUGHT HER, I TRIED MY BEST TO POINT THE WAY.

I EVEN NAMED HER DES-I-RÉE.

BUT I SEE NOW THAT I COULD NOT POSSIBLY HAVE APPRECIATED ITS DISILLUSIONED INSIGHTS INTO MORTALITY AND DESIRE.

LIKE THE REST OF THE AUDIENCE, I WAS NOT ALLOWED BACKSTAGE. YET THIS BACKSTAGE PHOTO OF MOM IS A DEEPLY FAMILIAR IMAGE.

SHE APPLIED HER EVERYDAY MAKEUP WITH THE SAME TRANSFIXED CONCENTRATION.

THE FIRST PAPER OF WINNICOTT'S THAT I READ WAS THIS ONE, WRITTEN IN 1967.

# 9 Mirror-role of Mother and Family in Child Development[1]

In individual emotional development *the precursor of the mirror is the mother's face.* I wish to refer to the normal aspect of this and also to its psychopathology.

GHASTLY!

NO, YOU'RE NOT!

ONE OF HIS CLINICAL ILLUSTRATIONS IS OF A MOTHER OF THREE BOYS WHO WAKES IN A STATE OF DESPAIR EACH MORNING UNTIL SHE CAN "PUT ON HER FACE." WINNICOTT SAYS SHE HAD SOME UNCERTAINTY ABOUT HER OWN MOTHER'S SIGHT OF HER AND WAS LOOKING IN THE MIRROR FOR REASSURANCE.

213

IF SHE'D HAD A DAUGHTER, HE WROTE, IT MIGHT HAVE HELPED. BUT A DAUGHTER COULD HAVE BEEN DAMAGED BY THE BURDEN OF HAVING TO REASSURE THE MOTHER.

YOU KNOW I DON'T LIKE YOU WATCHING ME.

MY MOTHER WOULD NOT BE SEEN WITHOUT HER "FACE." SHE STARTED WEARING TANGEE LIPSTICK AT AGE ELEVEN OR TWELVE. HER FATHER "LIKED MAKEUP ON A WOMAN."

I DON'T KNOW WHY YOU'RE ALWAYS SO PALE. YOU LOOK PEAKED.

WHEN I WAS EIGHT, I BEGAN SNEAKING MOM'S BLUSHER.

I WAS ALWAYS CAREFUL TO PUT THE COMPACT BACK PRECISELY WHERE I HAD FOUND IT.

I LIKED HOW HALE AND HEARTY I LOOKED WITH PINK CHEEKS. LIKE A REAL CHILD.

I DISCOVERED THAT I COULD RETOUCH MY FACE IN MY SCHOOL PHOTOS WITH A CRAYON, SMOOTHING OUT THE WAX WITH MY FINGERNAIL.

I WAS MORTIFIED WHEN I REALIZED THAT MOM HAD FOUND OUT ABOUT THE BLUSHER. NOT ONLY THAT, SHE SEEMED TO THINK I WAS ENGAGED IN SOME SORT OF GIRLISH EFFORT TO LOOK PRETTY.

ALISON'S BEEN EXPERIMENTING WITH MY MAKEUP.

RELAXED BY TWEEZING HER EYEBROWS.

IN HIS 1914 BOOK *ON NARCISSISM*, FREUD SAYS:

uded by a short summary of the paths leading to the an object.

A person may love: —

(1) According to the narcissistic type:
    (a) what he himself is (i.e. himself),
    (b) what he himself was,
    (c) what he himself would like to be,
    (d) someone who was once part of himself

(2) According to the anaclitic (attachment) type:
    (a) the woman who feeds him,
    (b) the man who protects him,

nd the succession of substitutes who take their plac nclusion of case (c) of the first type cannot be justifie ter stage of this discussion. [P. 101.]

The significance of narcissistic object-choice for

THE FACT THAT THE MOTHER IS THE ORIGINAL LOVE-OBJECT FOR BOTH MALES AND FEMALES PRESENTS FREUD WITH A STICKY WICKET.

HE HAS TO EXPLAIN WHY IT IS THAT WOMEN DO NOT, IN GENERAL, GROW UP TO FALL IN LOVE WITH WOMEN IN THE WAY THAT MEN, IN GENERAL, DO.

DAD, WE'RE GONNA MISS THE FIRST ACT!

BRONZING STICK

THIS LEADS HIM INTO SOME ODD CONTOR-TIONS, INCLUDING THE IDEA THAT WOMEN AND HOMOSEXUAL MEN TEND TOWARD THE NARCISSISTIC TYPE OF LOVE.

IS THAT WHAT YOU'RE WEARING?

215

SOME FEMALES, FREUD CONCEDES, ARE CAPABLE OF THE ATTACHMENT TYPE OF LOVE BECAUSE "BEFORE PUBERTY THEY FEEL MASCULINE" AND "DEVELOP SOME WAY ALONG MASCULINE LINES."

YOU LOOK LIKE A GAS STATION ATTENDANT IN THAT SHIRT.

I ADMIT THAT AT FIRST GLANCE MY FAMILY APPEARS TO BE A CASE STUDY FOR THESE DUBIOUS CONCLUSIONS.

BUT THE LIBIDINAL FORCES SWIRLING ABOUT OUR HOUSE WERE NOT QUITE THAT SIMPLE.

WE HAVE A FIXED AMOUNT OF "LIBIDO," OR PSYCHIC ENERGY, FREUD THEORIZED, WHICH WE INVEST IN OBJECTS LIKE OUR PARENTS AND "THE SUCCESSION OF SUBSTITUTES WHO TAKE THEIR PLACE."

IN MY FAMILY, BOYS WERE GOOD AND GIRLS WERE BAD.

MY BROTHERS WERE ALL SWEET AND INNOCENT. I WAS THE BAD SEED.

"CATHEXIS," AS IT TURNS OUT, IS THE TECHNICAL TERM FOR THIS PROCESS OF INVESTING LIBIDINAL ENERGY IN AN OBJECT.

I HAD SERIOUSLY *CATHECTED* JOCELYN BY THE TIME OF THIS MOMENTOUS SESSION, ABOUT ONE YEAR INTO OUR WORK TOGETHER.

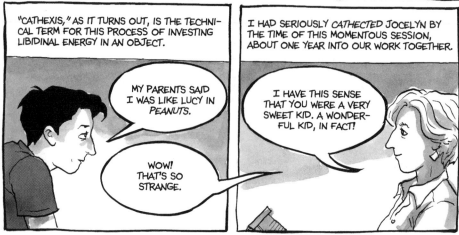

MY PARENTS SAID I WAS LIKE LUCY IN *PEANUTS.*

WOW! THAT'S SO STRANGE.

I HAVE THIS SENSE THAT YOU WERE A VERY SWEET KID. A WONDERFUL KID, IN FACT!

BECAUSE, AS AN ADULT... AND THIS WILL PROBABLY EMBARRASS YOU...

...YOU'RE REALLY ADORABLE.

JOCELYN KEPT TALKING, BUT I COULDN'T HEAR HER. MY HEAD WAS REVERBERATING WITH THE THING I HAD APPARENTLY BEEN LONGING TO HEAR FOR MY WHOLE LIFE.

IN A NARCISSISTIC CATHEXIS, YOU INVEST MORE ENERGY INTO YOUR IDEAS ABOUT ANOTHER PERSON THAN IN THE ACTUAL, OBJECTIVE, EXTERNAL PERSON.

LIAISONS...

"NARCISSISM" IS WHAT HAPPENS WHEN YOU CATHECT YOUR OWN EGO INSTEAD OF AN EXTERNAL OBJECT.

WHAT'S HAPPENED TO THEM...

THE JARGON REALLY GETS IN THE WAY.

IN THE MIRROR-ROLE PAPER, WINNICOTT GIVES A CRYSTAL-CLEAR DESCRIPTION OF NARCISSISTIC CATHEXIS WITHOUT RESORTING TO A SINGLE TECHNICAL TERM.

So the man who falls in love with beauty is quite different from the man who loves a girl and feels she is beautiful and can see what is beautiful about her.

WHATEVER WAS GOING ON BETWEEN MY PARENTS, I SUPPOSE THAT MY FANTASY OF SELF-SUFFICIENCY, MY HEAVY INVESTMENT IN MY OWN MIND, IS ALSO A KIND OF NARCISSISTIC CATHEXIS.

I EVEN NAMED HER ...

E-FLAT

A-FLAT

E

IMPOSSIBLE!

MOM NAMED ME AFTER A MIDDLE-ENGLISH POEM SHE LEARNED IN COLLEGE.

FROM ALLE WYMMEN MY LOVE IS LENT, AND LYHT ON ALISOUN.

THE SUBJECT OF THE POEM DESIRES ITS OBJECT. HE'S "SEIZED WITH LONGING."

...ICHOT FROM HEVENE IT IS ME SENT...

HE'LL GIVE UP LIVING IF ALISOUN WON'T HAVE HIM.

...AND LYHT ON ALISOUN.

THE REFRAIN IS TRANSLATED AS "MY LOVE HAS BEEN WITHDRAWN FROM ALL WOMEN AND SETTLED ON ALISOUN."

THE ECONOMIC ANALOGY IS THE SAME ONE FREUD USED TO DESCRIBE CATHEXIS. LIBIDO IS INVESTED IN AN OBJECT, WITHDRAWN, INVESTED IN ANOTHER.

218

MOM'S ROLES THAT SUMMER BEFORE I LEFT FOR COLLEGE--A MATCHMAKER AND A COURTESAN--GIVE A LITERAL TWIST TO THE FINANCIAL METAPHOR.

I WAS GOING HUNDREDS OF MILES AWAY TO A PRIVATE LIBERAL ARTS SCHOOL. MOM'S ONLY OPTION HAD BEEN THE STATE TEACHERS COLLEGE DOWN THE STREET.

MOM AND I DIDN'T HUG OR KISS GOODBYE. WE HADN'T TOUCHED IN YEARS.

SEE YA!

I SET OUT FOR ADULTHOOD WITH LITTLE MORE FUSS THAN IF I HAD BEEN GOING TO THE DENTIST.

WINNICOTT POSITS A CONNECTION BETWEEN MATERNAL MIRRORING IN INFANCY AND WHAT HAPPENS AS WE ENTER INTO EROTIC RELATIONSHIPS AS ADULTS.

To return to the normal progress of events, when the average girl studies her face in the mirror she is reassuring herself that the mother-image is there and that the mother can see her and that the mother is *en rapport* with her. When girls and boys in their secondary narcissism look in order to see beauty and to fall in love, there is already evidence that doubt has crept in about their mother's continued love and care.

I'M ALWAYS TRYING TO DISCERN A PATTERN IN THE CHECKERED HISTORY OF MY OWN LIAISONS.

BUT THE ONLY CONSTANT I CAN FIND IS THAT AS SOON AS I'M SURE THE OTHER PERSON HAS CATHECTED ME, TOO, I WANT TO FLEE.

ELOISE WAS AT LEAST AS AMBIVALENT AS I WAS ABOUT INTIMACY, WHICH GAVE OUR COURTSHIP A CERTAIN COMPELLING URGENCY.

WHEN SHE WENT TO NICARAGUA FOR SIX MONTHS, WE AGREED IT WAS OKAY TO SEE OTHER PEOPLE. AND WE BOTH DID SO.

THE PERSPECTIVE IS REALLY SOMETHING FROM HERE.

WHEN SHE RETURNED, WE ENDED THESE DALLIANCES, BUT REMAINED LIVING APART. SHE WOULD VISIT ME IN THE CITY, I WOULD VISIT HER IN THE COUNTRY.

SEE?

OUR RELATIONSHIP PROGRESSED WITH EXTREME DELIBERATION.

IT WAS A FULL YEAR, FOR EXAMPLE, BEFORE WE REACHED THIS PARTICULAR BENCHMARK:

WHAT?

I LOVE YOU.

AND EVEN THEN, I WAS ACUTELY UNCLEAR WHAT I MEANT BY IT.

IT GOT HARDER AND HARDER TO BE APART.

AS I GREW MORE DEVOTED TO ELOISE, I BEGAN TO FEEL ANOTHER KIND OF DEVOTION.

IF YOU COULD LEND ME $1500, I SHOULD BE OKAY FOR A COUPLE MONTHS.

IN DECEMBER, AT AGE TWENTY-FOUR, I QUIT MY JOB TO TRY TO MAKE MY WAY AS A CARTOONIST.

OKAY. I'LL SEND YOU A CHECK.

THANK YOU, MOM!

I ALREADY HAVE A JOB DOING SOME ADS FOR A TYPESETTER.

MY MOTHER DID NOT QUESTION THE WISDOM OF THIS PLAN.

SHE DID NOT BALK AT THE FACT THAT I WOULD BE LOSING MY HEALTH INSURANCE.

OVER THE NEXT YEAR SHE WOULD WRITE CHECK AFTER CHECK, GIVING--NOT LOANING-- ME A TOTAL OF $5200.

I WAS DRAWING.

BUT I WAS ALSO SPENDING A LOT OF TIME WITH ELOISE.

DON'T GO.

I ALREADY SKIPPED ELECTRICAL SYSTEMS! I CAN'T MISS MY DRIVE-LINE EXAM AT THREE.

AFTER THREE YEARS IN BROOKLYN, I HAD FINALLY MADE IT TO MANHATTAN AND DIDN'T WANT TO LEAVE. ELOISE HAD GROWN UP IN NEW YORK AND DIDN'T WANT TO LIVE THERE AGAIN.

MOVE TO MASSACHU-SETTS!

I CAN'T YET.

A VERY CONFUSING PERIOD WAS ABOUT TO BEGIN.

BEING IN LOVE WITH ELOISE, I DISCOVERED, DID NOT PREVENT ME FROM BECOMING ATTRACTED TO SOMEONE ELSE.

COME PICK ME UP!

DONNA WAS A PHOTOJOURNALIST I WORKED WITH AT THE PAPER. SHE WAS VERY GOOD.

SHE HAD A REMARKABLE ABILITY TO CAPTURE THE PRECISE INSTANT THAT REVEALED EVERYTHING.

JESUS, DONNA. THIS ONE'S AMAZING.

THAT'S THE WALL STREET PROTEST.

223

MY GIRLFRIEND GOT ARRESTED AT THAT.

HUH.

OMIGOD, THAT'S HER! UNDER THE BARRICADE!

A FEW WEEKS LATER, DONNA AND I KISSED AND SLEPT TOGETHER BUT DID NOT HAVE SEX.

I'M IN A MONOGAMOUS RELATIONSHIP.

I THINK I'M ATTRACTED TO YOU BECAUSE YOU'RE UNAVAILABLE.

I TOLD ELOISE, OMITTING SOME DETAILS.

I'M SO FUCKED UP.

I THINK IT'S ABOUT MY CONFLICT OVER WHETHER TO MOVE OR NOT.

THE NEXT TIME SHE CAME TO THE CITY, WE HAD A BAD FIGHT.

MAYBE IT WOULD HELP IF I HAD A SHELF HERE FOR MY STUFF.

A SHELF?

ELOISE SUGGESTED THAT WE SEPARATE FOR THREE WEEKS WHILE I FIGURED THINGS OUT.

OKAY.

I LASTED LESS THAN THREE DAYS.

I WANT TO BE WITH YOU.

I SPENT THE NEXT WEEKEND IN THE COUNTRY.

BUT AS SOON AS I GOT BACK TO THE CITY, I HAD SEX WITH DONNA.

I LIED EXPERTLY TO ELOISE.

OH...I HAD TO GO OVER TO THE DOJO. SUE LOST HER KEY.

I SLEPT WITH DONNA AGAIN, BUT REFRAINED FROM HAVING SEX.

I'M SO FUCKED UP.

I KNEW I WAS BEHAVING BADLY ALL AROUND. I HAD TO CONFESS.

BUT ELOISE HAD A CONFESSION, TOO.

ANN FROM WORK A COUPLE TIMES. AND ALSO DEE.

DEE WHO WAS IN *NICARAGUA* WITH YOU?

NATURALLY, I WENT RIGHT OVER TO DONNA'S.

FOR SOMEONE HAVING THIS MUCH SEX, I FELT CURIOUSLY IMPOTENT.

LIKE I WASN'T REALLY THERE.

IF I WAS LOOKING FOR A REFLECTION, ELOISE PROVIDED ONE ON HER NEXT VISIT.

YOU DON'T HAVE A JOB. YOU CAN'T COMMIT TO ME. YOU'RE JERKING DONNA AROUND.

TAKE SOME RESPONSIBILITY FOR YOURSELF!

THAT SAME AFTERNOON, I HAD A PLAN WITH DONNA. SHE'D BEEN WANTING TO TAKE PICTURES OF ME DOING KARATE.

I WAS LOOKING FORWARD TO SEEING THEM. I KNEW MY FORM WAS PRETTY GOOD.

SHE GAVE ME THIS PRINT A COUPLE WEEKS LATER, AFTER I'D MADE THE DECISION TO MOVE TO MASSACHUSETTS.

IN DONNA'S MIRROR I AM SLACK, LOST, AND ODDLY PRETTY.

SHE TITLED IT "ALISON IN-BETWEEN."

THE PHOTO IS BLACK AND WHITE, BUT MY SKIN IS TINTED WITH RETOUCHING INK. MY CHEEKS ARE PINK, LIKE IN MY HAND-COLORED SCHOOL PHOTOS.

A FEW WEEKS AFTER THIS, I WAS HAVING ONE OF MY USUAL CONVERSATIONS WITH MOM.

UH HUH.

I DETERMINED THAT AT THE NEXT PAUSE, I WOULD TELL HER SOMETHING ABOUT MY LIFE.

UH HUH.

HEY! I GOT PAPERS IN PHILADELPHIA AND CHICAGO TO CARRY MY COMIC STRIP.

FOR MONEY.

HMNH.

I HAVE TO GET THE PLUMBER TO COME BACK, THAT PIPE IS STILL LEAKING.

I FORCED MYSELF TO KEEP TALKING.

PLUS I MET WITH THAT PUBLISHER. I SIGNED A CONTRACT TO DO A BOOK OF CARTOONS.

YOU MEAN YOUR LESBIAN CARTOONS?

YEAH.

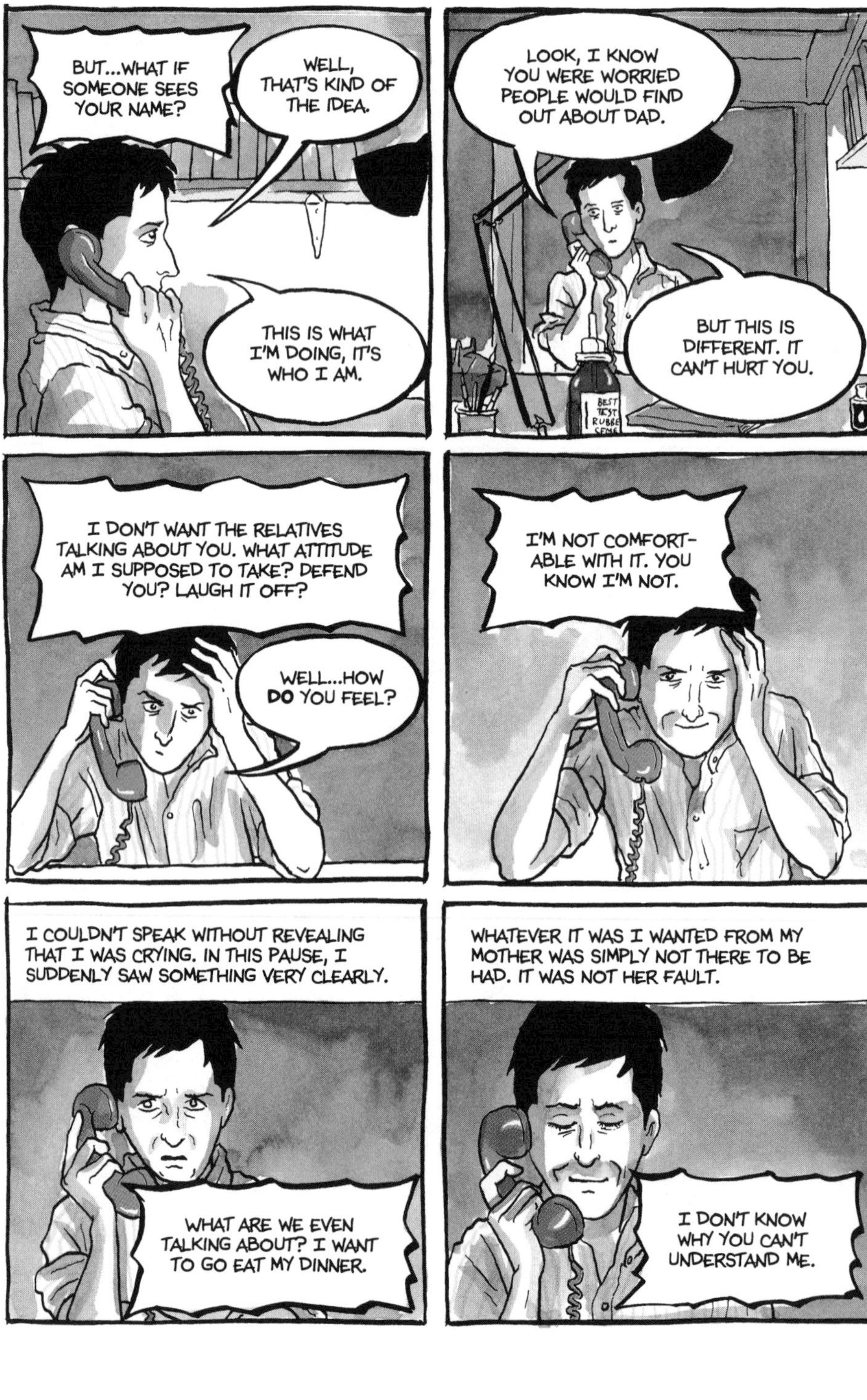
BUT...WHAT IF SOMEONE SEES YOUR NAME?
WELL, THAT'S KIND OF THE IDEA.
THIS IS WHAT I'M DOING, IT'S WHO I AM.
LOOK, I KNOW YOU WERE WORRIED PEOPLE WOULD FIND OUT ABOUT DAD.
BUT THIS IS DIFFERENT. IT CAN'T HURT YOU.
I DON'T WANT THE RELATIVES TALKING ABOUT YOU. WHAT ATTITUDE AM I SUPPOSED TO TAKE? DEFEND YOU? LAUGH IT OFF?
WELL...HOW **DO** YOU FEEL?
I'M NOT COMFORT-ABLE WITH IT. YOU KNOW I'M NOT.
I COULDN'T SPEAK WITHOUT REVEALING THAT I WAS CRYING. IN THIS PAUSE, I SUDDENLY SAW SOMETHING VERY CLEARLY.
WHAT ARE WE EVEN TALKING ABOUT? I WANT TO GO EAT MY DINNER.
WHATEVER IT WAS I WANTED FROM MY MOTHER WAS SIMPLY NOT THERE TO BE HAD. IT WAS NOT HER FAULT.
I DON'T KNOW WHY YOU CAN'T UNDERSTAND ME.

AND IT WAS THEREFORE NOT MY FAULT THAT I WAS UNABLE TO ELICIT IT.

CAN YOU UNDERSTAND?

I KNOW SHE GAVE ME WHAT SHE COULD.

SHE HAD JUST SENT ME ANOTHER $1500 CHECK, FOR GOD'S SAKE, WHILE I PURSUED A CALLING SHE WAS NOT HAPPY ABOUT.

YET I DID NOT FEEL GUILTY ABOUT HANGING UP.

HER CHECK WOULD SEE ME THROUGH UNTIL I MOVED AND GOT A PART-TIME JOB IN SEPTEMBER TO SUPPLE-MENT MY CARTOONING INCOME.

MOM HAD SUPPORTED ME FOR NINE MONTHS.

THE SIGNIFICANCE OF THIS PARTICULAR LENGTH OF TIME DOES NOT ESCAPE ME.

THINGS HAD ONCE BEEN MUCH SIM-PLER BETWEEN US.

ABOUT A YEAR BEFORE THE HANG-UP CONVERSATION, MOM TOLD ME AN INTERESTING STORY.

YOU WERE AROUND A YEAR AND A HALF. WE WERE AT THE FUNERAL HOME.

"THERE WAS A HALL STAND WITH A MIRROR ON THE LANDING OF THE STAIRS."

"YOU MUST HAVE CLIMBED UP ON IT. I HEARD A TERRIBLE CRASH."

"I WAS SURE YOU WERE DEAD. I RAN AND HID IN THE BATHROOM."

"BUT DAD PICKED YOU UP AND THERE WAS NOT A SCRATCH ON YOU."

I WAS MOVED BY THIS IMAGE OF MOM'S VISCERAL CONCERN FOR ME.

AT THE BEGINNING OF HIS MIRROR-ROLE PAPER, WINNICOTT ACKNOWLEDGES THAT HE HAS BEEN INFLUENCED BY ANOTHER PAPER.

JACQUES LACAN'S "THE MIRROR STAGE AS FORMATIVE OF THE FUNCTION OF THE 'I.'"

BOTH PAPERS OUTLINE THEORIES OF HOW WE COME TO THINK OF OURSELVES AS SELVES.

LACAN STARTS BY TOSSING DESCARTES'S "I THINK, THEREFORE I AM" OUT THE WINDOW. THE "I" IS NOT NEARLY SO SOLID, NOR SO EASILY APPREHENDED, HE IMPLIES.

WHEN A BABY IDENTIFIES HERSELF FOR THE FIRST TIME IN A MIRROR, THERE'S A "FLUTTER OF JUBILANT ACTIVITY," A "LEANING-FORWARD."

THE REFLECTION IN THE MIRROR IS YOU...BUT NOT EXACTLY. IT'S BACKWARDS, FOR ONE THING.

AND IT'S ALL OF A PIECE, UNLIKE THE DIFFUSE WAY YOU'VE EXPERIENCED REALITY UNTIL THIS MOMENT.

NOW YOU CAN SEE THAT YOU'RE SEPARATE FROM EVERYTHING ELSE.

THAT THERE'S AN INSIDE AND AN OUTSIDE.

IN THIS MOMENT YOU IDENTIFY WITH YOUR IMAGE, YOUR DOUBLE, AN UNATTAINABLE IDEAL.

BUT FOR WINNICOTT, THE SELF IS NOT ALIEN AND ILLUSORY. IT'S COHERENT AND AUTHENTIC...

...AND, IF ALL GOES WELL, FEELS "REAL."

In other words the mother is looking at the baby and *what she looks like is related to what she sees there.* All this is too easily taken for granted. I am asking that this which is naturally done well by mothers who are caring for their babies shall not be taken for granted. I can make my point by going straight over to the case of the baby whose mother reflects her own mood or, worse still, the rigidity of her own defences. In such a case what does the baby see?

MAYBE THE MOTHER MANAGES TO BE A MIRROR ONLY PART OF THE TIME. IN SUCH "TANTALIZING" CASES, SOME BABIES LEARN TO WITHDRAW THEIR OWN NEEDS WHEN THE MOTHER'S ARE EVIDENT.

WINNICOTT OFFERS HIS OWN TWIST ON DESCARTES'S *COGITO*.

# When I look I am seen, so I exist.

THE DAY I HUNG UP THE PHONE ON MOM WAS THE LAST TIME SHE MADE ME CRY.

THINGS GOT EASIER AFTER THAT.

WHEN I THINK ABOUT MOM'S ACTING CAREER, IT OCCURS TO ME THAT WE'RE NOT SO DIFFERENT.

IT'S JUST THAT INSTEAD OF PLAYING A CHARACTER, I'M PLAYING MYSELF.

I KNOW SHE WISHES I WEREN'T WRITING THIS BOOK ABOUT HER.

THE IRONY IS THAT IF IT WEREN'T FOR HOW EFFECTIVELY SHE MODELED CREATIVE RISK-TAKING, I WOULD PROBABLY NOT BE WRITING IT.

HER COURAGEOUS SOLO IN *A LITTLE NIGHT MUSIC*, HER DETERMINATION THE NIGHT SHE NEARLY FAINTED IN *THE MISER*...

...SHE HAS TRANSMITTED SOME OF THAT DRIVE TO ME.

AFTER THE SUMMER I WAS SIXTEEN, I DIDN'T SEE MOM ONSTAGE AGAIN UNTIL I WAS THIRTY-THREE.

THIS SEEMS ODD TO ME NOW, GIVEN HOW MANY PLAYS SHE DID OVER THE YEARS.

BUT SHE DIDN'T LIKE VISITORS WHILE SHE WAS WORKING ON A SHOW.

IN FACT, THE ONLY WAY I MANAGED TO SEE HER IN *THE ROYAL FAMILY* WAS TO TAKE HER BY SURPRISE.

AMY AND I DROVE NINE HOURS FROM VERMONT, CHECKED INTO A MOTEL, THEN RACED TO THE THEATER, LATE.

A FRIEND OF MOM'S AT THE BOX OFFICE TOOK OUR FLOWERS TO GIVE HER AFTER THE SHOW.

TO BE APPEARING WITH YOUR MOTHER! QUITE AN EVENT, QUITE AN EVENT IN THE THEATER.

I WAS NOT USED TO PERPETRATING ANY SORT OF DECEPTION ON MOM. I WAS AFRAID TURNING UP LIKE THIS WOULD UPSET HER.

*THE ROYAL FAMILY*, WRITTEN IN THE 1920S, IS A PARODY OF THE BARRYMORES.

YOU'RE ABOUT TO ENTER INTO YOUR GREAT INHERITANCE, COME BEFORE THE PUBLIC AS THE MEMBER OF A DISTINGUISHED FAMILY.

THAT SPEECH NEEDS CUTTING, BERTIE.

MOM PLAYED THE MATRIARCH, FANNY CAVENDISH.

ONE WEEKEND WHEN I WAS FIFTEEN, MOM AND I TOOK THE BUS TO NEW YORK SO SHE COULD SEE THE 1976 REVIVAL OF THE PLAY ON BROADWAY.

AN ELDERLY EVA LE GALLIENNE PLAYED FANNY, ROSEMARY HARRIS HER DAUGHTER.

I ELECTED TO ATTEND A JULES FEIFFER PLAY INSTEAD. MY SHOW ENDED FIRST, SO I WAITED FOR MOM OUTSIDE HER THEATER.

THE USHERS OPENED THE DOORS. I HEARD WILD APPLAUSE AND COULD SEE ROSEMARY HARRIS TAKING A CURTAIN CALL.

WHEN MOM CAME OUT SHE WAS SWOONING.

I CAN'T SPEAK. DON'T TALK TO ME.

I WAS CURIOUS TO SEE IF MOM'S ACTING WAS AS GOOD AS I REMEMBERED. SHE DIDN'T HAVE MUCH TO WORK WITH--THE OTHER ACTORS WERE AWKWARD AND THE SHOW DIDN'T QUITE GEL.

THE THRILL YOU GET OUT OF DOING YOUR WORK IS BIGGER THAN ANY OTHER SINGLE THING IN THE WORLD!

YOU LOVE IT! YOU COULDN'T LIVE WITHOUT IT!

THE MOTHER AND GRAND-MOTHER TRY TO CONVINCE THE DAUGHTER NOT TO LEAVE THE STAGE TO GET MARRIED.

IMPASSIONED, FANNY BEGINS TO RELIVE THE MOMENTS BEFORE THE CURTAIN GOES UP.

HALF HOUR, MISS CAVENDISH! GREASEPAINT, ROUGE, MASCARA.

FIFTEEN MINUTES, MISS CAVENDISH!

MY COSTUME...MORE ROUGE...WHERE'S THE RABBIT'S FOOT!

OVERTURE!

SUDDENLY SHE GOES LIMP AND COLLAPSES.

MOTHER! MOTHER, WHAT'S THE MATTER!

BUT IT'S JUST A FAINTING FIT.

SHE'S REALLY GOOD!

SHE DOESN'T ACTUALLY DIE UNTIL THE END OF THE THIRD ACT.

WE WENT AROUND TO THE STAGE DOOR. MOM WAS NOT UPSET BUT DELIGHTED TO SEE US.

I CAN'T BELIEVE IT!

AT HER HOUSE, I MADE DINNER WHILE SHE GOSSIPED ABOUT THE SHOW.

TONY WAS STILL ON BOOK AT THE DRESS REHEARSAL!

I WAS GIDDY. I FELT LIKE I HAD FINESSED A TRICKY RITE OF PASSAGE.

TO THE THEATAH!

I HAD AN EXPERIENCE SIMILAR TO THIS MUCH MORE RECENTLY.

I JUST WATCHED THE MOVIE VERSION OF *A LITTLE NIGHT MUSIC*, WITH ELIZABETH TAYLOR AND HERMIONE GINGOLD!

REMEMBER THE SUMMER YOU PLAYED MADAME ARMFELDT?

I WAS HOPING FOR SOME GOOD MATERIAL.

I DON'T EVEN WANT TO THINK ABOUT IT.

IN ONE SCENE THE BUTLER LIFTS HER UP OUT OF HER WHEELCHAIR AND CARRIES HER...DID YOU GET CARRIED OFFSTAGE?

NO...I THINK HE JUST WHEELED ME OFF. BUT HE COULD HAVE CARRIED ME! I WEIGHED 108 THEN.

I REMEMBER THE DIRECTOR INSISTED THAT I WEAR THE SAME DRESS I WORE IN ANOTHER PLAY.

I CHOOSE A **PERFUME** FOR EACH CHARACTER I DO! I CERTAINLY DIDN'T WANT TO WEAR THE SAME DRESS. BUT HE OVERRULED ME.

OH, DIRECTORS CAN BE BITCHES.

YOU KNOW, IT'S ON BROADWAY RIGHT NOW. ANGELA LANSBURY'S GETTING GREAT REVIEWS AS MADAME ARMFELDT, BETTER THAN CATHERINE ZETA-JONES AS HER DAUGHTER!

LET'S GO SEE IT!

WE CAN DRIVE INTO THE CITY WHEN I COME TO VISIT YOU NEXT MONTH!

OH, BOB AND I ARE GOING IN ON THE BUS ON THE 27TH. I CAN SEE IT THEN.

OH.

BUT WHEN WE SPOKE AGAIN THE NEXT DAY...

I TOLD BARBARA* YOU WANTED TO TAKE ME AND SHE SAID THAT I SHOULD GO WITH YOU, THAT I SHOULD JUST TELL BOB I WANT SOME "TIME TO BOND" WITH YOU! HAHA!

*HER BFF

UH...

OR I COULD WRITE BOB A REAL SCHMALTZY, SENTIMENTAL E-MAIL ABOUT HOW I FEEL LIKE I NEED TO SPEND MORE TIME WITH YOU!

HA!

WELL, I'LL LET YOU GO. I HAVE TO SEE IF THE RECYCLING GOT PICKED UP.

THERE MATTERS MAY HAVE REMAINED, IF I HADN'T BEEN ON MY WAY TO THERAPY.

IT'S LIKE, NEITHER OF US CAN JUST SAY, "I WANT TO SPEND TIME WITH YOU." WE HAVE TO USE PROXIES, THEN ACT LIKE IT'S A BIG JOKE!

WELL, IF THE PLAY DOESN'T WORK OUT, YOU SHOULD STILL DO SOMETHING FUN TOGETHER.

"FUN"? LIKE WHAT? GO GET PEDICURES?

240

EVENTUALLY, MOM AGREED TO COME TO THE PLAY WITH ME. BUT REVERSALS OF FORTUNE CONTINUED TO BEFALL MY PLAN, LIKE WHEN BOB DECIDED HE WOULD ACCOMPANY US.

BUT AT THE LAST MINUTE HE COULDN'T COME, AND WE ARRIVED IN MANHATTAN ON OUR OWN.

WE PARKED DOWNTOWN AND TOOK THE SUBWAY TO TIMES SQUARE. A TRAIN CAME AND WENT AS I FUMBLED WITH THE METROCARD MACHINE.

"COME, DEAR! WE HAVE MISSED..." OH! WHAT WAS IT...?

HAH!

"WE HAVE ALREADY MISSED FIVE, IF NOT SIX, TRAINS!"

THIS HAD BEEN ONE OF MOM'S LINES IN *THE IMPORTANCE OF BEING EARNEST.*

THE SUMMER I WAS THIRTEEN, I HELPED HER RUN LINES FOR IT.

LADY BRACKNELL IS SPEAKING TO HER DAUGHTER, GWENDOLYN.

"TO MISS ANY MORE MIGHT EXPOSE US TO COMMENT ON THE PLATFORM!"

MY THERAPIST HAD URGED ME NOT TO "WRITE" DURING THIS TRIP, BUT TO SIMPLY BE PRESENT WITH MOM.

BUT I WOULD ARGUE THAT FOR BOTH MY MOTHER AND ME, IT'S BY WRITING...

...BY STEPPING BACK A BIT FROM THE REAL THING TO LOOK AT IT, THAT WE ARE MOST PRESENT.

HOW COULD I HAVE FORGOTTEN THAT THE PLAY ENDS WITH MADAME ARMFELDT'S DEATH?

THE MOVIE VERSION HAD SKIPPED THIS SCENE.

BUT I WOULD HAVE SEEN MY MOTHER DIE SEVERAL TIMES IN THE ROLE THE SUMMER BEFORE I LEFT HOME.

242

I MADE NO ATTEMPT TO HIDE MY TEARS.

NOT THAT MOM WOULD HAVE NOTICED. SHE WAS COMPLETELY TRANSPORTED.

I HAD PULLED IT OFF.

I SUPPOSE IT ONLY MAKES SENSE THAT I FEEL CLOSEST TO MY MOTHER WITH NOT JUST A PLAY BETWEEN US, BUT A PLAY ABOUT ACTING. A SELF-REFLEXIVE MISE-EN-ABÎME.

WINNICOTT ENDS HIS MIRROR-ROLE PAPER WITH THIS ODD OBSERVATION ABOUT ACTUAL MIRRORS.

1960a). Nevertheless, when a family is intact and is a going concern over a period of time each child derives benefit from being able to see himself or herself in the attitude of the individual members or in the attitudes of the family as a whole. We can include in all this the actual mirrors that exist in the house and the opportunities the child gets for seeing the parents and others looking at themselves. It should be

THE HOUSE I GREW UP IN HAD AN ENTRY VESTIBULE, A SMALL ROOM BETWEEN TWO SETS OF DOORS—ONE TO THE OUTSIDE AND ONE TO THE INSIDE OF THE HOUSE.

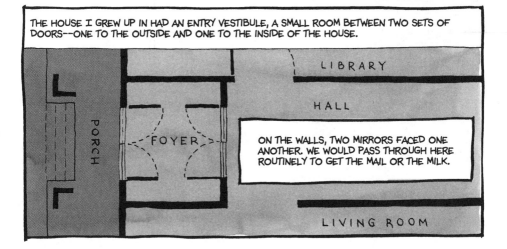

LIBRARY

HALL

PORCH

FOYER

ON THE WALLS, TWO MIRRORS FACED ONE ANOTHER. WE WOULD PASS THROUGH HERE ROUTINELY TO GET THE MAIL OR THE MILK.

LIVING ROOM

243

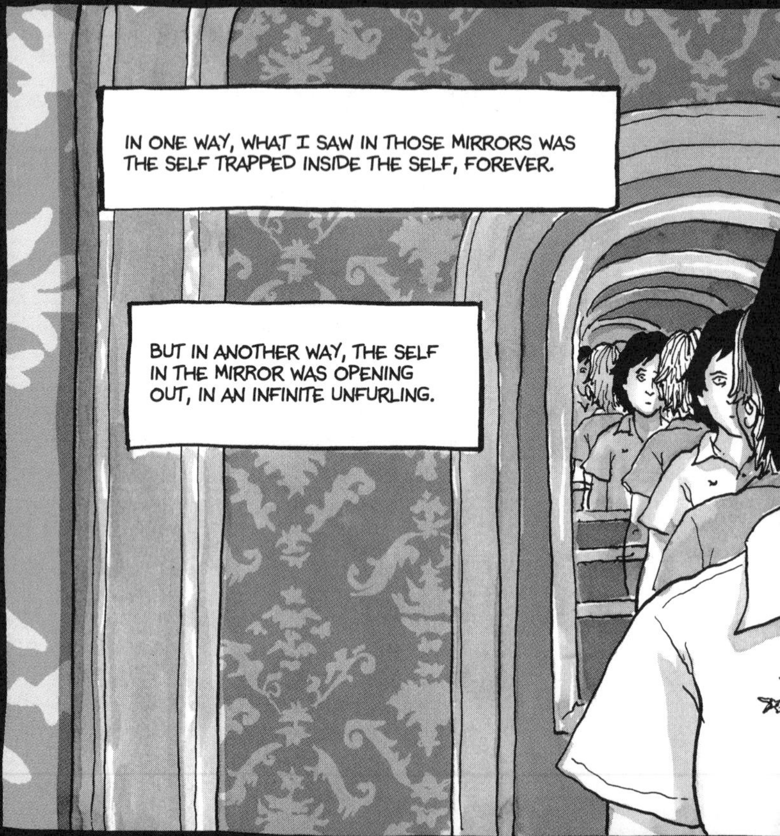
IN ONE WAY, WHAT I SAW IN THOSE MIRRORS WAS THE SELF TRAPPED INSIDE THE SELF, FOREVER.
BUT IN ANOTHER WAY, THE SELF IN THE MIRROR WAS OPENING OUT, IN AN INFINITE UNFURLING.

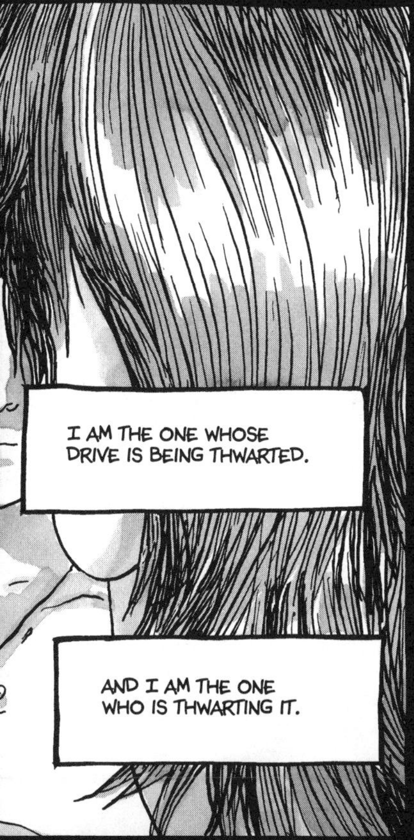
I AM THE ONE WHOSE DRIVE IS BEING THWARTED.
AND I AM THE ONE WHO IS THWARTING IT.

# 7

# The Use of an Object

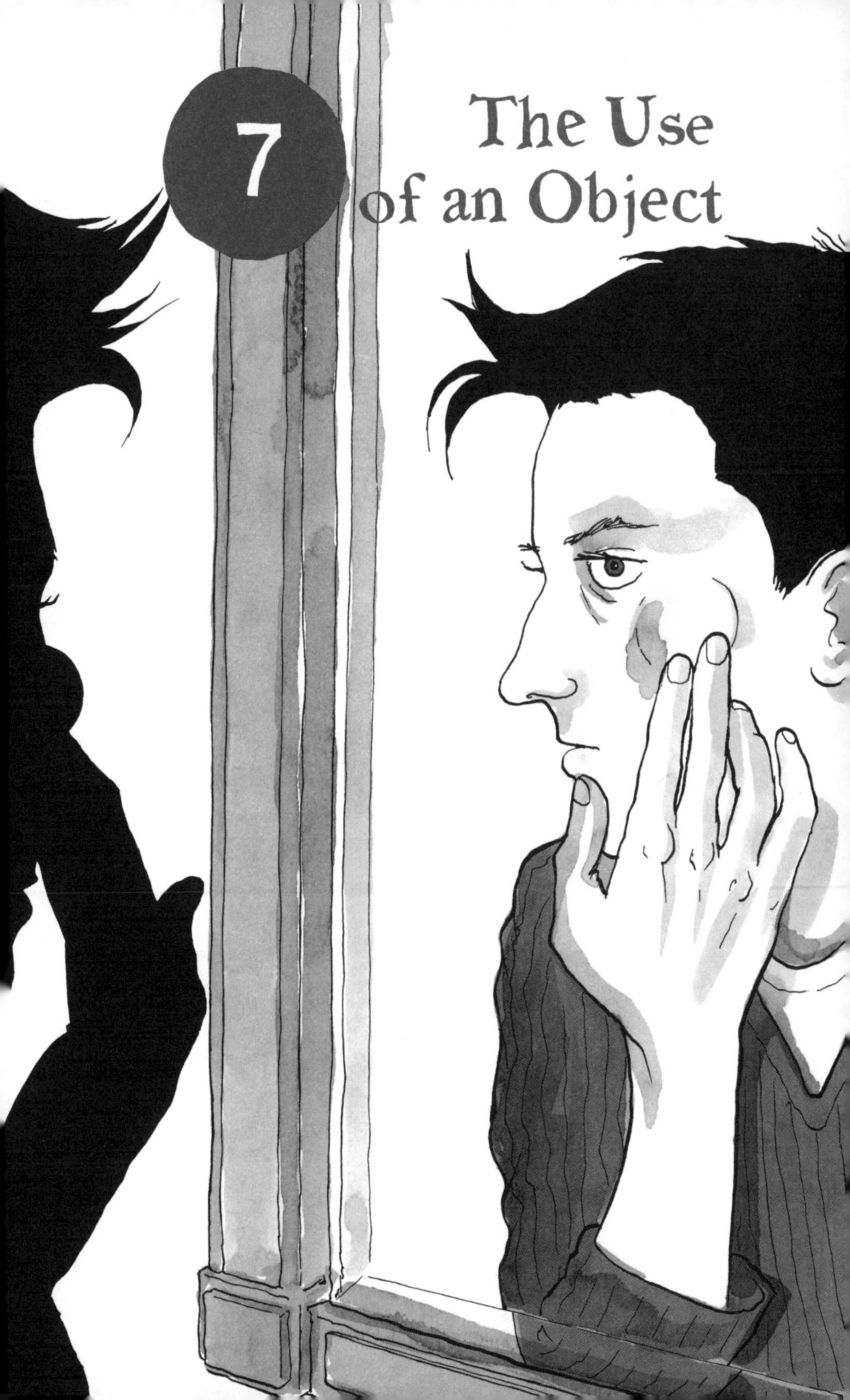

I JUST GOT BACK FROM A GRUELING WILDERNESS TREK. I HAVEN'T SEEN A MIRROR IN A WHILE.

I'VE HAD THIS PIMPLE ON MY CHEEK FOR YEARS. ONCE, WHEN IT WAS SMALLER, I TRIED TO POP IT.

NOW IT'S HUGE, AND AN ALMOST SURGICAL CUT HAS APPEARED IN THE SKIN OVER IT.

I CAN SEE THIS WHITE *THING* INSIDE. I TRY TO SQUEEZE IT OUT. BUT THAT DOESN'T WORK. I'M GOING TO HAVE TO REACH IN AND YANK ON IT.

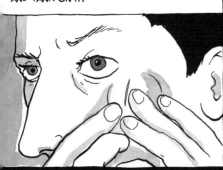

I FEEL REVULSION AND FEAR. I STEEL MYSELF.

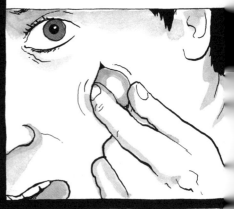

IT'S A TUMOR THE SIZE OF A GOLF BALL.

IT REMINDS ME OF WHAT I'VE HEARD ABOUT UTERINE FIBROIDS-- THAT SOMETIMES THEY HAVE TEETH AND HAIR.

I'M GIDDY WITH RELIEF. IT'S GONE. AND AMAZINGLY, THERE'S NO WOUND OR SCAR.

MOM! **MOM!**

THE MOST INCREDIBLE THING JUST HAPPENED!

BUT SHE WON'T EVEN TURN AROUND. SHE'S STILL MAD AT ME ABOUT THE BOOK.

WE'RE ON OUR WAY TO SEE STONEHENGE.

SOMEONE HAS SURROUNDED IT WITH A HOUSING DEVELOPMENT.

AS IF THIS ISN'T SACRILEGE ENOUGH, THE SHODDY CONDOS ARE BUILT WITH THEIR BACKS TO THE RING OF MEGALITHS.

BIG GREEN DUMPSTERS HANG FROM THE REAR SECOND-FLOOR DECKS, READY TO SPILL.

I HAD THE STONEHENGE DREAM THE NIGHT AFTER I BROKE DOWN AND CALLED MOM.

HI. IT'S ME.

IT HAD BEEN FIVE DAYS SINCE I'D RECEIVED HER E-MAIL ABOUT MY MANUSCRIPT.

WHERE **WERE** YOU?

WHAT?! DID YOU TRY TO CALL?

NO, BUT I SENT YOU THAT E-MAIL AND THEN I DIDN'T HEAR FROM YOU!

BUT YOU SAID YOU'D CALL OVER THE WEEKEND!

OH.

I GUESS I FORGOT.

I HAD THAT ARTIST PROFILE I HAD TO TURN IN. I'VE BEEN UNDER A LOT OF STRESS WITH THESE NEWSPAPER DEADLINES.

MAY 2002

TO MY GREAT RELIEF, MOM ONLY HAD A FEW SMALL DETAILS SHE WANTED ME TO CHANGE.

I DON'T MIND THE STUFF ABOUT ME AND DAD. TO BE HONEST, YOU'RE NOT CLOSE TO MY STORY THERE. IT'S YOUR PERCEPTION, WHICH IS FINE.

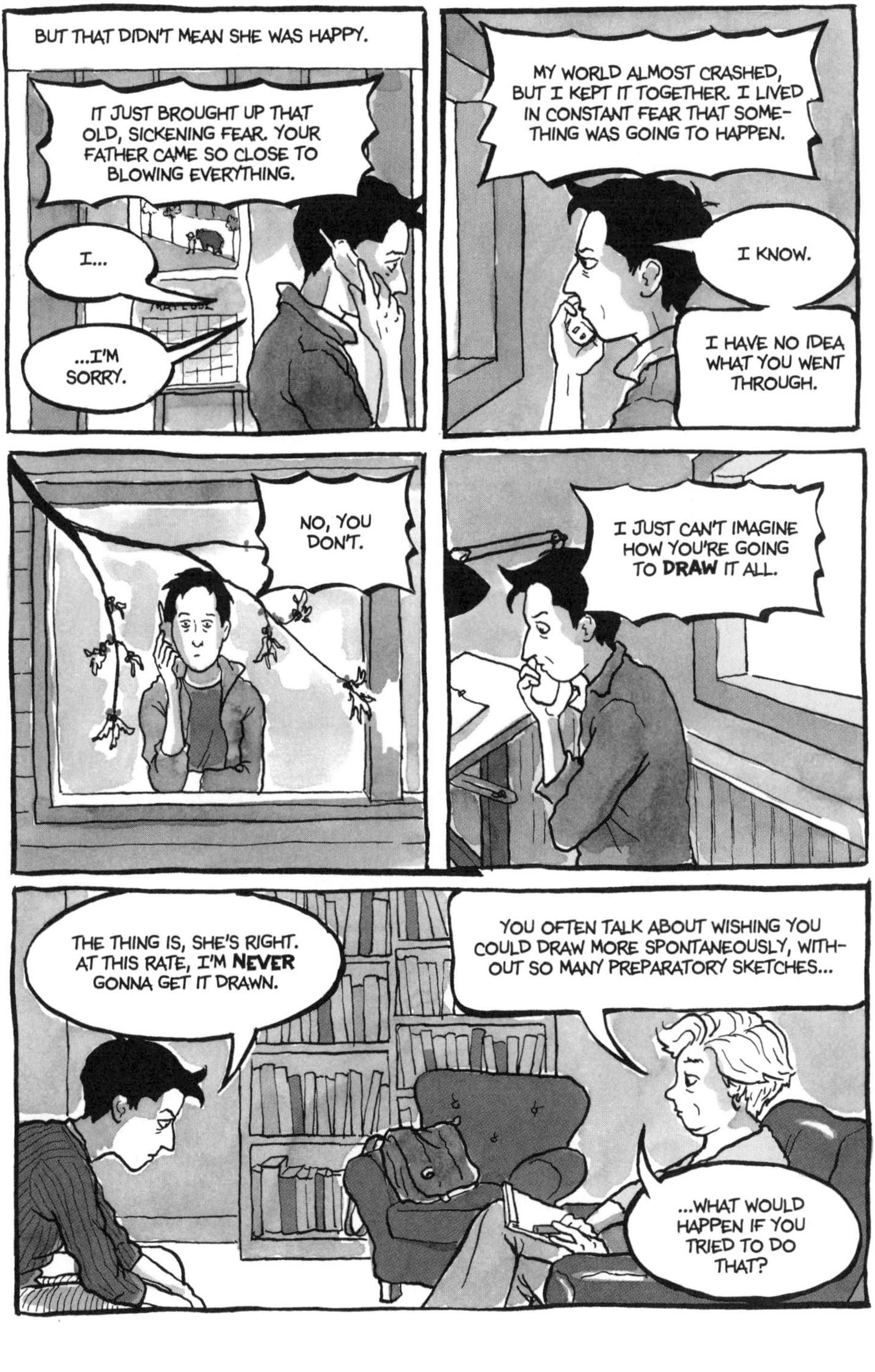
BUT THAT DIDN'T MEAN SHE WAS HAPPY.
IT JUST BROUGHT UP THAT OLD, SICKENING FEAR. YOUR FATHER CAME SO CLOSE TO BLOWING EVERYTHING.
I...
...I'M SORRY.
MY WORLD ALMOST CRASHED, BUT I KEPT IT TOGETHER. I LIVED IN CONSTANT FEAR THAT SOMETHING WAS GOING TO HAPPEN.
I KNOW.
I HAVE NO IDEA WHAT YOU WENT THROUGH.
NO, YOU DON'T.
I JUST CAN'T IMAGINE HOW YOU'RE GOING TO **DRAW** IT ALL.
THE THING IS, SHE'S RIGHT. AT THIS RATE, I'M **NEVER** GONNA GET IT DRAWN.
YOU OFTEN TALK ABOUT WISHING YOU COULD DRAW MORE SPONTANEOUSLY, WITHOUT SO MANY PREPARATORY SKETCHES...
...WHAT WOULD HAPPEN IF YOU TRIED TO DO THAT?

THAT'S IMPOSSIBLE!

THE KIND OF DRAWING I DO HAS TO BE METICULOUSLY PLANNED, EVERY LINE HAS TO CONVEY SPECIFIC INFORMATION.

I WONDER IF YOU'RE TRYING TO PROTECT YOUR SPONTANEOUS, "PURE" DRAWING.

AS IF MAKING IT PUBLIC MIGHT CONTAMINATE IT, OR AT LEAST MAKE IT VULNERABLE TO CRITICISM.

HUH...LIKE, THE SPONTANEOUS DRAWING IS MY ID, AND THE ANAL, LABORIOUS DRAWING IS MY SUPEREGO?

IT'S LIKE MY DREAM!

THE STONEHENGE DREAM?

YEAH! STONEHENGE IS MY TRUE SELF! AND IT'S OBSCURED FROM VIEW BY... BY...WHUDDAYA CALL IT...

...MY MOTHER'S NARCISSISTIC CATHEXIS!

THE WEEKS FOLLOWING THE DREAM WERE A PERIOD OF INTENSE CREATIVE FERMENT. I WAS NOT ONLY WORKING ON THE DAD BOOK, AND MY COMIC STRIP...

(CURIOUSLY, IN THE EPISODE OF MY STRIP THAT I WAS DRAWING AT THIS TIME, ONE OF MY CHARACTERS HAD JUST GOTTEN PREGNANT.)

...BUT I WAS ALSO SPENDING LONG HOURS WRITING DOWN MY DREAMS AND READING ABOUT PSYCHOANALYSIS.

I FELT A PIERCING LUCIDITY, AS IF THE HOOD ON MY LIFE HAD BEEN LIFTED AND I COULD SEE ITS INNER WORKINGS.

I SEE NOW THAT MY HEIGHTENED STATE WAS THE CONCEPTION, THE VERY FIRST STIRRINGS, OF THIS BOOK ABOUT MY MOTHER.

BUT I WOULD NOT SIT DOWN AND BEGIN WRITING IT FOR FIVE MORE YEARS, UNTIL AFTER THE DAD BOOK WAS PUBLISHED.

253

EARLY IN MY RESEARCH, WINNICOTT'S MIRROR PAPER LED ME TO LACAN'S MUCH MORE CRYPTIC MIRROR PAPER.

AS I WAS PLODDING THROUGH THIS FOR PERHAPS THE SIXTH TIME, THE MISTS PARTED AND ONE SENTENCE EMERGED, STARK AS A STANDING STONE ON SALISBURY PLAIN.

Correlatively, the formation of the *I* is symbolized in dreams by a fortress, or a stadium, its inner arena and enclosure, surrounded by marshes and rubbish tips, dividing it into two opposed fields of contest where the subject flounders in quest of the lofty, remote inner castle whose form (sometimes juxtaposed in the same scenario) symbolizes the id in a quite startling way,

IN THE "CONTEST" WITH MY MOTHER, I HAD LIBERATED MY SELF.

FREUD USED OTHER METAPHORS BESIDES THE ECONOMIC ONE OF INVESTMENT TO DESCRIBE CATHEXIS.

HE ALSO USED A MILITARY ONE, OF OCCUPATION.

IN THE DREAM I UPROOT MY MOTHER'S ENCAMPMENT.

PERHAPS THIS IS WHAT VIRGINIA WOOLF WAS TALKING ABOUT WHEN SHE WROTE, "I DID FOR MYSELF WHAT PSYCHO-ANALYSTS DO FOR THEIR PATIENTS."

IN THE FIRST SECTION OF *TO THE LIGHTHOUSE*, LILY BRISCOE ASKS THE RAMSAY'S OLDEST SON WHAT HIS FATHER'S BOOKS ARE ABOUT.

"Oh, but," said Lily, "think of his work!"

Whenever she "thought of his work" she always saw clearly before her a large kitchen table. It was Andrew's doing. She asked him what his father's books were about. "Subject and object and the nature of reality," Andrew had said. And when she said Heavens, she had no notion what that meant. "Think of a kitchen table then," he told her, "when you're not there."

So now she always saw, when she thought of Mr Ram...

in t...

char...

focu...

THE JOKE IS THAT THIS VAST AND POMPOUS-SOUNDING TOPIC IS ALSO WHAT *TO THE LIGHTHOUSE* IS ABOUT.

tree, or upon its fish-shaped leaves, but upon a phantom

IN HER EARLY NOTES FOR THE BOOK, WOOLF DRAWS A DIA-GRAM OF ITS FORM: "TWO BLOCKS JOINED BY A CORRIDOR."

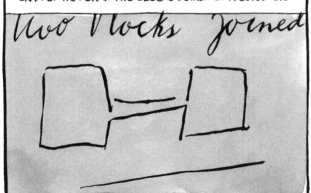

THE FIRST AND LAST SECTIONS DESCRIBE SINGLE DAYS TEN YEARS APART, BEFORE AND AFTER THE GREAT WAR.

THE BRIEF MIDDLE SECTION COMPRESSES THOSE TEN YEARS OF PROFOUND SOCIAL UPHEAVAL, LOSS, AND "THE GRADUAL DISSOLU-TION OF EVERYTHING" INTO FEWER THAN TWENTY PAGES.

THE "BREAK IN UNITY" OF THIS DESIGN WAS A PROBLEM WOOLF NEEDED TO SOLVE, JUST AS LILY BRISCOE STRUGGLES THROUGHOUT THE BOOK WITH HER OWN DESIGN PROBLEM.

SHE'S TRYING TO WORK OUT THE RELATION OF SHAPES IN HER PAINTING, BUT SHE'S ALSO TRYING TO UNDERSTAND THE RELATION BETWEEN MR. AND MRS. RAMSAY.

LIKE MANY OF THE OTHER CHARACTERS, LILY LOVES MRS. RAMSAY AND FEARS MR. RAMSAY.

MR. RAMSAY IS A HARSH BUT FAIRLY ACCURATE PORTRAIT OF WOOLF'S FATHER, EXHAUSTING HIS WIFE WITH HIS RAGES AND NEEDINESS. BUT MRS. RAMSAY IS MORE IDEALIZED.

SHE'S NOT AS STRICT, FOR ONE THING. AND ALTHOUGH YOU CAN IMAGINE HER SIGNING A PETITION AGAINST FEMALE SUFFRAGE, LIKE WOOLF'S REAL MOTHER DID...

YOU KNOW DAD DOESN'T TELL ME WHAT TO DO, RIGHT?

UH HUH.

...SHE DOES NOT NEGLECT HER DAUGHTERS IN FAVOR OF HER SONS.

WE'RE EQUALS.

*they could not paint or write or do anything Ever: so that, being a man*

THE WORD "FEMINIST" APPEARS THREE TIMES IN WOOLF'S DRAFT OF THE DINNER PARTY SCENE WHERE LILY AND MR. RAMSAY'S STUDENT, CHARLES TANSLEY, TRY TO MAKE SMALL TALK.

*break; & then ~~she would~~ come up cringing. Down she went: horror & despair; annihilation, nonentity; sure enough, they arched crashed over her stooping form; & yet — & yet. Opening her eyes in the pale world of daylight again, profound small trophy retriev would sew to the inside of her dres*

THE WORD HAS BEEN EDITED OUT OF THE FINAL VERSION, WHICH IS KIND OF FUNNY GIVEN LILY'S OWN ANXIETY ABOUT IT.

*matter) ~~not are enduring, indeed ever lasting~~ no*
*matter;) & opening her eyes she was* Elated *so joyous in her freedom*
*& did* mark *a something*

LILY "COULD NOT BEAR TO BE CALLED, AS SHE MIGHT HAVE BEEN CALLED HAD SHE COME OUT WITH HER VIEWS, A FEMINIST."

*...sley to whom she had no*
*in port...* *to be be called,*
*(Suppos... wish* *come out with her*
*militancy in her, ~~dist & could no~~ & was & easier, less*
*as she might have been called had she*
*Views a feminist;*
*agitating*
*threatening to accept thi*
*& after all, ~~half one's fee~~*

LILY IS STRUGGLING TO HANG ON TO HERSELF IN THE FACE OF MR. TANSLEY'S STATEMENT THAT WOMEN CAN'T PAINT OR WRITE. "DOWN SHE WENT; HORROR & DESPAIR; ANNIHILATION; NONENTITY..."

AND SHE SUCCEEDS. SHE REMEMBERS THE PROBLEM SHE'S ENGAGED WITH IN HER PAINTING AND FEELS "JOYOUS IN HER FREEDOM."

*...rite* *& one* *above*
*...hat one meant* ~~the last~~ *she* ~~last~~
*...e light house built? did he really think it would*
*was longing to go to the lighthouse;* *& rough*
*be too rough?*
*Certainly said Mrs R...*
*Charles Tansley turned in his ...*

IN CONTRAST TO MRS. RAMSAY'S APPARENT SELFLESSNESS, LILY IS TRYING TO BECOME A SELF, A SUBJECT.

*~~It wa~~* *~~he said~~; always have been*

A SUBJECT IN THE SENSE OF *ONE WHO DOES*, NOT IN THE SENSE OF *ONE WHO IS DONE TO*, THE WAY MRS. RAMSAY IS MR. RAMSAY'S SUBJECT.

*Complete ...*
*the great Enemies of progress* *be tolerable on* *might 'o p...*
*With civilisation* *It is foolish to say*
*Mrs* *for Mrs Ramsay*

LANGUAGE GETS VERY CONFUSING AS IT APPROACHES THIS PLACE WHERE OUTSIDE AND INSIDE TOUCH.

*~~that a young man has way~~*

OR FAIL TO.

WINNICOTT DRAWS HIS OWN DIAGRAM OF RELATION, OF THE "TERRITORY BETWEEN THE OBJECTIVE AND THE SUBJECTIVE."

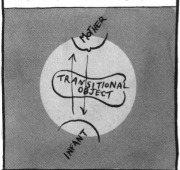

I FIND THE TRANSCRIPT OF AN INTERVIEW THAT CLARE WINNICOTT DID AFTER DONALD'S DEATH.

CLARE IS IN HER LATE SEVENTIES. THE INTERVIEWER'S LEADING QUESTIONS ANNOY ME. HE'S ASKING HER ABOUT WHAT DONALD LIKED TO READ.

> N:   Any [                    read? Biographies, mostly.
>                      1.   I mean, Freud admires Attila the Hun
> and Napoleon and so on.
>      Winnicott:   Freud?
>      N:   Yes. Freud obviously loves the men who conquer the world
> and so forth, which is quite telling. Did he admire Napoleon or any
> kind of all-conquering figure?
>      Winnicott:   No. No, I wouldn't say so, no. He much
> preferred the--I mean, he liked Virginia Woolf. He liked the
> intricate things. He liked the stream-of-consciousness stuff, you
> know? Interested in the loss (?). He liked poetry. And th

TO THE LIGHTHOUSE MAY BE AN INTRICATE DOMESTIC NOVEL. BUT IT ALSO CONQUERS THE WORLD--OR AT ANY RATE, THE PROBLEM OF THE OUTSIDE WORLD.

TO BE A SUBJECT IS AN ACT OF AGGRESSION. I PUT THE ODDS ON A PSYCHIC DEATHMATCH BETWEEN ATTILA THE HUN AND VIRGINIA WOOLF AT FIFTY-FIFTY.

IN MY FIFTH OR SIXTH SESSION WITH JOCELYN, SOMETHING INTERESTING CAME UP.

I HAD A **BAD** ANXIETY ATTACK LAST NIGHT.

I TRIED TO TELL WHERE IN MY BODY I WAS FEELING IT, LIKE YOU TOLD ME TO.

IT WAS IN MY STOMACH. IT'S LIKE, I'M AFRAID I'M GONNA THROW UP.

AND THROWING UP IS THE WORST THING IN THE WORLD TO ME.

DID YOU HAVE A BAD THROWING-UP EXPERIENCE?

NO. I HARDLY EVER THROW UP. UNTIL APRIL, I HADN'T THROWN UP SINCE I WAS TEN.

YOU THREW UP IN APRIL?

YEAH. UH...JUST BEFORE I GOT DEPRESSED.

I TOLD HER ABOUT A TERRIFYING BOUT WITH STOMACH FLU, AND HOW KIND ELOISE WAS.

WHAT HAPPENED THE TIME YOU WERE TEN?

I WOKE UP IN THE NIGHT AND DIDN'T FEEL GOOD. I WENT TO MOM.

MY STOMACH HURTS.

HMM. MAYBE YOU NEED TO POOP. HAVE YOU DONE THAT LATELY?

AT THE RISK OF OVERCOM-PLICATING MY NARRATIVE, I MUST ADMIT (THOUGH PERHAPS IT'S ALL TOO OBVIOUS) THAT I WAS AN ANAL-RETENTIVE CHILD.

GO TRY, AND I'LL COME CHECK ON YOU.

I WALKED INTO THE BATHROOM AND THREW UP A SMALL QUANTITY OF FLUID ONTO THE LINOLEUM.

I REMEMBER THE SPOT EXACTLY BECAUSE I SPENT THE REST OF MY TENURE IN THAT HOUSE AVOIDING IT.

MOM CAME QUICKLY AND LED ME TO THE TOILET, WHERE I THREW UP A LITTLE MORE.

YOU NEVER GET SICK!

HER TONE WAS KIND, SYMPATHETIC. NONE-THELESS, I SUSPECT THAT THIS WAS THE MOMENT IN WHICH MY PHOBIA CRYSTALLIZED.

I GUESS I FELT LIKE I'D FAILED HER. SHE HAD SO MANY DEMANDS ON HER...THE ONE THING SHE NEEDED FROM ME WAS THAT I NOT NEED ANYTHING FROM HER.

THAT'S A PRETTY BIG THING TO ASK.

A FEW WEEKS LATER, I TOLD JOCELYN HOW NERVOUS I WAS ABOUT AN UPCOMING TRIP TO PENNSYLVANIA TO SEE MOM. I ASSOCIATED TO THE TIME I HAD HUNG UP THE PHONE ON HER.

HOW DID YOU FEEL WHEN YOU HUNG UP?

SAD, I GUESS. I MEAN, I WAS CRYING.

UH...AND RELIEVED?

LIKE, FINALLY I COULD STOP BANGING ON THIS DOOR BECAUSE NOBODY WAS HOME.

YOU MUST BE VERY ANGRY AT YOUR MOTHER.

I THINK THAT'S WHAT YOUR ANXIETY IS ABOUT.

UHHH...

JOCELYN'S INTERPRETATION SOUNDED LIKELY ENOUGH, BUT I DIDN'T FEEL ANGER. I FELT COMPLETELY BLANK.

WINNICOTT'S LAST MAJOR PAPER, "THE USE OF AN OBJECT," BEGINS WITH AN INTERESTING ADMISSION.

patient's growing trust in the psychoanalytic technique and setting, and to avoid breaking up this natural process by making interpretations. It will be noticed that I am talking about the making of interpretations and not about interpretations as such. It appals me to think how much deep change I have prevented or delayed in patients *in a certain classification category* by my personal need to interpret. If only we can wait, the patient arrives at understanding creatively and with immense joy, and I now enjoy this joy more than I used to enjoy the sense of having been clever. I think I interpret mainly to let the patient know

[1] Based on a paper read to the New York Psychoanalytic Society, 12 November 1968, and published in the *International Journal of Psycho-Analysis*, Vol. 50 (1969).

IMMEDIATELY AFTER READING IT TO THE NEW YORK PSYCHOANALYTIC SOCIETY IN 1968, HE WAS HOSPITALIZED WITH THE HONG KONG FLU AND NEVER FULLY REGAINED HIS HEALTH.

"HE WAS SUBSEQUENTLY SEEN AS HAVING VENTURED INTO HOSTILE NEW YORK, FALLEN ILL, AND DIED," WINNICOTT'S BIOGRAPHER WRITES, BEFORE ATTEMPTING TO CORRECT THIS RECORD.

I WANT YOU TO TRY SOMETHING WHEN YOU'RE AT YOUR MOM'S.

OKAY.

261

IN FACT, IN THE REMAINING TWO YEARS OF HIS LIFE, WINNICOTT WOULD DO SOME OF HIS MOST PROFOUND THINKING AND WRITING.

ASK HER WHAT THE MAIN THING WAS THAT SHE LEARNED FROM *HER* MOTHER.

TELL HER NOT TO THINK ABOUT IT TOO MUCH, TO JUST SAY THE FIRST THING THAT POPS INTO HER HEAD.

"THE USE OF AN OBJECT" IS ABOUT "THE PATIENT'S ABILITY TO USE THE ANALYST." WINNICOTT DISTINGUISHES *USING* AN OBJECT FROM MERELY *RELATING* TO IT.

I HAD AN ANXIETY ATTACK THAT NIGHT AS I WAS PACKING FOR MY TRIP. I CONSIDERED JOCELYN'S IDEA THAT IT WAS SOMEHOW CONNECTED TO ANGER AT MY MOTHER.

I TRIED TO OBSERVE MY FEELINGS. BUT I COULD PENETRATE NO FURTHER THAN A THICK, CALLUSLIKE LAYER OF GUILT.

WINNICOTT SAYS THAT A BABY, WHEN IT STILL SEES THE MOTHER AS A PART OF ITSELF, CAN ONLY *RELATE* TO HER.

WE PROGRESS TO *USING* ANOTHER PERSON--TO BEING ABLE TO FULLY ASSIMILATE WHAT THEY HAVE TO OFFER US--ONLY WHEN WE UNDERSTAND THAT THEY'RE SEPARATE FROM US.

MOM WAS PUTTING OUR FAMILY HOME ON THE MARKET, SEVEN YEARS AFTER DAD'S DEATH. I CAN'T IMAGINE WHAT IT WAS LIKE FOR HER TO DISMANTLE THIS PLACE THEY HAD BUILT TOGETHER.

WE DIDN'T DISCUSS IT.

OKAY, I'M GONNA ASK YOU A QUESTION.

THE MAJOLICA COLLECTION

GOUGE FROM A PLATE DAD THREW

FLECKS FROM A JAR OF MAYONNAISE DAD THREW

DON'T THINK ABOUT IT, JUST SAY THE FIRST THING THAT COMES INTO YOUR HEAD.

OKAY.

WHAT'S THE MAIN THING YOU LEARNED FROM YOUR MOTHER?

THAT BOYS ARE MORE IMPORTANT THAN GIRLS.

SHE DID NOT SKIP A BEAT.

REALLY?

OH, YES. SHE WORSHIPED JOE AND ANDREW.*

*HER TWO OLDER BROTHERS

WINNICOTT GAVE A TALK ON FEMINISM TO THE PROGRESSIVE LEAGUE IN 1964.

BUT...BUT YOU WORSHIPED JOHN AND CHRISTIAN!

SOME OF WHAT HE SAYS IS VERY MUCH OF THAT ERA. "PENIS ENVY IS A FACT."

IF IT BOTHERED YOU THAT YOUR MOTHER DID THAT, WHY WOULD YOU DO IT?

BUT THEN WINNICOTT "REMINDS" THE AUDIENCE THAT "MALE ENVY OF WOMEN IS INCALCULABLY GREATER."

OH, I WASN'T NEARLY AS BAD AS SHE WAS.

WINNICOTT SEES BOTH MEN AND WOMEN AS FRUSTRATED BY MUTUAL ENVY.

Children find it difficult to allow for these things in their parents, but this just can't be helped. The forces may be so strong that there just have to be casualties among the off-spring when parents substitute plate-throwing for inter-course or separate to save the crockery.

NEAR THE END OF *TO THE LIGHTHOUSE*, LILY BRISCOE IS STILL TRYING TO FIGURE OUT WHAT WAS GOING ON BETWEEN MR. AND MRS. RAMSAY.

bedroom door would slam violently early in the morn-ing. He would start from the table in a temper. He would whizz his plate through the window. Then all through the house there would be a sense of doors slam-

SHE'S REFERRING TO ONE MORNING TEN YEARS AGO WHEN MR. RAMSAY, ANNOYED AT FINDING AN EARWIG IN HIS MILK, THREW A PLATE "FLYING THROUGH THE AIR TO THE TERRACE OUTSIDE."

THE SCENE IS PROBABLY INSPIRED BY THE STORY ABOUT WOOLF'S FATHER SMASHING A FLOWER POT AS A BOY. SHE RECOUNTS THIS IN *A SKETCH OF THE PAST.*

bad Wednesday. Even now I can find nothing to say of his behaviour save that it was brutal. If, instead of words, he had used a whip the brutality would have been no greater. How can one explain it? He had been indulged of course ever since he broke the flower pot and threw the fragments at his mother (whatever the truth of that story, it ran something like that). Delicacy excused that. Then as he grew

ABOUT A YEAR AND A HALF INTO MY WORK WITH JOCELYN, WE HAD ANOTHER PIVOTAL SESSION.

I'VE BECOME THIS **FISHWIFE!** NAGGING HER TO TELL ME WHERE SHE'S GOING, WHEN SHE'LL BE HOME.

YESTERDAY SHE TOLD ME SHE WANTS TO "TRAVEL."

ELOISE AND I HAD RECOVERED FROM HER AFFAIR WITH CHRIS SIX MONTHS EARLIER, BUT NOW THINGS WERE DETERIORATING AGAIN.

THE DEVELOPMENT OF A BABY'S ABILITY TO USE AN OBJECT IS NOT A GIVEN.

I GUESS I CAN'T BLAME HER. ALL I DO LATELY IS WORK.

AND HAVE ANXIETY ATTACKS.

THE GOOD-ENOUGH MOTHER MUST FACILITATE IT.

DO YOU SEE WHAT YOU'RE DOING?

YOU WANT ELOISE'S LOVE, AND WHEN YOU FAIL TO GET IT, YOU DECIDE IT MUST BE BECAUSE OF SOME FAULT IN YOU.

THE BABY WHO NEVER BECOMES ABLE TO USE THE MOTHER MAY LATER ENTER ANALYSIS IN HOPES OF FIXING THINGS.

DOES THAT REMIND YOU OF ANYTHING?

WHAT? MY MOTHER?!

BUT THERE'S A PROBLEM. HE OR SHE WILL BE UNABLE TO USE THE ANALYST.

LOOK AT YOU. YOU'RE A GOOD, KIND PERSON. YOU HAVE INTEGRITY AND TALENT. YOU WORK HARD. YOU'RE WILLING TO CHANGE.

IT'S THE ANALYSTS'S TASK IN SUCH A CASE TO GIVE THE PATIENT THE *CAPACITY TO USE* THE ANALYST.

YOU'RE ADORABLE.

AND THE ANALYST DOES THIS THE SAME WAY THE GOOD-ENOUGH MOTHER DOES...

MAYBE IF ELOISE WERE HAPPIER WITH HER JOB, SHE'D BE ABLE TO LOVE ME MORE.

...BY SURVIVING DESTRUCTION BY THE PATIENT/BABY.

DID YOU HEAR ANYTHING I JUST SAID?

YEAH, YEAH.

HERE'S THE VITAL CORE OF WINNICOTT'S THEORY:

THE SUBJECT MUST DESTROY THE OBJECT.

AND THE OBJECT MUST SURVIVE THIS DESTRUCTION.

I KNOW I'M GOOD AND KIND AND HARD-WORKING. LOTS OF PEOPLE ARE.

IF THE OBJECT DOESN'T SURVIVE, IT WILL REMAIN INTERNAL, A PROJECTION OF THE SUBJECT'S SELF.

IF THE OBJECT SURVIVES DESTRUCTION, THE SUBJECT CAN SEE IT AS SEPARATE.

FOR FREUD, HUMAN AGGRESSION WAS A REACTION TO REALITY, FRUSTRATION WITH THE FAILURE OF THE EXTERNAL WORLD TO INSTANTLY GRATIFY OUR NEEDS.

AND ADORABLE.

BUT FOR WINNICOTT, IT'S THE OTHER WAY AROUND. REALITY DOESN'T MAKE US FEEL AGGRESSION.

BUT, JOCELYN, IF I REALLY WERE ALL THOSE THINGS...

AGGRESSION MAKES US FEEL REAL.

...I WOULD DIE.

I WASN'T SURE WHAT I MEANT BY THIS, BUT IT SUDDENLY STRUCK ME AS THE TRUTH.

BECAUSE YOU'D RATHER DIE THAN FEEL ANGER AT YOUR MOTHER FOR NOT GIVING YOU WHAT YOU NEEDED?

UH...I CAN'T THINK...

THERE'S THIS...THIS LINE I SEEM UNABLE TO CROSS.

I KNOW.

268

THREE DAYS AFTER THIS SESSION, ELOISE WAS OUT LATE AGAIN. BY ONE-THIRTY I WAS CONVINCED SHE'D HAD AN ACCIDENT. IT WAS TOO LATE TO CALL ANY OF HER FRIENDS.

I FOUND HER INTACT CAR AT CHRIS'S PLACE.

WHAT'S GOING ON?

I COULD HEAR THE CLOCK TICKING. NO ONE ANSWERED.

AFTER A MOMENT OF LINGUISTIC AWE AT THE WAY THIS SILENCE EXPLAINED EVERYTHING, IT HIT ME.

IN THE WRETCHED WEEKS THAT FOLLOWED, I REALIZED I HAD TO LEAVE.

WHAT ABOUT THE VIRGIN ISLANDS?

WE HAD BEEN PLANNING A TRIP WITH ELOISE'S PARENTS OVER CHRISTMAS.

JESUS. I'M NOT GOING TO THE FUCKING VIRGIN ISLANDS.

TAKE CHRIS.

I HADN'T BEEN HOME FOR CHRISTMAS IN A COUPLE YEARS, BUT NOW I HAD NOWHERE ELSE TO GO.

WOW, NICE!

WHEN THE BOYS GET HERE TOMORROW WE CAN PUT THAT TREE UP.

MOM HAD MOVED TO A NEW HOUSE IN THE TOWN WHERE SHE TAUGHT HIGH SCHOOL.

I'M SURE I TOLD HER ABOUT THE BREAKUP WITH ELOISE, BUT I'M EQUALLY SURE WE DIDN'T DISCUSS IT ANY FURTHER THAN THAT.

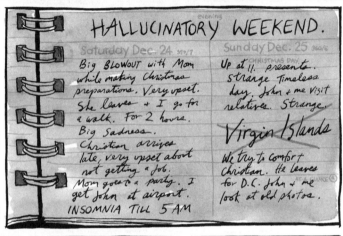

ON MONDAY I FLEW BACK TO THE MIDWEST.

MY MOTHER'S HOUSE WAS NOT MY HOME. THIS HOUSE WAS NO LONGER MY HOME.

IN FACT, THIS WAS NO LONGER MY DOG.

BUT I STILL HAD JOCELYN. I REMEMBERED THE HUG SHE HAD GIVEN ME A YEAR EARLIER, AFTER THE SESSION WHEN I HAD CRIED.

I CAME IN THAT TUESDAY DETERMINED TO ASK HER TO HUG ME AGAIN. BUT THE MINUTES TICKED BY, AND I COULDN'T DO IT.

WHY DO PEOPLE EVEN HAVE HOLIDAYS?

FINALLY, AFTER WE'D OFFICIALLY ENDED...

CAN I, UM, AM I ALLOWED TO ASK FOR A HUG?

SANTA FE CHAMBER MUSIC FESTIVAL

HMM. I WISH YOU'D BROUGHT THAT UP EARLIER. WE'D NEED TO TALK ABOUT IT, AND THERE'S NO TIME NOW. LET'S START HERE NEXT WEEK.

JOCELYN

I FELT LIKE SHE'D KICKED ME IN THE GUT. I SORT OF WISHED SHE HAD--AT LEAST WE'D HAVE MADE CONTACT.

AND THERE WAS NOTHING I WANTED MORE IN THAT MOMENT THAN THE CONTAINING PRESSURE, HOWEVER BRIEF, OF SOMEONE OUTSIDE MYSELF.

NOW THERE WAS NOTHING BETWEEN ME...

...AND NOTHING.

WINNICOTT ENUMERATES THE "UNTHINK-ABLE ANXIETIES" OF THE NEWBORN.

(1) Going to pieces.
(2) Falling for ever.
(3) Having no relationship to the body.
(4) Having no orientation.

THE GOOD-ENOUGH MOTHER STAVES THESE OFF BY LITERALLY HOLDING THE BABY TOGETHER.

THE ANALYST ALSO PROVIDES A *HOLDING ENVIRONMENT* FOR THE PATIENT...

...BUT THIS MEANS THE ANALYST'S ATTENTION, THE PHYSICAL ROOM, THE COUCH.

NOT ACTUAL TOUCH.

-15 DEGREES AT THREE PM.

FOR JOCELYN TO ACTUALLY HUG ME AT THIS TIME...

...WOULD HAVE BEEN TO DROP ME ANALYTICALLY.

AT MY "MIDLIFE CHECK-IN" A DECADE LATER, IT WAS STARTLING HOW IMMEDIATELY AND COMPLETELY I FELL BACK UNDER JOCELYN'S SPELL.

GOD, THIS IS SO BIZARRE.

IT'S LIKE I NEVER LEFT.

WE DISCUSSED THE ABRUPT NATURE OF MY TERMINATION, HOW IT WAS IN A WAY LIKE MY FATHER'S SUICIDE. I TOLD HER I WAS WRITING A BOOK ABOUT HIM.

BUT MOSTLY WE TALKED ABOUT THE INTENSITY OF MY TRANSFERENCE TO HER.

REMEMBER THE SESSION WHEN YOU SAID I WAS ADORABLE?

YES, I DO.

THAT MOMENT PATCHED UP THE HOLE.

HMM. BASED ON WHAT I'M LEARNING NOW IN MY PSYCHOANALYTIC TRAINING, SAYING THAT TO YOU WOULD BE AGAINST THE RULES.

BUT YOU KNOW WHAT?

I'D DO IT AGAIN.

THERE WAS ENOUGH IN YOU THAT WANTED A POSITIVE MOTHER FIGURE. YOU WERE ABLE TO TAKE IN MY GOOD FEELINGS ABOUT YOU.

BUT THE FEELING THAT YOU WERE BAD WAS STILL A PART OF YOU, SO YOU GOT OTHER PEOPLE TO CONFIRM IT.

ELOISE BY CHEATING ON YOU, DIANE BY BEING COOL AND DISTANT.

I GOT INVOLVED WITH THE FIRST PERSON WHO TOUCHED ME AFTER THE BREAKUP WITH ELOISE--DIANE, WHO I WENT TO FOR A MASSAGE.

THAT RELATIONSHIP DIDN'T LAST LONG, NOR DID THE NEXT ONE.

THEN I MET AMY. BUT AFTER THIRTEEN YEARS, WE BROKE UP.

MY PARENTS MADE IT TWENTY YEARS BEFORE MY MOTHER DECIDED TO LEAVE.

BUT OF COURSE IT WAS MY FATHER WHO LEFT FIRST.

A FEW MONTHS AFTER MY STONEHENGE DREAM, I WAS VISITING MOM.

LOOK! I THOUGHT THIS CLUMP OF THREAD WAS AN S-P-I.

I ALMOST HAD A HEART ATTACK!

YIKES!

MY MOTHER HAS ALWAYS HAD A TERRIBLE FEAR OF SPIDERS. WHEN I WAS LITTLE WE COULDN'T EVEN SAY THE WORD "SPIDER."

HEY, I JUST READ SOMETHING REALLY INTERESTING ABOUT PHOBIAS!

HANG ON, LEMME GET MY BOOK.

THIS GUY WRITES ABOUT A PATIENT WITH ARACHNOPHOBIA. A TEENAGE GIRL WHOSE PARENTS NEEDED HER TO BE REALLY GOOD ALL THE TIME. HE TELLS HER, "SPIDERS ARE GOOD TO HATE PEOPLE WITH."

ON KISSING TICKLING and BEING BORED
ADAM PHILLIPS

HE SAYS, "IN ORDER TO GET REALLY FURIOUS, SHE HAD TO FIND A SPIDER TO LET HER DO IT."

WELL, ALL I KNOW IS, I'VE HAD THIS EVER SINCE I WAS NINE.

"I WAS STANDING IN THE BACKYARD BY OUR PINK PEONY BUSHES. I SAW A GRASSHOPPER GET CAUGHT IN A SPIDERWEB."

"THEN A BIG BLACK SPIDER WITH YELLOW MARKINGS DARTED OUT AND SPUN A WEB AROUND AND AROUND THE GRASSHOPPER."

"AT FIRST THE GRASSHOPPER TRIED TO KICK ITS WAY OUT."

"BUT FINALLY IT WAS WRAPPED SO TIGHT, IT STOPPED MOVING."

I WAS IN THE MIDDLE OF REPORTING ALL THIS TO CAROL THE FOLLOWING WEEK...

...WHEN A SMALL SPIDER SUDDENLY RAPPELLED DOWN FROM THE CEILING.

276

WINNICOTT'S BIOGRAPHER F. ROBERT RODMAN DESCRIBES AN INTERPRETATION DONALD MADE NEAR THE END OF HIS LIFE IN A SESSION WITH AN ACUTELY ARACHNOPHOBIC PATIENT.

RODMAN MENTIONS IT AS EVIDENCE OF WINNICOTT'S "CONTINUING ABILITY TO REACH DEEP INTO HIS IMAGINATION FOR EXPLANATORY IDEAS."

I THINK THAT SOMEWHERE IN YOUR EARLY DEVELOPMENT...WHEN YOU HADN'T QUITE SEPARATED OUT FROM YOUR MOTHER...YOU HALLUCINATED HER.

THAT IS, YOU HALLUCINATED THE SUBJECTIVE OBJECT, THE BREAST OR WHATEVER, EXPECTING TO BE MET. BUT YOU WEREN'T.

THERE WAS A GAP.

A DARK LACK...AN ABSENCE. AND AS AN INFANT YOU DEALT WITH THIS IN THE ONLY WAY YOU WERE ABLE, BY PUTTING LEGS 'ROUND IT.

AND THEN IT BECAME A SPIDER AND YOU BECAME AFRAID OF IT.

277

WINNICOTT DIED ON THE TWENTY-SECOND OF JANUARY, 1971. HE'D GOTTEN UP IN THE NIGHT, AS HE ALWAYS DID, TO USE THE LOO.

THIS WAS NOT AN UNUSUAL POSITION. "WE NEVER SAT ON CHAIRS. WE ALWAYS SAT ON THE FLOOR," CLARE SAID.

BUT THIS TIME HE WAS GONE LONGER THAN USUAL.

CLARE FOUND HIM LEANING ON A CHAIR, ALREADY DEAD.

ONE MONTH LATER, IN FEBRUARY 1971, I BEGAN KEEPING MY DIARY. DAD STARTED ME OFF, TO SHOW ME HOW TO DO IT.

WEDNESDAY
Ash Wednesday
24
55
THURSDAY

Dad is reading Th
Swan. I h
saw San
Hospital
John is
SANDY
Mothe

THEN I BACKFILLED AS FAR AS I COULD REMEMBER, TO FEBRUARY 12TH.

Feb. 1971

SUNDAY
14
MATT had a party today.

MONDAY
Washington's Birthday
15
Today I was sick. I watched T.V.

TUESDAY
16
Today was Tuesday. Whoopee!

278

WHAT IS THE LINK BETWEEN MY PHOBIA AND MY MOTHER'S?

I WONDER IF THROWING UP IS SOMEHOW A MARKER OF FEMININITY.

LIKE, IT STANDS IN FOR THINGS THAT COME OUT OF THE FEMALE BODY.

MENSTRUAL BLOOD, VAGINAL LUBRICATION, EVEN A BABY.

THIS SESSION WAS IN AUGUST 2009, JUST AFTER I'D HAD MY LAST PERIOD.

I THINK YOUR MOTHER HAS SOME RESENTMENT ABOUT BEING FEMALE THAT GOT PASSED ON TO YOU.

THERE'S NO WAY TO KNOW, OF COURSE, WHETHER A PARTICULAR PERIOD WILL BE YOUR LAST. YOU CAN ONLY TELL RETROSPECTIVELY.

IN HIS 1964 TALK ON FEMINISM, WINNICOTT SAYS SOMETHING HE'S BEEN SAYING ALL ALONG.

1. We find that the trouble is not so much that everyone was inside and then born, but that at the very beginning everyone was *dependent* on a woman. It is necessary to say that at first

WINNICOTT SEES THIS DEPENDENCE AS THE ROOT OF MISOGYNY--THOUGH HE NEVER USES THAT WORD. PERHAPS, LIKE WOOLF WITH "FEMINIST," HE FELT PLAIN LANGUAGE WAS MORE PERSUASIVE.

The awkward fact remains, for men and women, that each was once dependent on woman, and somehow a hatred of this has to be transformed into a kind of gratitude if full maturity of the personality is to be reached.

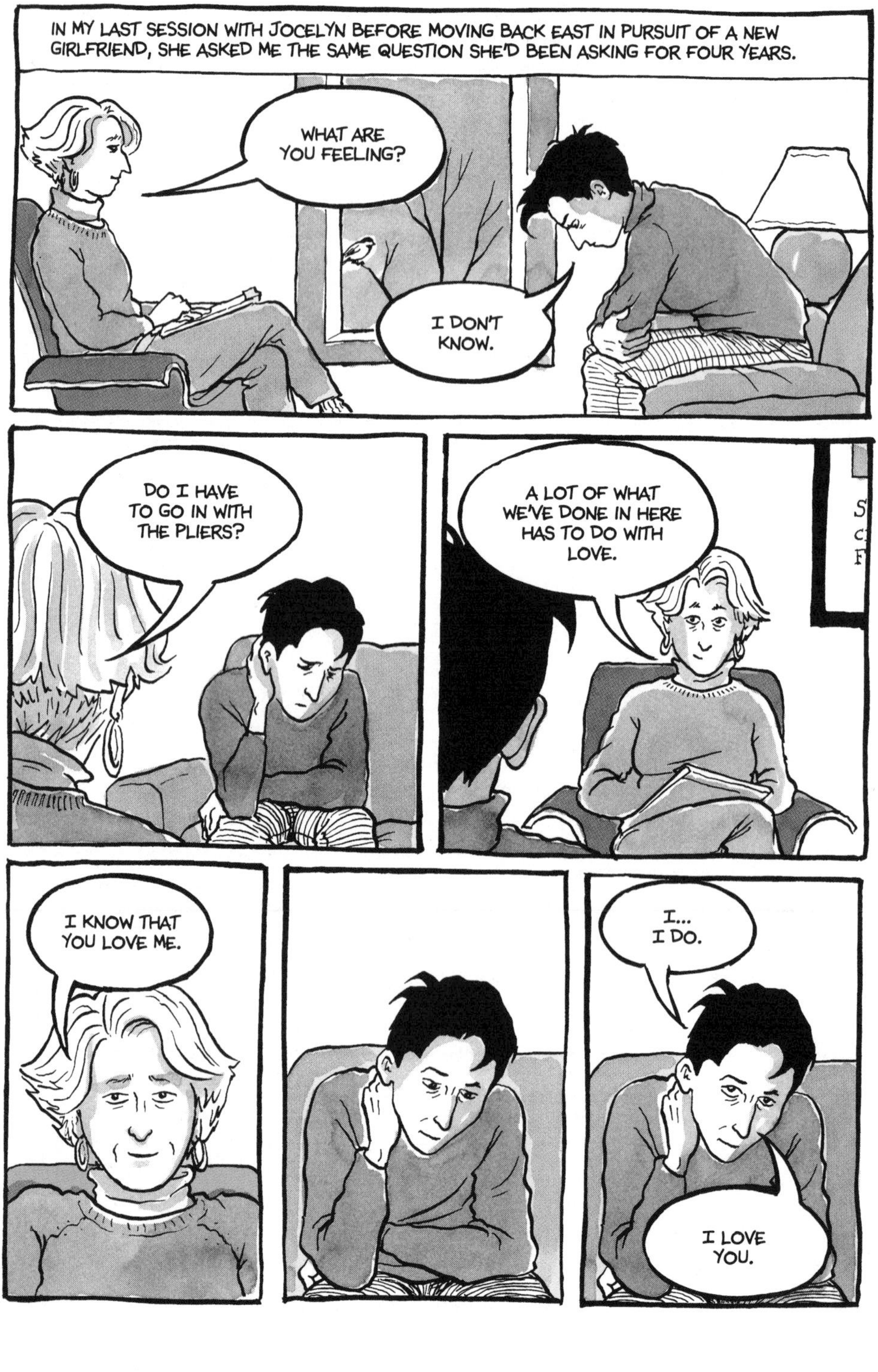
IN MY LAST SESSION WITH JOCELYN BEFORE MOVING BACK EAST IN PURSUIT OF A NEW GIRLFRIEND, SHE ASKED ME THE SAME QUESTION SHE'D BEEN ASKING FOR FOUR YEARS.
WHAT ARE YOU FEELING?
I DON'T KNOW.
DO I HAVE TO GO IN WITH THE PLIERS?
A LOT OF WHAT WE'VE DONE IN HERE HAS TO DO WITH LOVE.
I KNOW THAT YOU LOVE ME.
I... I DO.
I LOVE YOU.

I KNOW WHEN YOU ARE REALLY SHY...

... AND THAT IS WHEN YOU WANT TO TELL ME...

... THAT YOU LOVE ME.

"SHE WAS VERY POSITIVE IN HER GESTURE OF ASSENT," HE WRITES.

capacity to use an object is more sophisticated than a capacity to relate to objects; and relating may be to a subjective object, but usage implies t

This s **THE SURVIVAL OF THE OBJECT IS WHAT LEADS US TO THE WORLD OF "SHARED REALITY." TO "EXTERNALITY ITSELF."** t. (2) Object is ject in the world. (3) Subject destroys object. (4) Object survives destruction. (5) Subject can *use* object.

The object is always being destroyed. This destruction becomes the unconscious backcloth for love of a real object; that is, an object outside the area of the subject's omnipotent control.

Study of this problem involves a statement of the positive value of destructiveness. The destructiveness, plus the object's survival of the destruction, places the object outside the area of objects set up by the subject's projective mental mechanisms. In this way a world of shared

WHEN THE BOOK ABOUT MY FATHER WAS FINALLY PUBLISHED, I WAS EAGER TO SEND IT TO JOCELYN. WE HADN'T CORRESPONDED IN FIVE YEARS.

Tell me your snail mail address and I'll send you a copy.

AN E-MAIL FROM HER PARTNER ARRIVED NEXT DAY, INFORMING ME, AS GENTLY AS POSSIBLE, THAT JOCELYN HAD DIED TEN MONTHS EARLIER OF A RAPIDLY SPREADING CANCER.

THERE WAS A LINK TO A BLOG, A CURIOUS REVERSE CHRONICLE OF HER ILLNESS.

I READ EVERY WORD OF THIS AS IT PROCEEDED FROM DEATH TO DIAGNOSIS.

NOT ONLY WAS SHE DEAD, SHE HAD BEEN DEAD FOR NEARLY A YEAR.

THERE WERE SO MANY THINGS GOING ON IN MY LIFE AT THIS POINT, I DIDN'T HAVE TIME TO RECORD THEM.

JUST THE DAY BEFORE, AMY AND I HAD DIVIDED UP THE FURNITURE. SHE WAS ABOUT TO MOVE OUT.

A FEW DAYS LATER, I WOULD LEAVE ON A CROSS-COUNTRY TOUR FOR MY BOOK...

...AND BEGIN A FRAUGHT, LONG-DISTANCE RELATIONSHIP WITH "Z."

282

NEAR THE END OF THE BOOK TOUR, I WAS TALKING WITH MOM.

PEGGY HARRIS SAID SOMETHING TO BARBARA ABOUT THE BOOK, ABOUT HOW TERRIBLE IT WAS THAT YOU'D DONE THIS TO YOUR MOTHER.

HUH.

SHE HAD SHARED A FEW OF THESE SECON~ AND THIRD-HAND REPORTS FROM FRIENDS.

Y'KNOW, AT MY READINGS, SOMEONE ALWAYS ASKS, "WHAT DOES YOUR MOTHER THINK OF ALL THIS?"

RENTAL

REALLY?

YEAH. AND I SAY, WELL, YOU'RE NOT HAPPY ABOUT IT, BUT AT THE SAME TIME YOU HAVE A KIND OF AESTHETIC DISTANCE.

WAIT, I JUST READ SOME-THING INTERESTING ABOUT MEMOIR. HANG ON.

ARE YOU THERE?

UH HUH.

IT'S BY DOROTHY GALLAGHER.

"THE WRITER'S BUSINESS IS TO FIND THE SHAPE IN UNRULY LIFE AND TO SERVE HER STORY. NOT, YOU MAY NOTE, TO SERVE HER FAMILY, OR TO SERVE THE TRUTH, BUT TO SERVE THE STORY."

WOW!

MILY ED!

HA!

THE STORY MUST BE SERVED!

THIS IS NOT THE END OF THE STORY, OF COURSE.

THE STORY HAS NO END. BUT NOW IT'S FIVE YEARS LATER, AND I MUST MANUFACTURE ONE.

I TOLD THE CLERK AT THE BOOKSTORE MY DAUGHTER HAS A BOOK COMING OUT.

PERPETUAL CALENDAR ELOISE'S MOTHER GAVE ME IN 1984.

WE ARE HAVING THIS CONVERSA- TION ON THE FRIDAY BEFORE THE MONDAY I NEED TO TURN MY TEXT IN TO THE COPY EDITOR.

I RECENTLY SENT MOM THE FIRST FOUR CHAPTERS OF THIS BOOK--ALL I'VE MANAGED TO GET DRAWN SO FAR.

SHE ASKED WHAT IT WAS ABOUT, AND I SAID, "ME!"

SHE SHOWED THE CHAPTERS TO BOB FIRST, SO HE COULD WARN HER IF THERE WAS ANYTHING TOO UPSETTING.

SHE SAID SHE COULD GET ME INTO A WITNESS PROTECTION PROGRAM.

SO FAR SHE HASN'T COMMENTED MUCH EX-CEPT TO SAY, IN WHAT WAS POSSIBLY AN ACCUSATORY TONE, "YOU MUST HAVE A PRETTY GOOD MEMORY."

I MIGHT NEED A WITNESS PROTECTION PROGRAM IF I DON'T GET IT DRAWN BY THE DEADLINE.

BUT TODAY SHE SEEMS TO WANT TO SAY SOMETHING POSITIVE.

WELL, IT COHERES.

THERE ARE CLEAR THEMES.

I DON'T HAVE ENOUGH DISTANCE TO KNOW ANYTHING ABOUT ITS MARKETABILITY.

IT'S...IT'S A METABOOK.

YEAH! IT IS!

AT LAST, I HAVE DESTROYED MY MOTHER, AND SHE HAS SURVIVED MY DESTRUCTION.

OH, TOMORROW'S DON GIOVANNI!!

LA CI DAREM LA MANO...

MOM GOES REGULARLY TO THE METROPOLITAN OPERA SIMULCASTS AT A LOCAL MOVIE THEATER.

I JUST READ A REVIEW OF THE PRODUCTION. THE SET HAS A WHOLE LOT OF DOORS.

SO IN THE CATALOG ARIA WHEN THE SERVANT LISTS ALL DON GIOVANNI'S CONQUESTS, THE DOORS POP OPEN AND THERE ARE ALL THESE GIRLS!

DON GIOVANNI IS IN PERPETUAL PURSUIT OF HIS MOTHER, TOO.

HER NAME, INEZ, IS A FREQUENT CROSSWORD PUZZLE ANSWER.

OKAY, I'M GONNA GO DO MY PUZZLE.

OKAY. TALK TO YOU LATER.

I AM ALTERNATELY ENVIOUS AND CONTEMPTUOUS OF PEOPLE WHO FINISH THEIR PHONE CONVERSATIONS WITH A ROTE "I LOVE YOU!"

MY MOTHER AND I KNOW THIS; THERE'S NO NEED TO JABBER ABOUT IT.

ALISON, GET OFF THE FLOOR!

I CAN'T! I'M CRIPPLED!

I HAVE ALWAYS THOUGHT OF THE "CRIPPLED CHILD" GAME AS THE MOMENT MY MOTHER TAUGHT ME TO WRITE.

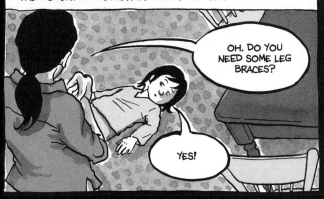

OH. DO YOU NEED SOME LEG BRACES?

YES!

I DON'T REMEMBER THE PARTICULARS OF OUR PLAY. I'M INVENTING THIS DIALOGUE WHOLESALE.

WHAT I REMEMBER IS A FEELING OF INEBRIATION. THE FURTHER I MOVED INTO THIS IMAGINARY SPACE, THE MORE IT OPENED UP.

BUT I'M SURE MOM INDULGED MANY SUCH PLAY SCENARIOS WITH ME. WHY IS THIS THE ONE THAT I RECALL?

AND SPECIAL SHOES!

OKAY. LET ME LACE THEM UP.

I CAN ONLY SPECU-LATE THAT THERE WAS A CHARGE, AN EXCHANGE, A MUTUAL CATHEXIS GOING ON...

SHE COULD SEE MY INVISIBLE WOUNDS BECAUSE THEY WERE HERS, TOO.

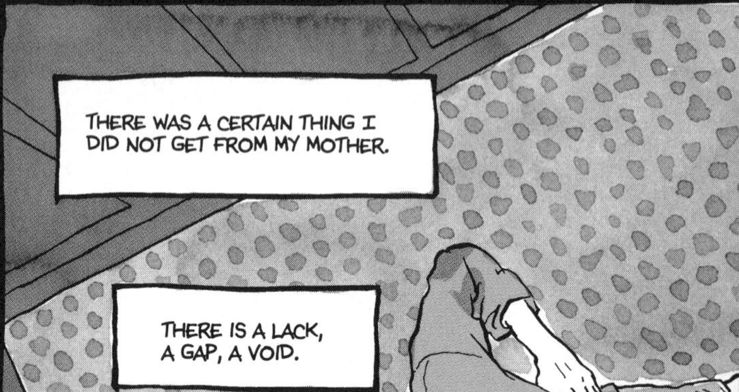
THERE WAS A CERTAIN THING I DID NOT GET FROM MY MOTHER.
THERE IS A LACK, A GAP, A VOID.
HOW'S THAT?
BUT IN ITS PLACE, SHE HAS GIVEN ME SOMETHING ELSE.

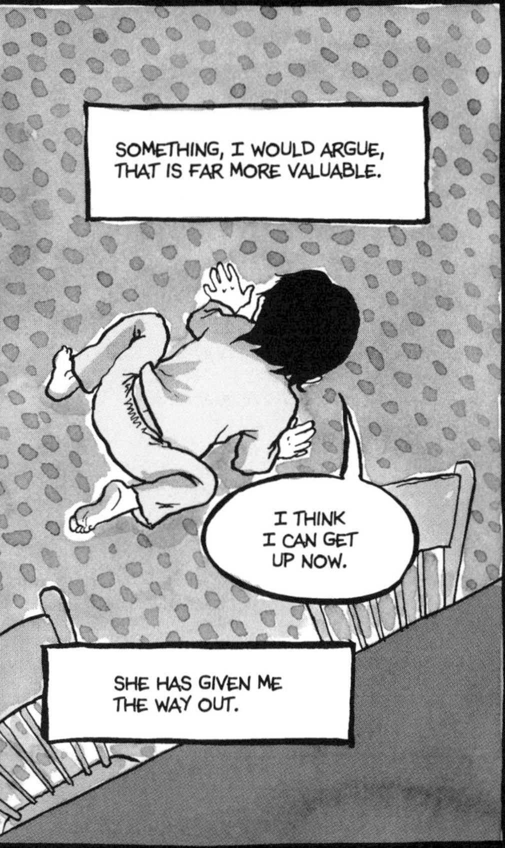
SOMETHING, I WOULD ARGUE, THAT IS FAR MORE VALUABLE.
I THINK I CAN GET UP NOW.
SHE HAS GIVEN ME THE WAY OUT.

# ACKNOWLEDGMENTS

THANK YOU TO VAL ROHY, HILLARY CHUTE, LUCY JANE BLEDSOE, ALISON PRINE, RUTH HOROWITZ, AND JUDITH LEVINE FOR READING VARIOUS EARLY BITS AND PIECES OF THIS BOOK. THEIR CRITIQUES AND INSIGHT HELPED IT TO FINALLY COHERE.

I HAVE HAD THE UNIMAGINABLE GOOD FORTUNE OF WORKING ON TWO BOOKS IN A ROW WITH THE SAME AMAZING EDITOR, DEANNE URMY. HER INCISIVE MIND AND EMOTIONAL INTELLIGENCE PROVIDED A FIRM RUDDER TO MY WAVERING COURSE. I'M ESPECIALLY GRATEFUL FOR HER DEDICATION TO THIS STRANGE PROJECT AS IT BEGAN TO EXTEND WELL PAST THE INITIAL DEADLINE.

WITHOUT THE FAITH AND VISION OF MY AGENT, SYDELLE KRAMER, I WOULD HAVE HAD TO GET A JOB LONG AGO. I'M ESPECIALLY INDEBTED TO HER FOR HER OBSERVATION, FOUR YEARS INTO THE WORK ON THIS BOOK, THAT IT WASN'T MAKING ANY SENSE.

REBECCA VAN DYKE, MALINA LESLIE, AND CHARLES FORSMAN PROVIDED SUPERLATIVE TECHNICAL ASSISTANCE WITH COLORING AND PRODUCTION, SPOTTING AND FIXING HUNDREDS OF PROBLEMS AND ERRORS. SPECIAL THANKS TO BECCA FOR HER LONG COMMITMENT, TO MALINA FOR HER METICULOUSNESS, AND TO CHARLES FOR HIS CALM IN THE FACE OF MY FREQUENT PANICS. LAURA TERRY ALSO PROVIDED EARLY ADVICE ON THE PRODUCTION PROCESS. I'M INDEBTED TO THE CENTER FOR CARTOON STUDIES IN WHITE RIVER JUNCTION, VERMONT, FOR TEACHING LAURA AND CHARLES HOW TO DO ALL THIS NEWFANGLED STUFF. AND I AM ETERNALLY GRATEFUL TO JESSICA ABEL FOR TELLING ME ABOUT INDESIGN.

THANKS TO ROSEMARY WARDEN FOR ALLOWING ME TO FEEBLY IMITATE HER BEAUTIFUL SUMI-E PAINTING, *FISH IN REEDS*, AND TO JEB (JOAN E. BIREN) FOR HER PERMISSION TO BASE MY DRAWING OF ADRIENNE RICH ON A PHOTO FROM HER 1987 PHOTOGRAPHY BOOK, *MAKING A WAY: LESBIANS OUT FRONT*.

BETH FULLER'S COPY EDITING OF MY WORDS AND MY DRAWINGS MADE ME TREMBLE WITH DELIGHT. CHRISTOPHER MOISAN WENT WAY ABOVE AND BEYOND THE CALL OF DUTY IN WHAT WAS TO ME A STAGGERINGLY COMPLEX DESIGN AND PRODUCTION PROCESS.

I'M PROFOUNDLY GRATEFUL FOR THE GENEROSITY OF AMY RUBIN, ELOISE, AND CHRIS FOR ALLOWING ME TO PILFER SCENES FROM OUR LIVES.

WITHOUT HOLLY RAE TAYLOR'S PATIENT SUPPORT AND FROLICSOME COMPANIONSHIP I WOULD NEVER HAVE FINISHED THIS BOOK. SHE IS AN EXPANSIVE, ENLIVENING FORCE.

AND WITHOUT JOCELYN AND CAROL -- NOT THEIR REAL NAMES -- I WOULD NEVER HAVE BEGUN THIS BOOK. MY GRATITUDE TO EACH OF THEM IS BOUNDLESS.